WHY
STARTUPS
FAIL

WHY STARTUPS FAIL

A New Roadmap for Entrepreneurial Success

TOM EISENMANN

CURRENCY
NEW YORK

Published in the United States by Currency, an imprint of Random House, a division of Penguin Random House LLC, New York.

CURRENCY and its colophon are trademarks of Penguin Random House LLC.

LIBRARY OF CONGRESS CATALOGING-IN-PUBLICATION DATA
Names: Eisenmann, Thomas R., author.
Title: Why startups fail / Tom Eisenmann.
Description: New York : Currency, [2020] | Includes bibliographical references and index.
Identifiers: LCCN 2020047464 (print) | LCCN 2020047465 (ebook) | ISBN 9780593137024 (hardcover ; alk. paper) | ISBN 9780593239391 (alk. paper) | ISBN 9780593137031 (ebook)
Subjects: LCSH: New business enterprises. | Business failures. | Success in business. | Entrepreneurship.
Classification: LCC HD62.5 .E446 2020 (print) | LCC HD62.5 (ebook) | DDC 658.1/1—dc23
LC record available at https://lccn.loc.gov/2020047464
LC ebook record available at https://lccn.loc.gov/2020047465

Hardback ISBN 978-0-593-13702-4
International ISBN 978-0-593-23939-1
Ebook ISBN 978-0-593-13703-1

Printed in the United States of America on acid-free paper

crownpublishing.com

9 8 7 6 5 4 3 2 1

First Edition

Book design by Victoria Wong

For Jill, Caroline, and Jack

Contents

WHY
STARTUPS
FAIL

Introduction

Why do the vast majority of startups fail? That question hit me with full force several years ago—when I realized that I couldn't answer it. In quick succession, I had witnessed the demise of two startups that I knew well, both founded by former students of mine. You'll meet these entrepreneurs and learn about their experiences later in the book. The first, Triangulate, had assembled a talented team to create and operate online dating sites. The second, Quincy, had come up with a terrific idea: to sell stylish, affordable, better-fitting work apparel for young professional women. I'd encouraged my students to launch both of these ventures, and I was also an investor in Quincy. Yet, despite their strong promise, both of these startups failed. Why? In each instance, I could list many possible reasons, but I couldn't pinpoint the root cause.

This was unnerving: Here I was, an academic expert teaching some of the country's brightest business minds how to give their future companies the best shot at success, yet I was a failure at explaining how they could avoid failure. And, since more than two-thirds of new ventures fail, that left a lot of explaining to do!

For the past twenty-four years, I've been a professor at Harvard Business School, where I've led "The Entrepreneurial Manager," a required course for all of our MBAs. At HBS, I've also drawn on my research, my experiences as an angel investor, and my work for startups as a board director to create fourteen electives on every aspect of launching new ventures. HBS is a startup factory: Our alumni have founded more than thirteen hundred venture capital–backed startups since 2006. We've seen our fair share of successes. Over the past ten years, nineteen HBS startups have achieved "unicorn" status—a valuation in excess of $1 billion—including Stitch Fix, Cloudflare, Oscar Health, and Zynga. Many of the unicorns' founders were my students; I provided guidance and feedback on their venture plans—as I've done with at least two thousand other HBS students and alumni.

At the same time, we've had plenty of failures. Most were promising ventures founded by bright, committed entrepreneurs. Many of these founders followed our playbook for startup success diligently and executed it flawlessly. They identified a gap in the market, devised a differentiated product to meet that need, and validated market demand using the best Lean Startup techniques. They chose a proven business model, sought out advisers, and hired employees with the experience their startup needed. By all accounts, these ventures *should* have succeeded. And yet . . .

My inability to explain why these high-potential companies failed to live up to their promise cast doubt on whether the playbook I was teaching at HBS was as bulletproof as I thought. Was the advice I'd given to countless founders unsound? And if I couldn't sufficiently explain the causes of startup failure, how could I be confident that I was teaching my students to achieve startup success?

That's when I became determined to do everything in my power to really get to the bottom of this question of *why startups fail*. By isolating the behaviors and patterns that often lead to failure, I hope to help entrepreneurs avoid fatal missteps, and thus spare them, and their teams, a great deal of pain. Failure hurts! And if it's due to avoidable errors, it doesn't just hurt, it also wastes time and capital that could be better spent elsewhere—to the benefit of not only entrepreneurs, employees, and investors but also society at large. Society needs entrepreneurs to solve a spate of problems and can't afford to have talent and resources tied up in ill-considered, ill-fated ventures. But, at the end of the day, if an entrepreneur's startup does fail, despite her best efforts, I want to equip her with tools to learn more from the experience and bounce back stronger. With those goals in mind, I launched the multiyear research project that culminated in this book.

Decoding Defeat

To get started, I delved into research on failure in other settings, such as medicine, sports, and military combat. I'd already learned that it was difficult to diagnose the factors behind a startup's demise. Now I wondered: Was this true in other fields, too? In those fields, what stood in the way of making sense of failure? Did startups share those handicaps? Had experts in other fields devised solutions for anticipating and avoiding failure? If so, could such solutions work for entrepreneurs, as well?

My inquiry yielded some good news: Across domains, from philosophy to firefighting, experts agree that we can learn a lot from failure.

"If you cannot fail, you cannot learn." That statement by Lean Startup guru Eric Ries echoes a big idea from Karl Popper, one of the twentieth century's greatest philosophers of science. If you're confident in your assumptions about how things work, and everything goes according to plan, then you don't learn anything new. But if plans go awry, it forces you to reexamine your assumptions; in effect, you've tested your assumptions and found them wanting. In other words, you've conducted an experiment that's failed to validate your original hypothesis. When that happens, you've gained a valuable new insight.

By studying failure in other realms, I discovered that we learn from setbacks in two distinct ways: from direct personal experience and vicariously—that is, by observing others' mistakes. Direct experience can be a powerful teacher when individuals reflect on what went wrong and what they might have done differently. This works best when feedback cycles are frequent and fast, when cause-and-effect relationships are stable and well understood, and when stakes are modest enough that strong emotions won't muddle thinking. Weather forecasting fits this profile. Startups do not.

By definition, first-time founders have no direct experience with startup failure; even serial entrepreneurs have at most a few personal data points from which to glean feedback. Also, since they're offering something new, entrepreneurs inevitably face uncertainty about cause and effect: that is, whether their actions will lead to intended outcomes. Finally, a founder's identity becomes so fused with that of her venture that failure sparks strong emotions like frustration, guilt, and sadness—on top of the financial loss incurred.

Fortunately, vicarious learning from others' mistakes can substitute for direct personal experience. This was familiar ground for me, because Harvard Business School is built around a model of learning through company case studies. These cases, I found, are a powerful tool for helping entrepreneurs foresee and forestall failure.

Better yet, it turns out that vicarious learning from *near failures* is especially effective—this is why the National Traffic and Safety Board issues reports on aircraft near misses. Accounts of near failures provide insight not only into the mistakes made by responsible parties but also into the decisions and actions that helped them ultimately avoid a disaster. Accordingly, this book draws on case studies of both failures and near failures.

Studying failure in other domains also showed me why it can be so difficult to understand startups' stumbles. Humans are wired to oversimplify explanations for both good and bad outcomes through what philosophers call the *single cause fallacy*. We shine a spotlight on one big reason for a calamity—say, a failed presidential bid ("neglect of a key swing state") or a sports team's late-season collapse ("the star pitcher's torn hamstring")—when the outcome is actually a result of multiple factors.

Furthermore, we're prone to make what psychologists call the *fundamental attribution error*. Research shows that when we observe others, our explanations for their behaviors tend to overemphasize *dispositional* factors—their personality type and the values we assume they have—while downplaying *situational* factors, such as social pressures or environmental circumstances. By contrast, when explaining our own behaviors, we tend to attribute good outcomes to dispositional factors—in particular, our skill and diligence—and bad outcomes to situational ones. This is why we perceive the BMW driver who just cut us off to be a self-centered jerk, while he blames his car's blind spot. And it's why, when a new venture falters, investors and team members often blame the founder's shortcomings—whereas the founder frequently points her finger at external circumstances ("a soft economy") or other parties ("our VCs, who pushed too hard for growth").

The result is that both first- and third-party explanations for why a startup failed may not be reliable. So rather than accept those explanations at face value, I would need to develop an independent and objective view of the startup's value proposition, team members' capabilities, investors' objectives, founders' motivations, and so forth. And luckily, my role at HBS gave me access to hundreds of alumni entrepreneurs who trusted me enough to do this.

My Research Approach

Studying failure in other settings pointed me toward comprehensive case studies to explain why startups falter. However, that meant I couldn't rely much on past scholarly work, because it was based mostly on theoretical models, econometric analysis, and large-sample surveys—and rarely was informed by rigorous interviews or careful case study research. Consequently, I'd need to get out into the field to study failed startups firsthand.

I interviewed dozens of founders and investors to understand why the new ventures they'd launched or backed did not succeed. I also read scores of first- and third-person published accounts of entrepreneurial setbacks, all with the goal of identifying recurring problems and patterns.

The MBA classroom proved to be my most productive source of insight. Over the past several years, I've written and taught twenty detailed case studies about failed ventures, each of which fueled a fascinating student debate over what went wrong and whether different approaches might have led to a better outcome. Founders were typically in attendance when I taught the cases, affording students the opportunity to probe the founders' explanations and explore counterfactuals ("What if you'd hired a different chief technology officer?").

As I kicked my research into high gear, I decided to launch an MBA elective entirely focused on entrepreneurial failure. I did worry that encountering failure after failure might depress students and sap their energy. But just the opposite happened. In each class, my students were galvanized by the intellectual puzzle: Why did this promising startup fail despite its strong product, talented team, and savvy, deep-pocketed investors? Exploring the topic with smart students sharpened my thinking and expanded the repertoire of cases I draw upon in the chapters that follow.

The final component of my research was a survey comparing the decisions and attributes of failed or struggling startups to those of their more successful counterparts. The founders of 470 new ventures answered a broad range of questions about their products, customers, competition, teams, funding, and so forth. I used this survey data to validate hypotheses gleaned from my interviews and case studies, and to shed light on which startup failure patterns are most pervasive.

Startup Failure Patterns

My research revealed six distinct patterns that explain a large portion of startup failures. I briefly describe the patterns below, and later I devote a full chapter to each. These patterns run counter to oversimplified accounts that tend to pervade the popular mythology; for example, the penchant of venture capitalists to blame "bad jockeys" for a startup's misfortunes. (VCs often describe the opportunity that a startup pursues as "the horse" and its founder as "the jockey"). Part I of this book, "Launching," focuses on three failure patterns common among early-stage startups. In Part II, "Scaling," I analyze three more patterns that explain the failure of many resource-rich, late-stage startups. For each of the failure patterns, I'll provide examples of ventures that fell prey to them and describe actions that other entrepreneurs took to avoid similar mistakes.

Early-Stage Failure

Good Idea, Bad Bedfellows. The fate of many early-stage companies I studied showed that entrepreneurs could identify a promising opportunity yet still fail. Put another way, those companies made clear that a great concept is necessary, but not sufficient, for startup success. As noted above, many venture capitalists think that a talented jockey is more important than a fast horse. So, VCs look for founders with the right stuff: grit, vision, an industry insider's acumen, and experience leading startup teams.

But focusing solely on founders neglects the other parties whose contributions are crucial to a new venture. As we'll see, problems with a broad set of stakeholders, including employees, strategic partners, and investors—not just the founders—all can contribute to a venture's downfall. In studying early-stage startup failures, I saw this pattern of dysfunctional relationships with key resource providers repeated regularly; I've labeled it *Good Idea, Bad Bedfellows.*

False Starts. When the information service CB Insights identified determinants of failure for scores of recent startups, the most common problem—cited nearly half of the time—was "no market need." That baffled me. After all, Lean Startup methods have been widely understood and embraced by entrepreneurs for almost a decade. Through experiments and iteration, any founder following these methods should have been able to identify and pivot to an attractive opportunity. But the landscape has been littered with roadkill in the form of self-proclaimed Lean Startups that never found a market. Why? Was something missing from Lean Startup's dogma?

I've been a Lean Startup apostle since 2010, when I first met the movement's progenitors. That year, Steve Blank presented his seminal ideas to my students and Eric Ries became an Entrepreneur-in-Residence at HBS. But as I dug deeper into case studies of failure, I concluded that Lean Startup practices were falling short of their promise. It's not that the methodology isn't sound, it's that many entrepreneurs who claimed to embrace Lean Startup logic actually embraced only *part* of the Lean Startup canon. Specifically, they launched minimum viable products (MVPs)—the simplest possible offering that would yield reliable customer feedback—and iterated on them in response. By putting their MVP out there and testing how customers responded, these founders should have been able to avoid squandering too much time and money building and marketing a product that no one wanted. Yet by neglecting to research customer needs *before* commencing their engineering efforts, they ended up wasting valuable time and capital on an MVP that was likely to miss its mark. These were *False Starts;* the entrepreneurs were like sprinters who jumped the gun—too eager to get a product out there. The rhetoric of the Lean Startup movement actually encourages this "ready, fire, aim" behavior.

False Positives. Excessive optimism about market demand, based on a strong response from a startup's first customers, also can lead some founders to pursue a flawed opportunity, burning through cash reserves in the process. Lean Startup gurus caution entrepreneurs to be wary of deceptive signals about the strength of demand for their solution. But entrepreneurs—like all of us—are prone to see what they hope to see. *False Positives* occur when entrepreneurs, beguiled by the enthusiasm of a few early adopters, incorrectly extrapolate strong demand to the mainstream market and step on the gas. When the next wave of marketing gets a tepid response, the team may be able to course-correct and pivot to an offering that appeals to mainstream customers. But pivots can be costly. The firm must reengineer its product and reeducate the market. Prospective buyers may be confused by the changes and skeptical of an unproven new product. Early adopters may be alienated by the changes and abandon the product.

Both the False Start and the False Positive patterns boost the odds of failure because they send the startup down the wrong path. But these patterns stem from very different mistakes. With a False Start failure, a team builds the wrong product—one that fails to meet customers' needs—because they skipped up-front research. With a False Positive failure, a team builds a product that meets the needs of the wrong customers: focusing too much on early adopters and not enough on mainstream customers.

Late-Stage Failure

Startups that withstand Bad Bedfellows, False Starts, and False Positives go on to confront the growing pains of adolescence. Mortality rates do decline once startups make it through their infancy. To my surprise, however, I learned that VCs still lose money on about one-third of their investments in *late-stage* startups. What was going on here?

Speed Trap. As I studied late-stage failures, I found many that had gained considerable traction before going off the rails. Notable examples included Fab.com, profiled in this book, along with Groupon, Nasty Gal, and Beepi. Their demise followed a similar pattern, one that I call a *Speed Trap*. Ventures that fall victim to a Speed Trap have identified an attractive opportunity. Early adopters embrace the product and spread the word about it. This attracts more customers without any investment in marketing. The rapid early growth also lures enthusiastic investors. To justify the high price they paid for equity, investors push for aggressive expansion. Not that entrepreneurs need much prodding; they're eager to grow, too.

After marketing intensively, the startup eventually saturates its original target market, meaning that further growth requires broadening the customer base to encompass new segments. This next wave of customers, however, doesn't find the company's value proposition nearly as compelling as the early adopters did. The new customers don't spend as much and they are less likely to repurchase.

Similarly, they are less likely to provide word-of-mouth referrals. Consequently, to keep growing, the firm must spend heavily on marketing, which raises the average cost of acquiring a customer.

Meanwhile, the startup's rapid early growth attracts rivals. Seeking an edge, competitors cut prices and pour money into promotions. At some point, new customers begin to cost more for the startup to acquire than they are worth. As the venture burns through cash, investors become reluctant to commit more capital. In response, the CEO may slam on the brakes, slowing growth and cutting head count to stem cash outflows. The startup may survive, but its share price will plummet, and investors will incur big losses.

Help Wanted. With a Speed Trap, the relentless quest for growth leads to a steady erosion in product-market fit as successive waves of new customers find the startup's offering less appealing. With another late-stage failure pattern, which I've labeled *Help Wanted,* hypergrowth leads to problems of a different kind. These startups do manage to sustain product-market fit while adding legions of new customers. But, as with the early-stage failure pattern Good Idea, Bad Bedfellows, these late-stage startups stumble due to resource shortfalls of two types.

The first relates to *financing risk*. Sometimes an entire industry sector suddenly falls out of favor with venture capital firms, as with biotech in the early 1990s or cleantech in the late 2000s. In the extreme, even healthy startups caught in a downdraft cannot attract new funds: Babies go out with the bathwater. Funding droughts take investors and entrepreneurs by surprise and can last for months or even years. If one of these dry spells commences just as a fast-growing startup is trying to raise a new funding round, and if that startup cannot rapidly reduce its spending, the venture may not survive.

The second type relates to *gaps in the senior management team*. Scaling startups typically need senior executives with deep functional expertise who can manage rapidly expanding pools of employees in engineering, marketing, finance, and operations. Delaying the hiring of these executives or recruiting the wrong individuals can lead to strategic drift, spiraling costs, and a dysfunctional culture.

Cascading Miracles. In marked contrast to ventures that grew rapidly before falling prey to the Speed Trap or Help Wanted failure patterns, some late-stage startups never achieved much traction, despite having raised hundreds of millions of dollars from VCs and having hired hundreds of employees. Each pursued an incredibly ambitious vision, and in doing so faced multiple challenges, including most or all of the following: 1) persuading a critical mass of customers to fundamentally change their behavior; 2) mastering new technologies; 3) partnering with powerful corporations who'd prospered from the status quo; 4) securing regulatory relief or other government support; and 5) raising vast amounts of capital. Each challenge represented a "do or die" proposition: Missing the mark on any of them would doom the venture. Assuming a 50 percent chance of a good outcome for any given challenge, the probability of getting five out of five good outcomes is the same as the odds of picking the winning number in roulette: 3 percent. To win such a gamble, these entrepreneurs were betting on *Cascading Miracles.*

Some late-stage startups that followed the Cascading Miracles pattern were legendary flops, including Iridium, Segway, and Webvan. More recent examples include Joost, a YouTube competitor from Skype's founders; numerous Initial Coin Offerings; and a venture I'll profile, Better Place, whose charging stations for electric cars used robots to rapidly swap depleted batteries with fully charged replacements. Such ventures are often launched by charismatic founders who seduce employees, investors, and strategic partners with an opportunity to help usher in a dazzling future.

With the benefit of hindsight, it's possible to see why startups that relied on Cascading Miracles failed. But in the moment, it can be difficult to determine whether a founder's "change-the-world" vision is delusional. In the early 1970s, for example, many people thought Fred Smith was crazy for trying to raise what at the time was the biggest VC round in history to fund the nascent Federal Express. As I write this, skeptics are asking similar questions about Elon Musk's sanity, and Tesla's long-term viability. There is no foolproof method for avoiding the Cascading Miracles failure pattern, but I'll present some early-warning signs that a late-stage startup might be heading toward this treacherous path.

How to Fail (Better)

My postmortem interviews with founders put the human cost of entrepreneurial failure into sharp focus. In this regard, Quincy Apparel's demise stood out for me. When they launched the company, co-founders Alex Nelson and Christina Wallace vowed not to let conflict over the business threaten their close friendship. Yet two years later, after clashing over whether to shut the company down, they were no longer on speaking terms.

I'd counseled many other entrepreneurs who were deciding whether to call it quits—and had seen the immediate aftermath of that decision. There was always plenty of raw emotion on display in these conversations: anger, guilt, sadness, shame, and resentment. In some cases, I sensed that these founders were in denial; others just seemed depressed. Who could blame them, after having had their dreams dashed, relationships frayed, and self-confidence shattered? Many were also concerned about what the flop would do to their reputation, how they'd pay their bills, and what they'd do next. At ground zero, failure *really* hurts.

Observing these reactions, I wondered if there were ways to mitigate personal pain in the wake of a startup's failure. Part III of the book, "Failing," explores this challenge, shifting the focus from *why* startups fail to *how entrepreneurs handle failure*. Specifically, how can founders preserve relationships when shutting down? And, how can they heal and bounce back from the experience?

One source of needless pain often comes from *Running on Empty*—another startup failure pattern rooted in the fact that the decision to pull the plug on a struggling venture is so nettlesome. Many founders are inclined to persist, past the point where the odds of a turnaround have become minuscule, even though postponing the inevitable is costly for them and those around them. The result: pointlessly burning through capital that investors will never get back. Team members invest time that could be spent searching for a new project. Relationships are strained as pressure mounts, hope dims, and promises are broken.

But how to know when to keep going and when it's time to call it quits? Over the years, dozens of founders have sought my advice about whether their startup showed enough promise to warrant more time and toil. My uncomfortable admission: While I could assess upside potential and downside risk, I couldn't confidently give them an answer. Why was this choice so difficult?

For one, failure is typically a slow-motion affair, with a mix of ups and downs. Growth sputters, and prospective investors hedge with "We need more time to think this over." This can make it difficult to determine whether the situation truly has become hopeless. Similarly, founders are constantly told that great entrepreneurs are gritty and that tenacity pays off. They are fed myths about pivots, and they are reminded of the tenacious founders of Twitter, Slack, and YouTube. These outsize successes were spawned from, respectively, initial failures with podcasting software, a videogame, and a dating site. So, founders are predisposed to slog it out. Hope springs eternal: "Our new product features will surely turn sales around." "Our new marketing VP will crack the code on subscriber acquisition." "Our competitor will fail before we do, and we'll get their customers."

Part III explores how to navigate the decision to pull the plug and offers advice for managing a shutdown once the decision is made. Importantly, we'll look at how founders should approach tough choices that could have serious consequences for their reputation—perhaps even ethical implications. For example, should they run the venture's bank balance down to zero while searching for a new investor, even if running out of cash means not being able to pay employees or vendors who are owed money?

At the same time, founders shouldn't overlook the matter of how to deal with the emotional and professional fallout from failure. My inquiry into this phase of the founder's journey was informed not only by interviews with entrepreneurs but also by psychological research on learning from failure and on coping with loss. Since a founder's identity is inextricably intertwined with her venture's performance, absorbing lessons from the demise of one's own startup is challenging. To gain insight, founders can benefit from techniques that therapists use to help patients manage grief, heal, and find meaning after a life-altering loss. To that end, Part III offers guidance for founders on how to manage their emotions, make sense of what happened, and use that insight to guide them in whatever they do next.

CHAPTER 1

What Is Failure?

The news that Jibo would shut down broke some hearts. Indeed, it was a sad day for many in March 2019 when he announced, "The servers out there that let me do what I do are going to be turned off soon. I want to say that I really enjoyed our time together. Thank you very, very much for having me around. Maybe someday, when robots are way more advanced than today, and everyone has them in their homes, you can tell them that I said hello." Then, for the last time, Jibo did one of his signature dances.

Jibo was a social robot, engineered to create an emotional connection with humans. Spawned in the laboratory of MIT Media Lab professor Cynthia Breazeal, who pioneered the field of social robotics, he had a six-inch-wide stationary conical base that was topped by another cone, and then by a hemispherical head. Each segment of his body could swivel and tilt independently, allowing the twelve-inch-tall robot to move in expressive ways. Jibo could twerk! His head featured a flat touch screen that normally displayed a blinking, glowing white orb, akin to a single eye. The overall design was sleek and minimalist; Jibo wasn't designed to resemble a human, but in many ways he could communicate like one.

Festooned with cameras, microphones, and speakers, Jibo was an engineering marvel with the personality of a clever, helpful twelve-year-old boy. Jibo spoke responses to voice prompts (e.g.,

"Hey Jibo, what's the weather?"), and his screen could also display requested information (e.g., "It's fifty degrees and sunny") or icons for menu options. A blue ring around Jibo's waist lit up when he was listening. The robot also employed sophisticated software that recognized faces and voices. Coupled with his ability to rotate fluidly around his base, these features allowed Jibo to keep his eye directed at an individual as she walked around a room or to turn from one person to another as they conversed.

Jibo could serve up basic information such as news, sports scores, and stock prices. He could tell jokes, play music, set a timer, and read email. But Jibo had other capabilities, too. For example, Jibo was programmed to initiate conversations—say, greeting a family member upon his arrival home ("Hey, Tom, before you left this morning, I warned you that traffic would be heavier than normal. How was your commute?"). He could also interact with a child and display images while reading her a story; take family photos; and, of course, dance on command. More such applications were under development, including the ability to engage a home-alone pet by recognizing that he was in the room and even speaking to him ("Stop chewing that shoe, Rover"). The team was also close to launching a videoconferencing feature that could identify and zoom in on whoever in the room was speaking—perfect for a call to Grandma during a family dinner, if she had a Jibo, too.

For two decades, Breazeal's research teams had studied how robots can provide companionship for the elderly, encourage autistic children to engage in social interaction, and spark collaborative creative learning, among other useful functions. In 2013, she and cofounder Jeri Asher, a healthcare entrepreneur, raised $2.2 million in seed funding to commercialize these inventions. To serve as CEO, they recruited Steve Chambers, then president of Nuance Communications, the leading provider of natural language understanding and speech recognition software.

Because Breazeal's research had shown how social robots could contribute to seniors' emotional wellness, the team initially pitched Jibo as a companion for the elderly. However, mainstream VCs interested in consumer electronics and complex systems like robots weren't interested in the elderly market, and the small set of investors who funded new ventures for aging consumers—accustomed to simpler concepts like cellphones with large keypads—were daunted by the program's technological vision.

So, the team decided to pivot and refocused its pitch on how Jibo could help build family cohesion. The idea was, if Jibo sat in the kitchen, he might spark conversation between, say, squabbling siblings, or surly teenagers and their harried parents. VCs with children could relate to this target consumer, and they were intrigued by cutting-edge consumer hardware in the wake of Facebook's $2.3 billion acquisition of the virtual reality headset maker Oculus Rift—which, like Jibo, was a breakthrough fusion of hardware and software, targeted to consumer markets. And, having witnessed the explosive growth of platforms like Facebook, Amazon, and Salesforce.com, VCs liked that Jibo would be a platform, hosting applications from a wide array of third-party software developers and information services.

Before investing, however, the VCs wanted evidence of market demand for this novel innovation, along with proof that it could actually be built. To gauge consumer interest, the VCs insisted that Jibo launch a crowdfunding campaign, which commenced in July 2014. An Indiegogo campaign allowed consumers to pre-order a Jibo for $599, with delivery slated for "holidays 2015." When the campaign ended three months later, the startup had sold 4,800 units, beating a 3,000-unit goal. Concurrently, to demonstrate that the robot could be built, Jibo's engineering team delivered what Chambers described as "a Frankenbot—a functional but not beautiful prototype." In January 2015, Jibo closed a $27 million Series A round.

Flush with cash, Jibo's team commenced product development in earnest. But engineering the robot turned out to be enormously difficult. After raising another $28 million, they finally launched the product in September 2017—nearly two years late—at a price of $899, 50 percent higher than the Indiegogo offering. Chambers later recounted that when trying to figure out how much extra capital to raise, he'd assumed that the product's component costs and development time might exceed original projections by 2.5x and 2x, respectively. Yet actual component costs and development time each turned out to be 4x greater than projected. Why?

The problem wasn't with manufacturing; in fact, devices with physical components like these had been built before. Chambers explained, "People assume that we had manufacturing problems because the product seemed so novel, but that just wasn't the case. The hardware wasn't cold fusion. We used off-the-shelf screens, motors, sensors, and chipsets that were produced in mass volumes."

Chambers said that the big delays stemmed from two problems. "First, many components included in our original cost analysis weren't adequate to fulfill our vision. We used sensors tuned to office environments, but we learned that lighting in a typical home is very different. Upgrading sensors and adding processing power to run them added to the product's cost."

Second, Jibo's engineers struggled to develop "middleware"— the layer of software that processed inputs from sensors (the robot's "eyes and ears"), made it available to applications, and then sent instructions back to the operating system (essentially Jibo's "brain"). The software had to track faces, localize sounds, detect emotions, generate expressive body motions, and so forth—sophisticated tasks that had to be done in real time. But at the time, cloud services that support real-time interactivity were just arriving on the scene. So, almost all of Jibo's software had to be embedded in the device, along with powerful processors to run it. "We lost more than a year sorting out the right balance between embedded and cloud systems," Chambers recalled.

Then, in May 2017, as Jibo was gearing up for launch, Chambers was diagnosed with leukemia and had to leave the company immediately to undergo emergency treatment. Jibo's CTO moved into the CEO role. After almost a year, Chambers recovered fully, but too late to rejoin his colleagues.

In the meantime, something happened that no one saw coming.

In November 2014 Amazon launched the Echo, its $200 smart speaker, along with the Alexa voice assistant. Now, users who wanted a device that could deliver the news, music, weather, and so forth in response to voice prompts could get that basic functionality at a much lower cost from the Echo.

Customers who wanted companionship and an emotional bond loved Jibo, but there just weren't enough of them to keep Jibo afloat. As a result, year one revenue reached only $5 million, one-third of what Jibo's team had expected. Meanwhile, the startup had burned through its venture capital and couldn't raise more. Management tried to sell the company but couldn't find a buyer willing to continue operating it. Most of Jibo's employees were laid off in June 2018, and the company's intellectual property and other assets were later sold to an investment firm.

So, why did Jibo fail? The immediate cause of death was that Jibo ran out of cash—but that's not terribly helpful. It's like a coroner saying someone died from loss of blood. A better explanation: Jibo couldn't attract enough customers. But this is akin to a forensic investigator saying someone died of a gunshot wound. Was he the victim of a jealous spouse, or was he an innocent bystander during a gang shooting?

Before we can get to the heart of why Jibo failed, we need to ask ourselves what exactly we mean when we say that a startup has failed. The answer is less obvious than it might seem, as I discovered when my students hotly debated whether or not Jibo *was* in fact a failure.

One camp maintained that Jibo had obviously failed because the startup, despite having raised a total of $73 million in venture capital, was unable to generate enough sales after the expensive and long-delayed launch of its product.

Another group acknowledged that Jibo's leaders had made mistakes but believed that the startup's demise had resulted not from mistakes or missteps but rather from misfortune—that is, from events that were difficult to predict and impossible to control—in particular, the launch of Amazon's Echo. These students also argued that Jibo was a "good" failure—one with a bright silver lining—because it paved the way for a new generation of robot companions for the elderly.

A final contingent viewed Jibo as a success despite shutting down because it was a brilliant technological achievement that fulfilled its inventor's vision of a home robot that forged an emotional bond with humans—a unique innovation that delighted many customers.

I saw merit in each of these arguments, and since I didn't have a clear answer, I let the debate rage on. But this classroom experience made one thing clear to me: We needed a standard for labeling a startup a failure.

Defining Entrepreneurial Failure

So, what exactly do we mean when we talk about entrepreneurial failure? How do we define "entrepreneurship," and what constitutes "failure"? Both of these words mean different things to different people.

Who Is an Entrepreneur? Some define entrepreneurship as the earliest stage in an organization's life cycle. For others, it's a reflection of company size. In this view, all small businesses are run by entrepreneurs, and "corporate entrepreneurship" is an oxymoron.

For some, entrepreneurship represents a specific role for an individual; they define an entrepreneurial venture as one that is run by a founder or owner-manager. Yet others view entrepreneurship as a constellation of personality attributes, in particular, a predisposition for risk-taking and an independent streak.

For the past thirty years at Harvard Business School we've defined entrepreneurship as *pursuing novel opportunity while lacking resources*. Entrepreneurs must create and deliver something new—a solution to a customer's problem that's better than, or costs less than, current options. That's the *opportunity*. And, at the outset, entrepreneurs do not have access to all of the *resources*—skilled employees, manufacturing facilities, capital, etc.—required to exploit that opportunity.

This definition views entrepreneurship as a distinctive way of managing, rather than a reflection of a company's age, its size, its leader's role, or the leader's personality. Hence, it rejects the popular notion that every small business is an entrepreneurial venture. After all, once they have matured, many small companies continue to offer only the "same old, same old"—and they have enough talent and capital on hand to do so.

Conversely, this definition allows for the possibility of entrepreneurship within big corporations, government agencies, and nonprofit organizations. For instance, it would classify Amazon's Kindle as an entrepreneurial venture, but not Google Drive. When the Kindle launched, the market for eBook readers was nascent, and Amazon had never before designed or manufactured physical products, so it needed a range of new resources and capabilities. By contrast, Google Drive targeted an existing and maturing market—its rivals Box, Mozy, Carbonite, and Dropbox had all launched years earlier—and Google had ready access to the resources required to enter this market, including marketing channels, data centers, and software engineers galore.

Because they are pursuing a novel opportunity without access to all required resources, entrepreneurs are, by definition, engaged in risky business. Entrepreneurial risk comes in four flavors.

- *Demand risk* relates to the willingness of prospective customers to adopt the envisioned solution. For Jibo: Did consumers in large numbers want a social robot in their home?
- *Technological risk* refers to the complexity of the engineering or scientific breakthroughs required to bring a solution to fruition. For Jibo: Could its engineering team build the crucial middleware layer that processed sensor inputs and application instructions?
- *Execution risk* hinges on the entrepreneur's ability to attract and manage employees and partners who can implement the venture's plans. For Jibo: Would third-party developers build applications before the robot had a big base of users?
- *Financing risk* is relevant when external capital is required.

Will capital be available on reasonable terms? For Jibo: After launch delays consumed its capital reserves, would existing investors commit more funds? Would new investors step in?

What Does It Mean to Fail? Because new ventures confront so much risk, we should expect many to fail. But what exactly does that mean? A standard definition of failure—an outcome that falls short of expectations—is too broad to be useful in identifying startup failures, because it begs two key questions. Which outcomes are pertinent? And, whose expectations are relevant?

When we think about failure, we often think of someone or something with little or no redeeming value. I will *not* use the term "failure" this way. All of the failed startups profiled in this book were conceived by smart and committed entrepreneurs, and all of the ventures showed promise—at least initially. True, all of the entrepreneurs made mistakes, but that doesn't mean they were inept. Far from it—given the uncertainty and resource constraints they face, most entrepreneurs make mistakes. Further, we'll see that some startups fail even when they largely avoid major mistakes. These ventures were smart bets that didn't pay off, and they come in two types. Some were based on plausible assumptions that were rigorously tested and yet ultimately proved untrue. Others were derailed by misfortunes that couldn't have been predicted. Which brings us to a third question: When a venture fails, is someone always at fault?

Which Outcomes Are Pertinent? When a company ceases operations, must it be considered a failure? Shutting down is often a sign of failure—but not always. For example, some entrepreneurs pursue projects that have a finite life span. Two hundred years ago, when agents organized whaling ventures, the captain, crew, boat owner, and financiers would split hoped-for profits from a single voyage. Today, in similar fashion, movie production companies recruit a director, cast, and crew. They shoot a film, edit it, and then disband, hoping for a hit. In cases like these, concluding the project after it has been completed could hardly be considered failure.

Moreover, some startups can melt down without ever shutting down. Bankrupt businesses often continue to operate rather than liquidating all assets. And many startups that don't go bankrupt become "zombies," generating just enough cash to keep going, but never enough to yield a payoff for their original investors.

This insight is central to the definition of entrepreneurial failure that I'll use in this book: *A venture has failed if its early investors did not—or never will—get back more money than they put in.*

Why *early* investors? Because, when a startup fares poorly, later investors may get all of their money back while early investors generally receive less than the full amount they invested—or nothing at all. Explaining why requires a short digression into the workings of venture capital. Startups that raise venture capital typically do so by issuing sequential rounds of preferred stock, labeled Series A, Series B, etc. Each new round of startup equity is generally granted a "liquidation preference" guaranteeing that, in the event of an "exit"— a merger or an initial public offering—shareholders in later rounds will get back their entire investment before shareholders in earlier rounds receive any exit proceeds.

Consequently, investors who hold Series A stock are often near the bottom of a "preference stack," which means that if the total proceeds realized upon exit are less than the total amount of capital a company has raised, the Series A investors will not get all of their money back. In cases where there has not yet been an exit, we can simply ask whether the total value of equity shares—if they could be sold—would be less than the total amount invested.

But what about *bootstrapped* ventures that never raise any equity from outside investors? A bootstrapping entrepreneur's investment equals the sum of 1) his "sweat equity," the gap between what he pays himself and what he could have earned by working elsewhere, and 2) the capital he personally contributed. If this investment exceeds the amount of cash the entrepreneur can ever expect to get back in the form of dividends or merger proceeds, then the venture has failed.

To recap, startups can be considered to have failed under the following conditions:

• *If a startup exited via a merger or an initial public offering,* and total proceeds received from the exit are less than the total amount of equity capital that investors contributed.

• *If a startup is still operating* and early investors would incur a loss upon selling their equity, if they were allowed to do so.

• *If a startup was bootstrapped* and its founder cannot expect to ever take more cash out of the company than the value of capital and sweat equity he contributed.

Whose Expectations Are Relevant? At this point you might be wondering why we use financial returns to investors as the only yardstick for entrepreneurial success and failure. What about founders' goals? After all, most founders are motivated by more than personal wealth. Some strive to invent a game-changing new product; others aspire to disrupt or transform an industry. Some are satisfied to have built a great team; still others simply want to prove they can ride the entrepreneurial roller coaster. If investors lost money but these goals were met, was the venture a success?

In my view, no—because entrepreneurship isn't only about founders and their goals. As a matter of fact, after raising a Series D round, fewer than 40 percent of startups still have a founder as their CEO. I will keep founders' personal goals in sharp focus throughout this book, but we shouldn't use founders' goal fulfillment as our main measure of success.

And what about a new venture's other stakeholders, in particular, employees and customers? Should we consider their expectations when asking if a startup was a failure? For instance, Jibo was so beloved by some owners that many of them, distraught at the loss of their robot companion, held wakes for him. *Wired* reporter Jeffrey Van Camp, who'd written a skeptical review of the robot's launch in late 2017, now wrote, "I've felt crushed knowing that every word the robot says to me could be his last. . . . My wife and I have made it a point to indulge Jibo more. . . . I couldn't help but feel that I owed him a little hospice."

Despite the immense joy that Jibo brought to many customers, however, it was clear that the startup couldn't attract *enough* of those customers, over time, to eventually generate healthy profits. Simply having some happy customers or employees isn't enough to label a startup a success.

Finally, before declaring a startup to be a failure, should we consider the payoff to society at large? This is complicated, because failed startups can generate spillover value that isn't captured by their investors. For example, failed ventures show other entrepreneurs who are trying to solve the same problem what *doesn't* work, thereby helping them avoid similar mistakes and hone their solutions—as Jibo did by providing inspiration and insights for a new wave of social robot startups that target the eldercare market.

Similarly, what about failed startups whose founders learned enough from their mistakes to avoid making such errors again—and perhaps guide others to sidestep them as well? Lots of learning is obviously better than a little learning, and a little learning is better than none at all. However, most entrepreneurs who preside over failed startups learn *something* from the experience, so if learning is what makes a failure a good one, then we'd have to give this label to almost all failed startups.

In theory, a startup could be deemed a success from society's perspective if it lost money for its investors but delivered *positive* spillover benefits to others that more than offset the investors' losses. For example, team members may acquire skills, insights, and experience at failed startups that they can apply elsewhere, like the alumni of GO Corp, a failed 1990s pen-and-tablet computing startup, who famously went on to lead many successful Silicon Valley technology ventures, including Intuit (Bill Campbell), VeriSign (Stratton Sclavos), and LucasArts (Randy Komisar). Conversely, startups that fit this book's definition of success—they made money for their early investors—might cause *negative* spillovers (accelerating ecological damage, exacerbating income inequality, and so forth), making them failures from society's point of view.

In practice, however, it's almost impossible to measure spillovers. So, we'll stick with the "investors lost money" definition of startup failure here, but recognize that from society's perspective, some failures deliver more value than others.

Who's to Blame? When a venture fails, our first instinct is generally to try to figure out what mistakes were made and who made them. But failures can usually be attributed to some combination of *misfortunes* that were outside the control of responsible parties and *mistakes* made by those parties.

Misfortune: Sometimes, a startup's demise is due *mostly* to misfortunes, rather than mistakes. When Covid-19 started paralyzing the U.S. economy, thousands of otherwise healthy new ventures couldn't raise funds and saw sales dry up; the same thing happened during the Great Recession of 2008. Other misfortunes are less universal, impacting only a single industry sector. During the 2000s, for example, clean tech startups were often predicated on rising fossil fuel costs, but the unexpected growth of fracking and the commensurate decline in fuel costs derailed many of those ventures. They were failures, but many were not blameworthy. They were simply smart bets on rising fuel costs that didn't pay off.

In the same spirit, some entrepreneurs get negative results even after running well-conceived and well-executed experiments. For example, following Lean Startup logic, an entrepreneur may formulate hypotheses about an opportunity and then test them rigorously, with minimal waste. If these hypotheses are refuted decisively, the entrepreneur might decide to shut down the venture rather than pivot and continue to test new assumptions. Again, that's a "good" failure, one that's not blameworthy.

However, many assumptions cannot be tested. For example, there is always intrinsic uncertainty about the future health of the economy; rivals' and regulators' behavior; whether a scientific breakthrough will be forthcoming and if so, how long it will take;

how long an investing bubble might float before it bursts; and many other factors. In such circumstances, having researched the issue and consulted experts, all one can do is make well-informed predictions and then hope for the best. An entrepreneur who does this may make no major mistakes. To deliver what's expected, he may assemble the right resources—employees, investors, and partners—but in the end, his core assumptions may simply turn out to have been wrong. This, too, we can categorize not as a mistake but, rather, as a smart bet that didn't work out.

Jibo's team was blindsided by two such misfortunes. The first was the CEO's sudden illness and departure. As investor and board member Jeff Bussgang explained, "The company was dependent on a visionary CEO who could fundraise in the face of long, delayed product development cycles; a market that didn't yet exist; and big competitors. Steve was that CEO and was absolutely brilliant with strategic partners. I believe that if he had remained healthy, Steve would have been able to guide Jibo through the speed bumps."

Second, Amazon's Echo truly came out of the blue. Industry consensus was captured by one tech news site: "Amazon just surprised everyone with a crazy speaker that talks to you." Of course, smartphone makers had been busy building voice assistants, but no one expected this technology to migrate into a stand-alone speaker. Since Jibo was positioned as both an assistant and a companion, this was a serious problem. Jibo suddenly faced a rival voice assistant with a big head start, a much lower price, and deep pockets.

Mistakes: Did Jibo's leadership also make mistakes that contributed significantly to the startup's demise? Probably, but the line between a mistake and a well-reasoned choice can get blurry, and some observers—like my students—might disagree about whether certain key decisions were flawed or, instead, were smart, calculated bets that simply didn't work out.

Consider Jibo's strategy in the wake of Echo's launch. Was it a mistake to continue developing the voice assistant component as originally planned, or should they have doubled down on the companionship features and simply ceded the voice assistant space to rivals? Lacking the ability to track faces, initiate conversations, and move expressively, Alexa, Siri, and Google Home couldn't match Jibo as a companion. But was there a big enough market for an expensive home robot that offered only companionship? And to justify spending $899 on a robot friend, did consumers also need him to be an egg timer and a weatherman? This was a tough decision, and one that the team at Jibo couldn't have anticipated.

Similarly, after the Echo was offered for $200, it seems reasonable to ask whether Jibo could have been redesigned to cost less. Chambers and his team did in fact consider many options along these lines, like whether the robot should have two segments capable of independent motion, rather than three. But as it turned out, the third axis added only $48 to the final price, and extensive testing showed that the expressive movement enabled by three axes versus two made a big difference to consumers. At the behest of their VCs, Jibo's team also considered incorporating the robot's software into a personal computer and shedding his body, but tests revealed that this design had no appeal whatsoever. Chambers concluded, "People like to say Jibo was overengineered. I don't know. He was the only consumer robot that ever really worked."

Did hiring mistakes contribute to Jibo's failure? Again, it's hard to be definitive, but product development was significantly delayed under the startup's first chief robot architect and its VP of development, despite the fact that they'd led advanced research and development teams at iRobot and Palm, respectively, and were highly qualified. Chambers eventually brought in a new chief technology officer who, within a few months, resolved the issues concerning embedded versus cloud architectures. If this CTO had been hired in the first place, instead of the original chief architect, or if the leadership changes had been executed sooner, might Jibo have cut its product development time in half? Maybe, but it also seems possible that anyone hired to lead Jibo's development would have needed to wrestle with messy engineering challenges for two years before solving them.

As with most failed startups, Jibo's demise was likely due to a mix of misfortune *and* missteps. In later chapters, we'll look closely at whether, what, and how entrepreneurs can learn from conducting a postmortem analysis of where and why they erred.

Horses and Jockeys

Entrepreneurs, investors, and academics often explain failure in one of two ways. The first emphasizes flawed venture concepts (i.e., "horses"), while the other focuses on founders (i.e., "jockeys") whose abilities didn't match the needs of their startup or who simply were inept. While there's support for both views, I would argue that an emphasis on horses or jockeys is not sufficient to explain why startups fail.

Blame the Horse? Not surprisingly, many founders are not inclined to admit that their own shortcomings led to their startup's failure. Instead, they point to problems outside of their control. For example, in a survey of failed founders, the top two reasons cited were "too much competition" and "changing market conditions."

It's reasonable to ask whether founders should be blamed for entering an overcrowded market in the first place. Perhaps, but it's often the case that a flurry of startups are drawn simultaneously to an emerging opportunity—as with food delivery, legal cannabis, and drones. Consequently a startup can have trouble predicting how many rivals it will ultimately face. In any case, given our penchant for attribution errors—that is, blaming our own failures on uncontrollable circumstances and others' failures on their personal faults—we should interpret founders' explanations for startup failure with care.

While most investors blame bad jockeys for startup failure, some see slow horses as the main problem. For example, billionaire entrepreneur and investor Peter Thiel says that "all failed companies are the same: they failed to escape competition." Paul Graham, founder of the elite accelerator Y Combinator, likewise holds that having a compelling solution to a customer's problem—a strong horse—is the key to success: "There's just one mistake that kills startups: not making something users want. If you make something users want, you'll probably be fine, whatever else you do or don't do. And if you don't make something users want, then you're dead, whatever else you do or don't do."

While these points are persuasive, explanations asserting that flawed venture concepts are the leading cause of startup failure do beg two questions. First, since jockeys pick their horses in the entrepreneurial race, shouldn't we question the jockey's judgment for selecting a slow horse? In other words, shouldn't entrepreneurs be faulted for failing to spot a flawed concept in advance? Second, if an entrepreneur discovers that his idea has shortcomings after it launches, why not pivot to a better one? Venture concepts are fluid, and, unlike a real-life jockey, a founder can change horses mid-race.

Blame the Jockey? So, are poor jockeys the main cause of a startup's demise? Many investors seem to think so. In a survey of venture capital partners, the top two reasons cited for startup failure were weak senior management and weak functional management. In another survey in which VCs were asked to identify differences between successful and failed startups, two of the three patterns that emerged pointed to management flaws. With the first pattern (accounting for 19 percent of failures, according to the survey), the senior team had adequate experience and market knowledge but no capacity for sustained effort, so they threw in the towel prematurely. With the second pattern (accounting for 49 percent of failures), the managers were perceived to be "hapless amateurs, inadequate in every way." The third pattern echoes Peter Thiel's point: For 32 percent of the failures, management had adequate market knowledge but never found competitive advantage.

If jockeys make all the difference, then some must be more skilled than others. There is some academic evidence for this. Research by my HBS colleagues Paul Gompers, Josh Lerner, and David Scharfstein and their former student Anna Kovner shows that 30 percent of serial entrepreneurs who were successful in their first venture succeeded in subsequent ventures, compared to 22 percent of serial entrepreneurs who failed in their first venture and 21 percent of first-time founders. These differences suggest that learning from experience isn't decisive. If it were, then unsuccessful serial entrepreneurs would presumably succeed with their second or third ventures at a substantially higher rate than first-time founders.

There are two possible explanations for why serial entrepreneurs whose first startup was a success are more likely to succeed again. First, prior to founding their initial venture, some serial entrepreneurs may have had advantages that other first-timers lacked: better skills or superior access to resources—perhaps due to their gender, race, or socioeconomic background. Second, funding and talent tend to flow to entrepreneurs with a track record of success, making the assumption that they'll succeed again a self-fulfilling prophecy. These explanations are not mutually exclusive; both could be true.

In what ways might some entrepreneurs be more skilled than others? They may have superior general ability—raw intellect, resilience, etc.—or they may have a wealth of relevant industry experience. These attributes are also not mutually exclusive.

General ability: The notion that successful entrepreneurs are simply smarter or psychologically better suited for the role than their failed counterparts has intuitive appeal. Unfortunately, researchers aren't much in agreement about this. In fact, certain qualities typically associated with successful founders, such as a very high level of confidence, might also increase entrepreneurs' odds of failure—a possibility we'll explore in later chapters.

Industry experience: Unsurprisingly, research shows that prior industry experience improves the odds of entrepreneurial success. Put simply, entrepreneurs with industry experience are better equipped to spot opportunities and formulate successful strategies for exploiting them. We'll explore the impact of industry experience in Chapter 3, when we examine the failure of Quincy Apparel.

In general, we should expect higher odds of failure for founders who are overconfident and who lack industry expertise. But it's important to note that these factors merely influence the *likelihood* of entrepreneurial success or failure. Entrepreneurs with pitch-perfect confidence and deep domain experience will still be vulnerable to the failure patterns described in this book—and must work hard to anticipate and avoid them. Moreover, as with analysis suggesting that flawed venture concepts are the chief cause of startup failure, explanations that focus on founders' shortcomings—poor jockeys—leave some questions unanswered. In particular, is it possible to spot an entrepreneur's shortcomings *before* he launches his company? For example, how does one distinguish between unwarranted over-confidence and the energy and enthusiasm that most founders bring to their ventures?

Horse, Jockey, or Both? How do we sort through these compet-ing claims about the factors behind startup failure that entrepre-neurs, investors, and academics have put forth? It's obvious that success is more likely when you have both a fast horse *and* a skilled jockey. Furthermore, as noted above, jockeys select their own horses in the startup race, so it's ultimately difficult to untangle the quality of a venture concept from the skill of its founding team.

In the end, I don't think horse versus jockey debates are particu-larly helpful. They provide a starting point, but they are oversimpli-fied ways of assigning blame. Oversimplification indulges our penchant for attributing a calamity to a single cause, when in fact many factors are at play. We'll examine those diverse factors more closely in the next chapter.

So, back to Jibo—was it a failure? Yes, by this book's definition: Early investors lost money. Could we label Jibo's failure a smart bet that didn't pay off? Yes, I believe we can. Some observers might con-strue management's decisions about product positioning and key senior hires to have been mistakes, but to my eye, these decisions were well considered. Furthermore, as befits its genesis in an MIT laboratory, the venture had many attributes of a well-run experi-ment: Jibo's team conducted extensive early research—focus groups, prototype testing, etc.—to validate demand and refine the robot. And, the venture was hit by a couple of big bolts out of the blue: the type of misfortune that's hard to foresee when making a smart bet.

Finally, was Jibo a "good failure," in the sense that society will ultimately benefit from insights gleaned from the venture? It's too soon to say, but Jibo is already the model for the next generation of eldercare robots. And, as Jibo said of social robots in his farewell message, I believe we'll see a day when "everyone has them in their homes."

PART I

LAUNCHING

CHAPTER 2

Catch-22

As I explained in the previous chapter, an entrepreneur is someone who pursues a novel opportunity while lacking resources. For early-stage startups—defined here as those that are less than three years old—this dynamic creates a Catch-22 situation, that is, a logical impasse equivalent to "You can't get a job without experience, and you can't get experience without a job."

From the outset, a founder is short on some, if not all, of the resources necessary to exploit a novel opportunity. These may include co-founders, team members with certain specialized skills, outside investors, and strategic partners who can provide technology or distribution. To mobilize the missing resources, the entrepreneur must convince multiple parties that committing to the new venture, with all its attendant risks, will deliver an attractive payoff.

Hence, the Catch-22: *A founder cannot pursue a novel opportunity in any meaningful way without resources, and she can't attract resources until she's actually pursued the opportunity*—at least to the point where she can demonstrate to resource owners that the risks are reasonable. To break through this impasse, early-stage entrepreneurs can employ one or more of four tactics to *reduce resource requirements* while respectively *resolving, shifting, deferring,* or *downplaying opportunity-related risks.* However, as I'll explain here and in the chapters that follow, every one of these tactics contains some potentially destructive downsides.

Tactic 1: Lean Experiments (Resolving Risk). Using minimum viable products that minimize resource commitments, founders can validate their assumptions about an opportunity and resolve uncertainty about the new venture's viability. As we'll soon see with clothing retailer Quincy, positive results for MVP tests can be persuasive when employees or investors are deciding whether to commit to a new venture.

- **The Hazards:** In their zeal to get started, early-stage entrepreneurs are vulnerable to *false starts*—that is, to bypassing crucial early research that informs their understanding of customer needs and whether their envisioned solution will meet them. We'll see this happen in Chapter 4 with Triangulate, a failed online dating service.

   Because we are primed to see what we want to see, founders are also prone to *false positives*—for example, early outcomes that suggest an opportunity is more attractive than it really is. We'll explore false positives and how to avoid them in Chapter 5, which profiles Baroo, a failed pet care startup.

Tactic 2: Partnering (Shifting Risk). Entrepreneurs may be able to "rent" resources from a strategic partner—for example, access to technology or distribution networks. The partner is often an established corporation that, by virtue of its greater scale and deeper pockets, is better able to bear risk than the startup.

- **The Hazards:** For early-stage startups that lack a track record and have dubious survival prospects, signing up strategic partners can be difficult; so can aligning both parties' interests once a partner has signed. As we'll see in the next chapter, Quincy struggled to get good service from its factory partners. Likewise, Chapter 5 will describe how Baroo's founder was disappointed with apartment building partnerships that were meant to steer tenants to her pet care startup.

Tactic 3: Staging (Deferring Risk). Venture capital–backed startups raise capital in stages, often taking in just enough funding in each round to meet their next set of major milestones, such as completing product development or launching the product. This approach defers risks because if the startup fails to meet a key milestone, investors can pull the plug and avoid future outlays.

- **The Hazards:** Entrepreneurs who struggle to raise initial funding—especially first-time founders who lack a track record—may take money from investors who don't add much value, whose preferences regarding risk/reward trade-offs are not aligned with those of the founders, and who lack the means to provide additional capital should the venture stumble. We'll see in the next chapter that Quincy's founders experienced all three of these problems with their lead investors.

Tactic 4: Storytelling (Downplaying Risk). By propagating a "reality distortion field"—that is, mesmerizing potential employees, investors, and strategic partners so they focus on a startup's world-changing potential rather than on its real-world risks—overconfident and charismatic founders in particular are able to persuade people to commit resources under terms favorable to their new venture. For strategic partners, this might mean granting the startup exclusive access to proprietary technology and forgoing the opportunity to license it to better-established companies. For employees, it might mean a willingness to work long hours or accept a below-market salary in exchange for the upside of stock options.

- **The Hazard:** A reality distortion field can reverse itself. Rather than bending reality to their will, overconfident founders may fail to perceive signals that their vision is a pipe dream. We'll see some examples of this in Part II, which examines failure patterns among late-stage startups—including Better Place, which lost $900 million trying to build a network of recharging stations for electric cars. An entrepreneur's reality distortion field can have a colossal negative impact on a late-stage startup that has hundreds of employees and hundreds of millions of dollars in invested capital. But early-stage entrepreneurs are at risk of self-delusion, too.

The Diamond-and-Square Framework

Armed with these tactics for avoiding the opportunity/resource Catch-22, an entrepreneur should be able to manage risk in ways that make it possible to attract enough resources to get started. But how can an aspiring entrepreneur know whether she has actually identified an *attractive* opportunity and determine what *types* of resources are required to successfully capitalize upon it? The *diamond-and-square framework* provides the answers. The framework's diamond breaks down the startup's *opportunity*—that is, the "horse"—into four constituent parts: its customer value proposition, technology and operations, marketing, and profit formula. The diamond is framed by a square whose corners denote the venture's key *resource providers:* its founders (that is, the "jockeys"), other team members, outside investors, and strategic partners.

An early-stage startup has promising prospects when the eight elements of the diamond-and-square framework are in alignment— that is, when they work together harmoniously. Furthermore, alignment must be *dynamic:* As the startup matures, its opportunity will evolve, as will the nature of the support needed from resource providers.

Misalignment can happen in various ways, and the diamond-and-square framework can be instrumental in identifying what's gone wrong. In some cases, elements within the diamond may be out of whack. For example, with a weak value proposition, a startup must spend more on marketing to attract customers, which in turn can cripple its profit formula. Likewise, the square's elements may not be synchronized. As we'll see in the next chapter, Quincy struggled because its team and investors failed to bolster co-founders who lacked apparel industry experience. Finally, diamond-and-square elements may be in conflict, as when Jibo's customer value

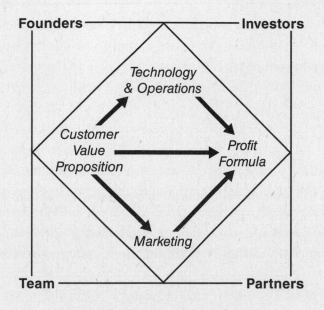

The Diamond-and-Square Framework

proposition and profit formula weren't strong enough to attract additional capital from investors.

I'll be using the diamond-and-square framework in the next three chapters to lay out a postmortem analysis of startups that fell victim to each of the early-stage failure patterns. But first, let's look at the framework's elements in greater detail.

Opportunity Elements

Customer Value Proposition

Of the four opportunity elements, an early-stage startup's customer value proposition is without question the most important. To survive, a new venture absolutely must offer a sustainably differentiated solution for strong, unmet customer needs. This point bears repeating: *Needs* must be strong. If an unknown startup's product doesn't address an acute pain point, customers aren't likely to buy it. Likewise, *differentiation* is crucial: If the venture's offering is not superior in meaningful ways to existing solutions, again, no one will buy it. Finally, *sustaining* this differentiation is important. Without barriers to imitation, the venture is vulnerable to copycats.

Such barriers—called "moats" by some entrepreneurs—come in two types: *proprietary assets* and *business model attributes*. Proprietary assets are either difficult to duplicate or are in scarce supply. Examples include trusted brand names, patents, a great location for a retail store, and preemptive access to a key raw material—like Beyond Burger's long-term contract locking up a large percentage of the world's supply of pea protein. Business model attributes are those that can confer an advantage in attracting and retaining customers, like high customer switching costs and strong network effects.

• **Switching costs** aren't just financial expenditures; they can also include inconveniences and risks incurred when a customer changes from one vendor to another. Consider, for example, the costs and risks when switching dog walkers. A family must trust the new walker with keys to their residence, must brief the new walker on their pet's patterns and preferences, and run the risk that their dog may not take to this new human in its life. Switching costs can be a double-edged sword. For example, to attract customers, Baroo had to overcome these barriers. However, once it did, Baroo retained customers because they faced the high cost of switching to a competitor.

• With **network effects,** a product becomes more valuable to any given user as it adds more users. Online dating is a prime example: A site that offers access to a greater number of potential romantic partners has more appeal. Due to strong network effects in online dating, startups like Triangulate struggle at the outset to attract users—another Catch-22, because they need users in order to get users. But if they can gain momentum, a flywheel kicks in, as new users attract more new users. After they reach critical mass, such businesses have an edge over rivals in attracting and retaining customers.

An early-stage startup has three important choices to make regarding its customer value proposition—choices that will have a big impact on its odds for success:

1. Target a Single Customer Segment? Upon launch, some ventures target multiple customer segments, each with distinct needs. For example, Jibo was aimed at consumers looking for functional utility from a voice assistant—managing a calendar, providing weather and traffic reports, etc.—*and* at those who sought companionship. More typically, startups focus on a single segment when they commence operations. Quincy, for example, elected to target young professional women, but not college students who'd need a work wardrobe after graduating.

Entrepreneurs face trade-offs when deciding how many segments to target initially. Obviously, a startup has the potential to earn more revenue if it can successfully sell to multiple segments. But creating a single product that meets the different needs of multiple segments can result in a bloated, unfocused offering—one that aims to be all things to all people but does not delight anyone. Likewise, marketing to multiple customer segments can be difficult and expensive because promotional messages must be tailored for each segment.

An alternative to targeting multiple segments with a single product is creating separate versions of the product, each with different features and branding. This solution takes care of positioning problems but boosts costs and complexity. Either approach to serving multiple customer segments—relying on one product or separate versions—poses the risk of product development delays, which can be detrimental, especially in fast-moving technology markets.

Many startups target a single segment upon launch because it speeds their time to market, and, by catering to a single segment's needs, allows them to capture a bigger share of a smaller market. It's easier to defend a stronghold like that and to expand from it. After launching, the startup can then try to modify its product and/or marketing approach in an effort to reach additional customer segments. We'll see examples of this kind of expansion in Part II.

	Single Segment	Multiple Segments
Benefits	• Quicker to market • Higher market share: easier to defend/expand from a stronghold	• More potential revenue
Risks	• Less potential revenue	• Too much complexity • Bloated, unfocused offering • Product development delays • Need to market to multiple segments

2. **How Much Innovation?** When designing their first product, founders must decide how much to innovate. Some entrepreneurs believe that more innovation is always better, but as we'll see, that mindset can get them in trouble.

Entrepreneurial innovation comes in three flavors: 1) *new business models,* as with Rent the Runway offering apparel for rent rather than sale; 2) *new technologies,* as with Solyndra, a failed maker of cylindrical solar panels built with a proprietary thin-film material; and 3) *combining existing technologies in new ways,* as with Quincy Apparel using a measurement system akin to that used for men's suiting to offer better-fitting clothing for women.

Some forms of innovation require changes in customer behavior. Such changes may incur switching costs: Consumers must learn how to use a new type of product and perhaps bear the risk that an unproven solution won't deliver on its promises. So, when innovation requires a change in behavior, the value delivered to customers must outweigh any switching costs they'll incur. For example, Quincy's innovation was clever because it promised a big benefit—better-fitting clothes—in exchange for a small change in customer behavior. Women were already accustomed to buying clothing online; they simply had to provide Quincy with a few additional body measurements, so their switching costs were minimal.

Often, applying new, innovative technology requires no change at all to customer behavior; customers can continue to exactly do what they've been doing, while enjoying lower cost, higher speed, or better reliability. For example, the original iPhone relied on Wi-Fi access points for location finding, which were less accurate than GPS. But once GPS chips were added to second-generation iPhones, consumers didn't need to change the way they used their iPhone or map applications in order to get better directions—the transition was seamless.

Customers are drawn to products that balance novelty with familiarity, so innovation poses a Goldilocks trade-off for entrepreneurs. Without enough of it, a startup's product will not be meaningfully differentiated from those of existing competitors. A startup that offers a "middling mousetrap"—rather than a better one—probably will fail. At the other extreme, a startup that attempts too much innovation can overshoot customers' needs. It will incur major marketing costs in an effort to persuade customers to try its radical solution. And it will risk product development delays if the innovation requires technological and engineering breakthroughs. By pioneering a fundamentally new product category—social robots for the home—Jibo confronted such challenges.

	Less Innovation	More Innovation
Benefits	• Low switching costs	• High differentiation
Risks	• Lack of differentiation	• Overshoot customer needs • High switching cost • Product development delays • High marketing costs

3. **Low- or High-Touch Solution?** Some startups offer a "one-size-fits-all" solution with bare-bones service; others deliver a more customized product with concierge-style service. Let's label these approaches "low touch" and "high touch," respectively. To contrast the two approaches, consider two different online services that help families find childcare providers. Care.com is a low-touch service: It provides access to an enormous list of providers but has parents do

the work of filtering the search results, reviewing profiles, and then contacting and interviewing candidates—time-consuming and anxiety-inducing tasks. Poppy, a failed startup we'll encounter in later chapters, offered a high-touch, "on-demand" solution for parents with ad hoc childcare requirements. If, for example, their regular nanny was on vacation, parents could simply text their request and a carefully vetted, trained childcare provider—a Mary Poppins on demand—would show up at their door. No need for the parents to screen the provider's qualifications.

For an entrepreneur, deciding whether to develop a low- or high-touch solution involves weighing a number of trade-offs. Because low-touch solutions are standardized—they look the same for every customer—they can be scaled up more readily. Standardization also facilitates automation, so the low-touch product can be delivered at a lower cost. That's imperative, because a low-touch solution, by its nature, lacks differentiation, and therefore cannot command a big price premium.

By contrast, a high-touch solution can charge a price premium because customers are understandably willing to pay more for 1) a solution that's customized to their specific needs, as with Quincy's better-fitting apparel; and/or 2) a solution that provides superior service, as with Poppy's ability to accommodate last-minute requests. That greater revenue is necessary to cover the extra costs incurred in delivering a high-touch solution. However, startups that offer a high-touch solution sometimes confront operational challenges that extra revenue cannot solve—and that preclude rapid scaling. Poppy, for example, found that a scarce supply of well-qualified care providers put the brakes on its plans to expand. Ultimately, Poppy could not achieve the scale that its founder aspired to, and she shut the startup down.

	Low Touch	High Touch
Benefits	• Easier to scale • Lower operating costs	• High differentiation • Commands price premium
Risks	• Lack of differentiation • Cannot command price premium	• Operational challenges • Difficult to scale • Higher operating costs

Technology & Operations

To survive, a startup must be able to fulfill its value promise, which entails actually inventing the product, building it, physically delivering it, and servicing it after it's been sold. Poor execution of any of these tasks can kill a venture.

Beyond the imperative for solid execution, most startups confront only one "do or die" decision about their technology and operations: whether to outsource key activities or undertake them internally. For example, an entrepreneur might face choices about whether to equip a new warehouse or instead rent an existing facility; whether to outsource customer service to a third-party call center operator; and whether to build software applications in-house or hire a contractor.

Such decisions involve significant risk, because a new venture's first investment round often provides just enough capital to run the business for twelve to eighteen months. If it takes four months to figure out that outsourcing product development to a contractor was a big mistake, and another three months to recruit a team of engineers to do that work in-house, an entrepreneur could have burned through half of the capital she raised—with little progress to show and no margin for additional errors.

The trade-offs inherent in these "build versus buy" decisions can be vexing. Developing capability internally can be slow and expensive, and it adds to organizational complexity. Outsourcing promises faster access to resources, usually with less fixed, up-front investment. But for a fledging startup, partners aren't always easy to come by. Internal development, on the other hand, may allow a startup to earn higher profits if its costs would match those of an outside vendor, since the vendor would charge a price that not only covers its costs but also tacks on some profit margin. Internal development avoids paying that profit margin and has two other big advantages: The startup can maintain control of mission-critical capabilities, and it can tailor activities to its specific needs. Later in this chapter, we'll explore the specific challenges that early-stage startups confront when seeking strategic partnerships.

	Build Technology & Operations	Buy Technology & Operations
Benefits	• Potentially higher profits • Control of mission-critical activities • Tailor activities to venture's needs	• Faster access to resources • Lower fixed, up-front investment
Risks	• Slow and expensive • Lack know-how • Operational complexity	• Less control • Challenging to find reliable partners

Marketing

Clearly, a new venture must make potential customers aware of what it's offering. On this front, the crucial decision for early-stage startups is how much to spend on marketing. It's another Goldilocks dilemma: Too little or too much can each have fatal consequences. Consider two extremes:

• **Build It and They Will Come.** This approach assumes that a great product will sell itself, specifically, that word-of-mouth referrals will spread virally and that press mentions will drive early customer acquisition. There are two advantages with this approach. First, minimizing its spending on marketing allows a startup to conserve scarce cash. Also, customers are typically more loyal when they've been acquired "organically"—that is, when they've sought out a product rather than being drawn to it through advertising.

But what if you build it and *no one* comes? VC Marc Andreessen commented on this possibility: "The number one reason that we pass on entrepreneurs we'd otherwise like to back is focusing on product to the exclusion of everything else. We tend to cultivate and glorify this mentality in the Valley. But the dark side is that it gives entrepreneurs excuses not to do the hard stuff of sales and marketing. Many entrepreneurs who build great products simply don't have a good distribution strategy. Even worse is when they insist that they don't need one or call no distribution strategy a 'viral marketing strategy.' "

There are some great products that, at the outset, do spread virally with no investment in advertising or other paid marketing tactics. Dropbox, Twitter, Pinterest, Instagram, and YouTube all come to mind. But such products are rare exceptions—we don't call them "unicorns" for nothing—and entrepreneurs should be wary of assuming they can follow that path. Also, no *paid* marketing by these viral hits doesn't mean *no marketing*. If you dig deeper, you'll invariably find that the startup invested manpower, if not capital, in dreaming up and executing savvy moves to stoke virality. For example, the video that Drew Houston made to introduce Dropbox was full of inside jokes for super-nerds (e.g., references to TPS reports from the movie *Office Space* or the 09 F9 key for decrypting Blu-Ray discs—a hacker crusade). These nerds became early adopters of Dropbox and then served as unpaid apostles for the product—as well as free tech support.

• **"Big Bang" Launch.** At the height of the late 1990s dot-com boom, startups often launched their products with massive advertising and public relations campaigns. That approach is less fashionable today, but we still see early-stage startups spending heavily on marketing, right out of the gate. A big, splashy launch, if it works, can propel a startup to a dominant position in a new market. But it's risky for a venture to invest aggressively in marketing before it has "product-market fit"—that is, before its product meets market needs and can be built and sold at a profit, at least in the long term. If demand turns out to be lower than expected, founders may pivot to a new value proposition, which will likely baffle existing customers. Heavy marketing investments made prior to a pivot are worse than wasted: They actually hurt the startup by confusing and alienating its existing and prospective customer base. Consistent with this risk, the Startup Genome Project, a research effort that surveyed the management practices of early-stage startups, concluded that premature scaling of marketing and product development efforts is a widespread cause of startup failure.

	Less Paid Marketing	More Paid Marketing
Benefits	• Conserve cash • More loyal customers	• Faster growth
Risks	• Failure to reach customers	• High cost • Wasted efforts if startup pivots

Profit Formula

A venture's profit formula is its plan for making money: How much revenue will it earn and what costs will it incur? In the profit formula, revenue and cost are each broken down into component parts. Revenue depends on the product's price and the number of units sold. Costs come in several types, each with different drivers. For example, *variable costs,* such as the components used to build each Jibo, increase in direct proportion to the number of units sold. *Marketing costs* vary with the number of new customers acquired. *Overhead expenses,* like executive salaries or office rent for the headquarters staff, are fixed—at least over the short term.

An entrepreneur doesn't really make decisions about her profit formula. Rather, the choices she makes about the other three elements of the venture's opportunity—its Customer Value Proposition, Technology & Operations, and Marketing—dictate revenue and costs. These decisions collectively determine who the venture will serve and in what numbers, how it will price its product, how it will attract new customers, whether it will employ a "high-touch" service approach and incur commensurate costs, and so forth.

A startup's long-term economic viability hinges on its performance with respect to many different metrics—but the following three are more critical than others:

• **Unit Economics:** When investors ask about a startup's "unit economics," they want to know how much profit the company will earn per unit sold. The relevant unit will differ by business. For example, for a manufacturer like Jibo, the unit would be the sale of one robot. A subscription service like Netflix or Spotify might track profit per subscriber per month. Note that "profit" in this context is defined as *gross profit*—that is, revenue per unit minus all variable costs directly incurred in producing and delivering the unit (for example, the cost to manufacture a single unit, warehouse labor for packing a unit, the cost of shipping each unit, fees paid to credit card companies on each unit, etc.). *Not* factored into the equation are marketing costs, allocations for overhead expenses, interest payments on debt, or income taxes. Deduction of these items would yield *net profit*.

Essentially, analysis of a startup's unit economics asks how much cash the firm earns—or loses—from a typical transaction. For a healthy business, cash earned per transaction multiplied by the number of transactions will yield sufficient total cash flow to cover 1) marketing costs and overhead expenses; 2) investments that must be made to support further growth—say, in inventory or factory equipment; 3) interest payments on any debt; 4) taxes; and 5) adequate profit for equity investors—that is, enough to encourage them to provide more capital, if needed. Since every business is different, we can't generalize about an amount of cash per transaction that would be "healthy." But a business that loses money on every transaction is probably in trouble—unless its managers have a clear plan for reversing the losses.

• **LTV/CAC Ratio:** A customer's lifetime value (LTV) equals the discounted present value of the gross profit earned over the life of a typical customer's relationship with the venture. "Discounted present value" accounts for the fact that a dollar received in the future isn't as valuable as a dollar received today, because you can put today's dollar in the bank and earn some interest until the future dollar arrives. Essentially, LTV deducts these forgone interest payments from future dollars earned.

Customer acquisition cost (CAC) reflects the average marketing cost incurred in acquiring a typical customer. An LTV/CAC ratio below 1.0 implies that a customer is worth less than it cost to bring her on board. If a startup's LTV/CAC ratio remains below 1.0 for an extended period, it is probably doomed because it won't earn enough gross profit to cover fixed overhead costs and earn a net profit. For this reason, many startups target an LTV/CAC ratio greater than three.

• **Break-even Point:** The LTV/CAC ratio is a key performance measure, but it's important to remember that cash flow from customers is earned over time, whereas the cost of acquiring customers is incurred up front. This implies that a startup with a healthy LTV/CAC ratio that is aggressively expanding its customer base could be burning through its capital reserves rapidly, meaning it may be at risk of violating the cardinal rule of entrepreneurship: Don't run out of cash!

To guard against that outcome, entrepreneurs need reliable cash flow projections, along with an understanding of when their startup will turn the corner and start generating, as opposed to consuming, cash. In other words, a startup has to reach its cash flow break-even point. That occurs when the venture's sales volume generates enough gross profit to cover all of its tax payments, marketing expenses, fixed costs, and new investments (e.g., additional equipment and inventory required to support the next wave of expansion).

My survey of early-stage founders shows that mastery of these profit formula metrics can improve a venture's odds for success (see Appendix for details). Founder/CEOs leading struggling startups were much less confident than their more successful counterparts in their estimates of unit economics, LTV/CAC ratios, and six-month cash flow projections.

Resource Elements

The four elements described above—the "diamond" in the diamond-and-square framework—collectively specify the *opportunity:* what the venture will offer and to whom; its plan for technology and operations; its marketing approach; and how the venture will make money. To capture this opportunity, the venture will need the right *resources* in the right amounts.

The "square" in the diamond-and-square framework specifies the four types of resource providers whose contributions are important for success in most startups. They include the venture's founders, other team members, outside investors, and strategic partners who may provide key technologies, operational capabilities, or access to distribution channels.

These four "square" elements should complement one another, so that an abundance of one resource can compensate for shortfalls of another. For example, a founder who lacks industry experience can be supported by senior team members or by investors who have such experience.

Founders

As I explained in the last chapter, *founder fit* can have a decisive impact on venture outcomes. Likewise, co-founder conflict can tear a startup apart. Some co-founders jointly conceive a venture concept and work together right from the start. Many other startups have one founder who was the sole "idea person"—she alone had the original insight to pursue the opportunity. This founder often recruits others to the founding team.

Whether the team was together from the start or it was assembled over time, there comes a time when both founders and investors should ask: Given the nature of the venture's opportunity and the capabilities of its original founders, should they recruit additional co-founders and/or jettison any current co-founders? When considering these decisions, three dimensions are especially important: industry experience, functional experience, and temperament.

- **Industry Experience.** Prior industry experience is more important in some settings than others. For example, it was clear to Jibo's co-founders that developing the robot and bringing it to market would pose a range of challenges beyond their capabilities, so they recruited as CEO Steve Chambers, a seasoned technology executive. But prior industry experience is not always a decisive factor. In the next chapter, I'll explore settings that make industry expertise important.

- **Functional Experience.** Founding teams should also have the right mix of business acumen and technical skills relevant to the opportunity the startup is pursuing. Shorthand often used for this kind of team is "hacker and hustler": referring to a talented engineer (hacker) and to someone with business know-how, especially the ability to sell (hustler). Of course, a founding team can compensate for any gaps by hiring senior managers with relevant skills.

A red flag: Beware founding teams whose members all have similar training and functional experience. Startups launched at business schools often fit this profile.

- **Temperament.** It takes a lot of confidence to be an entrepreneur who is setting out to do something that's never been done before. It's well documented that, when compared to members of the general public, entrepreneurs are, on average, more overconfident—that is, more likely to overestimate the accuracy of their predictions about uncertain outcomes. Fortunately, many attributes of highly confident founders improve the odds of startup success. For example, confidence fuels *resilience,* which is crucial for founders as they board the entrepreneurial roller coaster. Likewise, founders who project confidence are more persuasive when they pitch their vision to prospective employers and investors.

But as we'll see again and again, *too much* confidence can leave an entrepreneur vulnerable to taking on too much risk, especially when her passion prevents her from grasping the grim reality of her situation. At the other extreme, a founder's lack of confidence can also doom her venture, making it difficult to attract employees and investors. So, a founder's level of confidence should ideally lie somewhere on the middle of a spectrum that has *Too Headstrong* at one end and *Too Tentative* at the other. Either extreme can have fatal consequences.

Tentative founders—who may be short on self-confidence, lack passion for their concept, or underestimate the effort and stress associated with the founder role—will throw in the towel much more quickly than their headstrong counterparts. Job candidates and investors will sense their ambivalence and lack of a clear vision. The venture's strategy may drift as the founder "blows with the wind," repeatedly shifting course based on advice coming at her from different directions.

On the other hand, headstrong founders who are overconfident about an opportunity's attractiveness and/or their ability to compete are prone to launch ventures with too little capital, underestimate competition, and overstate their capability. If they survive the launch phase, headstrong founders, convinced that their original plan is sound, may be reluctant to pivot away from a flawed opportunity to what impartial observers would perceive as a better one. Headstrong founders can also be tough to work with. They may be defensive, judgmental (seeing colleagues as either heroes or idiots), reluctant to delegate, inclined to ignore advice, or insistent on "doing it my way." These behaviors can make it difficult for the venture to recruit and retain talented team members.

Given these risks, entrepreneurs should avoid bringing on or keeping founding team members positioned too far to either extreme on the headstrong-to-tentative spectrum. It's also important to ask, are co-founders' dispositions complementary? Two headstrong co-founders, for example, might repeatedly clash in dysfunctional ways, whereas a headstrong founder and tentative founder might balance each other out.

So, how does one figure out whether a founder is overconfident? Often, it's as simple as looking for signs like a lack of humility, a reluctance to listen, and defensiveness or inflexibility when challenged. One could ask a founder's former colleagues about her past behavior, but that's a double-edged sword: While she might have been problematic before, she could have learned from her mistakes. We'll see in Part III that some failed entrepreneurs are capable of self-reflection that leads them to change their management styles.

	Headstrong Founders	Tentative Founders
Benefits	• Resilience • Ability to attract investors	• Thorough risk assessment • Avoid impulsive decision-making
Risks	• Overconfidence about prospects • Can be arrogant, defensive, difficult to work with	• Lack of passion • Lack of persistence • Challenges with attracting employees and investors

Team

If other elements in the diamond-and-square framework are aligned, a weak team is unlikely to deal a death blow to a venture. But if the other elements are out of whack, then a weak team can be the straw that breaks the camel's back.

One decision about team composition that early-stage startups often wrestle with is whether to hire for attitude or skill. This is a delicate balance. If founders hire mostly for attitude, their team will be comprised of highly motivated, hardworking, jack-of-all-trade generalists who will shift readily between tasks as circumstances require. Hiring for cultural fit can yield similar results, attracting employees who embrace a venture's mission and feel a strong affinity to their teammates—and will move mountains out of a sense of duty to both. However, hard work alone may not get the job done if no one on the team has the skill to solve tough problems in marketing, engineering, or other functions.

Hiring mostly for skill can give early-stage startups a performance boost. But attracting talented specialists isn't always easy for an unknown, cash-strapped startup with questionable survival prospects. Also, founders without prior experience in a particular function will lack the right connections to help fill the recruiting pipeline. And even if they're able to attract some specialist candidates, these founders may find it difficult to separate the wheat from the chaff.

Hiring a team of skilled specialists does have its pitfalls. For example, specialists may be too quick to embrace solutions that worked for their prior employer but may not be suited for a nascent startup. Specialists may also display a "not my job" attitude when asked to help with work outside their area of expertise. Likewise, if accustomed to working in corporations with well-established processes that specify how work products and information flow from one function to another, specialists may find it hard to navigate the lack of process within a new venture. Finally, if an early-stage startup pivots to a new opportunity, the skills of some specialists may no longer be required, and the founder will face the difficult and demoralizing task of firing talented people.

	Hiring for Attitude	Hiring for Skill
Benefits	• Loyal, hardworking, flexible employees	• Performance boost
Risks	• Lack of critical domain expertise	• Challenges luring and retaining talent • Force-fit inappropriate prior solutions • "Not my job" attitude • Don't understand startup rhythms; can't navigate lack of process

Investors

In early-stage startups, founders must decide when to raise money, how much to raise, and from whom. Mistakes here can have grave consequences. Furthermore, founders who lack a track record may not have many degrees of freedom when making these choices. They may struggle to raise capital and be forced to cut corners, sacrificing "funder fit" in order to stay afloat.

• **When to Raise?** Deciding when to seek additional capital is a balancing act. An entrepreneur must predict when the venture will exhaust its current capital. That moment is known as the startup's "fume date"—the point at which its gas tank is empty and the enterprise is running on fumes. Backing up from the fume date, an entrepreneur must then estimate how long it will take to raise money, which hinges on two factors. First, investors will move faster if the startup has demonstrated strong traction through revenue growth, customer engagement, and/or the achievement of key milestones (e.g., product completion, beta test commencement, etc.), all of which can significantly boost the venture's valuation. Second, the entrepreneur must forecast investor sentiment. Investors move in herds, and as a result, venture capital is prone to boom-bust cycles. When a sector is hot, VCs scramble to add startups from that sector to their portfolio. But sentiment can turn sour—quickly—and when it does, investors may shun even healthy startups.

If a founder raises money too early, before key milestones are met, investors will insist on a lower price for equity shares because they must bear more risk that the startup will stumble. A lower valuation translates into more dilution of the founders' equity stake. To see why, assume that a founder raising her startup's first outside capital targets a $2 million seed round. If investors give the startup a post-money valuation of $8 million (which equals "pre-money" valuation + new equity—respectively, $6 million and $2 million in this example), then after raising capital, investors will own 25 percent of the equity (i.e., the $2 million they invested divided by the $8 million post-money valuation for the startup's equity) and the founder will own 75 percent. By contrast, if the startup manages to raise $2 million with only a $4 million post-money valuation, the founder will own just 50 percent of the equity after the financing.

At the other extreme, if a founding team waits too long to start fundraising, they run the risk that it may take longer to raise money than they expected—perhaps because their sector has fallen out of favor with investors, having entered the "bust" phase of a boom-bust cycle. If a startup runs low on cash during a funding drought, any new capital they can secure may come with adverse terms—again, resulting in a low price for the new shares, a low valuation, and considerable equity dilution for both management and any prior investors.

	Raising Early	Raising Later
Benefits	• Ability to capitalize on boom phase	• With more traction, raise funds faster and with less dilution of equity
Risks	• More dilution of equity • With less traction, it's more difficult to attract investors	• Adverse terms if it takes longer than expected to raise • Adverse terms if surprised by a bust phase

• **How Much to Raise?** The trade-offs involved in deciding the amount of capital to raise mirror those that pertain to the timing of fundraising. As my HBS colleague Bill Sahlman says, founders making these decisions can find themselves in a race between greed and fear. The greed: Founders (along with any existing investors) will suffer less dilution of their equity stake if they 1) delay fundraising until they've met more milestones, and/or 2) raise the absolute minimum amount of capital needed to meet the next set of milestones. The fear: If they delay fundraising or raise too little, they'll lack a capital buffer to carry them through any setbacks—for example, if they need to pivot to a new opportunity or get surprised by rivals. Without a buffer, the startup may be forced to raise what's called a "bridge" round under duress—and this is likely to be a "down round," that is, a reduction in share price. Down rounds can accelerate a startup's demise because they signal a sinking ship, making it challenging to attract new employees. Similarly, any current employees whose stock options are "underwater" will be more inclined to leave.

Given these trade-offs, some entrepreneurs subscribe to the dictum "Raise as much capital as you can, whenever you can." Indeed, having access to boatloads of capital can be a competitive weapon if a startup has to confront aggressive rivals. But raising a big round can damage a startup, too, if it allows management to spend in profligate ways. Marc Andreessen suggests that a startup that has raised too much money can "become infected with a culture of complacency, laziness, and arrogance." Resulting dysfunctions can include 1) over-hiring, with a commensurate slowdown in decision-making as too many managers get involved; and 2) schedule slippage, as employees say, "What's the urgency? We have all this cash."

In the same vein, raising money from investors who are willing to pay an enormous price for their shares results in less dilution of an entrepreneur's equity stake, but this can backfire. The price may be so high that it could be difficult to make enough progress to justify an even higher price for the next funding round. The result: a subsequent down round and the negative consequences described above.

	Raising Too Little	Raising Too Much
Benefits	• Less dilution of equity	• Buffer against surprises • "War chest" for opportunistic moves
Risks	• Lack of buffer against setbacks	• Profligate spending • If share price is too high, subsequent "down round" is more likely

• **From Whom?** Investors can add tremendous value to early-stage startups by providing good advice on strategic challenges; by steering job candidates to the firm; by coaching founders on their management and leadership style; and by providing introductions to help management raise their next round of capital. As successful *Shark Tank* contestants know, raising capital from elite investors signals that a startup has great prospects, so recruiting and fundraising benefits may accrue even if the investor doesn't take any direct action on the startup's behalf.

By contrast, flawed funder fit can wreak havoc on a startup in two ways. The first is the misalignment of risk/reward trade-offs. The business model of venture capital firms hinges on earning a huge payoff from a small percentage of their portfolio investments. In a successful VC firm, profits on a handful of big winners more than offset losses or barely break-even returns from the lion's share of their investments. Consistent with this model, most VCs push portfolio companies to pursue risky strategies that, if successful, will yield a large payoff. Many founders share this willingness to trade big risk for big rewards. Others, absent a push from their investors, would choose safer strategies that might yield more modest payoffs. In the chapters that follow, we'll see how these dynamics played out at early-stage startups Quincy and Baroo. Some scaling startups also echo the "we were pushed too hard by our VCs" theme in Part II.

A second problem with funder fit relates to an investor's ability and willingness to provide additional capital to a struggling startup that is running low on cash. Investors vary widely in this regard. If startups require more capital because they've missed product launch targets or they need more time to execute a pivot, they typically find it easier to raise additional funds from existing investors. While they may worry about "throwing good money after bad," existing investors will be more familiar than new investors with the startup's team, product, and market; the challenges the venture is wrestling with; and the upside if it succeeds. And, they might just be inclined to "double down" for emotional reasons—to demonstrate confidence in their initial investment decision. New investors, by contrast, will naturally be wary of a venture that has been missing its targets. For these reasons, early-stage founders—especially those who are "accident prone"—should seek investors that have a track record of providing bridge funding and have enough capital in their current fund to do so.

Most VC firms raise a new fund every few years. To avoid conflicts of interest, they rarely make follow-on investments in an existing portfolio company from a new fund. If they did, they'd be able to set the follow-on round's valuation in ways that steered profit to one fund at the expense of the other. Consequently, entrepreneurs should check to see if their investors have enough uncommitted capital left in their current fund to make follow-on investments.

Partners

As with decisions about team members, bad choices about partnerships rarely are the primary cause of a startup's demise. But they are more likely to boost the odds of failure by creating yet one more serious problem for management to deal with. At a certain point, management cannot bail water fast enough and the ship sinks.

Sticking with the maritime metaphor, Marc Andreessen likens a startup targeting a big company for a strategic partnership to Captain Ahab and Moby Dick, respectively. Spoiler alert, if you haven't read the book: It doesn't end well for Ahab. After chasing Moby Dick for decades, the obsessed Ahab finally harpoons the whale, who drags Ahab beneath the waves and drowns him. Andreessen explains: "The downside of dealing with a big company is that he can capsize you—maybe by stepping on you in one way or another and killing you, but more likely by wrapping you up in a bad partnership that ends up holding you back, or just making you waste a huge amount of time in meetings and get distracted."

As noted above in the discussion of outsourcing, partnering can provide fast access to resources without a fixed, up-front investment. However, consistent with Andreessen's concerns, it can be tough for an unknown startup with a dubious chance of survival to sign an established company as a partner. If that partner does come on board, the startup might still have trouble capturing its attention and keeping its interests aligned with those of the venture.

Along these lines, Dropbox founder/CEO Drew Houston described his frustrating early efforts to secure a distribution partnership: "Big companies sometimes seem happy to talk to a startup. They'll bring in twelve middle managers—none of whom have any authority—to kick the tires and learn all about your technology.

They'll spin your wheels for months. We got close to a deal with one of the anti-virus software providers. At the 11th hour they brought in a senior vice president who announced that they were going to bury our brand, contrary to everything we'd discussed to that point."

Partnerships can misfire for several reasons—and the larger the power imbalance between the players, the more likely a deal will never happen, or if it does, that it will eventually derail. In some cases, it can take a long time to secure commitment. As Houston suggests, some big companies are just "kicking the tires" to learn about a startup's technology and strategy—and maybe steal some ideas. For others who might be genuinely interested, the partnership is nevertheless low on the big company's priority list. Also, big company dealmakers often deliberately drag out negotiations to build bargaining advantage. They know that the startup is burning cash in the meantime and might make concessions out of desperation.

Once a deal is struck, partners may renege on promises. Big company politics can be opaque, and parties threatened by the partnership may seek to sabotage it. Or, the partnership's champion may exit the company, leaving the startup without internal support. In whatever way the relationship goes sour, the venture may still be stuck with that partner. If problems fester long enough, the odds of failure will rise inexorably. For example, the startup will burn through cash while scrambling to find an alternative, sacrificing quality and customer service in the meantime.

	Forging Partnerships
Benefits	• Fast access to resources without fixed, up-front investments
Risks	• Wasting time on deals that never happen • Risk of idea being stolen • Delays in dealmaking due to big company politics and priorities • Onerous terms due to asymmetry in bargaining power • Misalignment of incentives resulting in lack of partner commitment

. . .

Creating something from nothing is a daring act—one that requires not only vision and confidence but also countless difficult decisions. As explained above, many of the decisions confronting the founders of an early-stage startup can have a decisive impact on the new venture's odds of success. The diamond-and-square framework helps organize those decisions—and provides a tool for diagnosing what went wrong. We'll apply the framework to case studies of failed early-stage startups in the three chapters that follow. First up: a deeper dive into what can happen when founders identify a promising opportunity but cannot mobilize the resources required to bring that opportunity to fruition.

CHAPTER 3

Good Idea, Bad Bedfellows

In May 2011, when two of my former students came to me for feedback on their idea for a startup, I was intrigued. Alexandra Nelson and Christina Wallace had a promising concept: They wanted to produce affordable, stylish, and better-fitting work apparel for young professional women. Their "secret sauce" would be a sizing scheme that allowed customers to specify four separate garment measurements (waist-to-hip ratio, bra size, etc.)—akin to the approach used for men's suiting. They'd devised a novel solution for what seemed to be a strong, unmet customer need.

But instead of following the traditional playbook of trying to secure distribution in department stores or retail chains, Quincy's founders decided that theirs would be a direct-to-consumer brand—a business model gaining favor following the success of Bonobos and Warby Parker. Bonobos, in particular, provided a good prototype for Quincy: It sold "better fitting, better looking" men's pants online, and had raised $26 million in venture capital in its first three years.

I was impressed. As a next step, I encouraged Wallace and Nelson to do some legwork to prove that their target customers really wanted this product. The pair devised a textbook-perfect MVP: They held six trunk shows where women could try on sample outfits and place pre-orders. The response was promising: 50 percent of the young professional women who attended made purchases averaging $350.

Simultaneously, Nelson and Wallace conducted a survey, which revealed that 57 percent of respondents considered a garment's fit to be the most important factor when choosing work apparel and 81 percent had trouble finding clothes for work that fit well. They also learned that their target customers spent a total of $1.9 billion annually on work apparel. Buoyed by these consumer insights, the budding entrepreneurs quit their consulting jobs and launched Quincy Apparel.

Then Wallace and Nelson gave me a chance to put my money where my mouth was: They invited me to invest. That put my evaluation of their prospects in a whole new light. I liked both the concept and the founders: They were sharp and resourceful and brought complementary strengths to the venture. Wallace had a big vision and the charisma to sell it. Before HBS, she'd earned undergraduate degrees in math and theater studies from Emory, then worked at the Metropolitan Opera, managing divas—literally. Nelson, in turn, was deliberate and disciplined. She'd previously worked at Boston Consulting Group and had majored in mechanical engineering at MIT.

This seemed the perfect "outsider-insider" pairing, with one founder's temperament and skills being well suited for leading external efforts—fundraising, branding, partnerships, etc.—while the other's made her a natural for managing internal activities, including website development, warehouse operations, and customer service. I'd seen such founder pairs work well at several other startups launched by HBS alumni, including Birchbox (subscription beauty products), Cloudflare (Internet content delivery), and Rent the Runway (dress rental).

True, neither of Quincy's founders had prior experience in start-ups or in apparel manufacturing, but plenty of other HBS "fashion tech" entrepreneurs had succeeded without deep domain expertise—including the founders of Rent the Runway, Adore Me (lingerie), and Stitch Fix (subscription personal styling).

So, Quincy Apparel was a promising horse, with talented and hardworking jockeys at the reins. The decision was simple. I invested.

Determined to learn all they could from others' success stories,

Quincy's founders met with senior managers at Bonobos, who were generous enough to explain their strategy. Nelson, channeling Willie Wonka, called this Quincy's "golden ticket." Leveraging insights from these meetings, Nelson and Wallace came up with financial projections that showed Quincy earning $52 million in revenue and $18 million in pre-tax profit within four years. They then shared these projections with potential investors and raised $950,000 in seed capital—less than their $1.5 million target, but enough to launch spring and fall collections. The founders also wisely recruited a small team of fashion industry veterans—including a designer who'd appeared on the TV series *Project Runway*.

Initial sales were strong, as were repeat purchases: 39 percent of spring collection customers subsequently bought items from the fall collection. However, things soon began to unravel. It turned out that this strong growth required heavy investment in inventory, which depleted cash reserves. Meanwhile, production problems caused garments to fit poorly on some customers. This resulted in a 35 percent return rate—on par with rates for other online retailers that, like Quincy, offered free shipping and returns, but higher than the 20 percent return rate that Quincy's founders had targeted. Returns reduced profit margins, and correcting the production problems also cost money. They had been in business just nine months, and at the rate Wallace and Nelson were spending, Quincy would run out of cash in just two more months.

Wallace kicked into high gear and vowed to raise more capital. But after returning from investor meetings empty-handed, she saw the writing on the wall. Unless existing investors extended a loan, Quincy would have to halt operations. This became a big point of contention. Wallace wanted to shut down "gracefully," paying vendors in full and offering a modest severance package to employees. Nelson preferred to continue to search for new investors and in the meantime reduce operational complexity and inventory by offering a narrower range of garment sizes. But trimming the product line this way was at odds with Wallace's vision for Quincy as a brand that offered better-fitting clothing to women of *all* sizes.

After a tense boardroom showdown, Nelson's plan prevailed. Wallace was forced out of the company and proceeded to spend the next several weeks on her couch, despondent. Meanwhile, after only five weeks alone at the helm, Nelson saw that her plan wasn't working. New investments would not be forthcoming. She threw in the towel.

The untimely demise of Quincy Apparel kept me up at night because, on the surface, it shouldn't have happened. Their early trunk show tests—an impeccable application of Lean Startup methods—had demonstrated clear demand for their novel solution. And the market reconfirmed this demand after Quincy launched in March 2012: By November, monthly sales had reached $62,000, up from $42,400 the prior month. And, 17 percent of all Quincy customers had made repeat purchases, including the impressive 39 percent of customers who bought items from Quincy's first collection.

So, if Quincy's founders had identified a product that their target consumer clearly wanted, why did they stumble? Was its "better fit" promise too ambitious for founders who hadn't mastered the complexities of apparel production? Did the founders raise too little venture capital? Did they pick the wrong investors? Did weak leadership sink the ship? Was there co-founder conflict?

As I dug deeper, I found the root of the problem: Quincy hadn't assembled the resources required to capitalize on its promising opportunity. As a result, it fell victim to the early-stage startup failure pattern I call "Good Idea, Bad Bedfellows." In this context, "resources" doesn't refer simply to capital; we see the Good Idea, Bad Bedfellows pattern play out when a startup with a promising opportunity falters due to deficiencies and dysfunction among a range of key resource providers, including its founders, other team members, investors, and strategic partners. And, as we learned from the diamond-and-square framework introduced in the last chapter, problems originating with the resource square can ripple inward, wreaking havoc on one or more elements of the opportunity diamond.

In Quincy's case, three of the four opportunity elements were in place, at least initially. As the positive response to trunk show trials, early sales growth, and repeat purchase rates all made clear, Quincy's *Customer Value Proposition* addressed a strong unmet need in a differentiated manner.

Likewise, Quincy's problems did not stem from flawed *Marketing*. The startup relied principally on word of mouth from happy customers, "customer get customer" incentives (in the form of a $50 credit per referral), social media promotion, and press coverage. These marketing tactics worked as intended and attracted plenty of customers.

During its first year after launch, Quincy's *Profit Formula* was still unproven, but it was not patently unsound. Admittedly, the startup was rapidly burning through its capital reserves to produce the inventory needed to meet growing demand. And Quincy's gross margin was substantially lower than their target, because customers were returning their purchases at a higher-than-expected rate. Yet, despite these early miscalculations, the venture still had the potential to achieve long-term profitability. Priority customer segments accounted for almost half of Quincy's sales, and Nelson and Wallace had well-researched estimates that pegged the lifetime value of a priority customer at over $1,000—well in excess of the $95 to $125 projected cost to acquire such a customer.

Quincy *did* have major problems with the fourth opportunity element: *Technology & Operations*. The startup had an attractive value proposition, but it couldn't deliver the promised value consistently. Specifically, Quincy had trouble ensuring good fit—the crucial component in its promise to customers. The result was a return rate 15 percent higher than the founders had anticipated, with 68 percent of all returned purchases citing poor fit.

Unfortunately, as my postmortem revealed, Quincy had problems across all four elements of the resource square—founders, other team members, investors, and strategic partners. These "Bad Bedfellows" turned out to be the source of Quincy's operational problems and, ultimately, its failure.

Founders

Quincy's founders brought a version of "hacker-hustler" balance to the venture. Nelson, an MIT-trained engineer, took an analytical, disciplined approach to strategy and operational issues. Wallace, on the other hand, was charismatic; she could sell a bold vision for the startup. Notwithstanding these strengths, the co-founders had two key weaknesses: They lacked apparel industry experience and they failed to clarify "Who's the Boss."

Lack of Industry Experience. Although Nelson had been a consultant for various apparel retailers and had also worked on inventory optimization at Hermès the summer after her first year of business school, Quincy's founders had no prior hands-on experience with designing and manufacturing garments. Initially, they assumed that they could handle design themselves and could rely on a single production manager to coordinate manufacturing. Once this plan proved unrealistic, Nelson and Wallace hired a professional designer. Gradually, they learned about the many tasks required to design and produce a garment—and the many specialized roles involved in completing those tasks (e.g., technical designer, pattern maker, sample maker, fabric cutter, etc.). The more they learned, the more it became clear that they would have to create an entire production process from scratch—a daunting and time-consuming task.

"Learning by doing" also resulted in quality problems, such as not knowing that nearly identical fabrics could have different elasticities, which affected fit; not realizing that perspiration would bleed pink dye from the fabric they used to line jackets; and not anticipating that a garment's blouse cuffs would fail to fit most women because Nelson, who served as the fit model, had smaller-than-average wrists.

Founders' lack of industry experience is often at the core of the Good Idea, Bad Bedfellows failure pattern. After all, a promising idea will get you only so far if those running the show lack the knowledge and experience to execute it. Furthermore, the maxim "Ideas are cheap, but execution is dear" is especially true in sectors with greater operational complexity, causing founders who lack industry experience to struggle mightily. Quincy's operations were very complex: A range of activities—design, fabric procurement, pattern making, garment production, quality control, and shipping, among others—had to be closely coordinated. In Chapter 8, we'll see another example of online retailing, in this case, of home furnishings, which poses similarly onerous logistical challenges.

Founders who lack prior industry experience will also have more trouble attracting talent because they lack a professional network filled with promising candidates. And investors will be wary of a founding team that doesn't know where the land mines are buried. So, what can founders like Quincy's do to address such shortcomings?

• First, they can try to recruit another, more experienced cofounder or seasoned senior manager, but they'll likely run into a Catch-22. Nelson and Wallace *tried* to recruit a co-founder who knew the ins and outs of apparel product—but they were unsuccessful. It's easy to see why: Someone qualified to lead the design and production operations of an apparel startup is bound to have many attractive job opportunities, including founder roles with other promising new ventures. If they had more attractive options, would such candidates cast their lot with two MBAs who have a good idea but no relevant track record—and only enough capital to provide one year's worth of runway (that is, enough cash on hand to keep operating for one year, given projected revenue and costs)?

• Second, they can lean heavily on advisers to provide guidance on strategy and operations—and ideally also leverage the advisers' network connections to attract experienced managers. Again, Quincy's founders did have a few useful advisers—but they might have searched for more. They assumed that their lead investors brought fashion tech experience and contacts to the table but were ultimately disappointed with the help they got from their VCs.

• Finally, they can invest more time and effort into acquiring some specific industry knowledge themselves, while being aware that mastery can take years. It would certainly take that long for Quincy's founders to master the process of designing and manufacturing apparel. But if they'd spent more time researching the challenges of garment manufacturing and inventory management *before* launching, they might at least have learned enough to target their recruiting efforts more precisely. In her postmortem analysis, Nelson speculated that perhaps she and Wallace had left their consulting jobs prematurely. In retrospect, she realized that they should have continued to evaluate their concept while still employed full-time. "I could rely on my husband's income," she said, "but the minute that Christina quit her job, we needed to fund the business, and that put a lot of pressure on us." However, this slower approach may not be a viable option for entrepreneurs who suspect they have only a narrow window of opportunity—perhaps because another startup may soon spot the same idea.

Who's the Boss? In addition to lacking industry experience, Nelson and Wallace faced significant challenges in managing their own relationship. According to analysis by Noam Wasserman, dean of Yeshiva University's Business School, co-founder relationships are less stable—that is, more likely to end in breakup—when co-founders are family members or were close friends prior to launching a venture. There are many tempting reasons to start a business with your close friend or family member—for example, you share similar goals and values and already know each other's strengths, weaknesses, habits, and quirks. However, compared to those who were previously colleagues or strangers, co-founders with close personal bonds find it more difficult to have tough conversations about roles and strategies. They're afraid that the ensuing conflict might jeopardize their personal relationship.

Quincy's founders, best friends at Harvard Business School, were vulnerable to this dynamic. In fact, when they decided to launch a venture together, they vowed that they would never let disagreements over the business threaten their friendship. Thinking it would spare them from making painful choices about their roles in the venture, Wallace and Nelson from the outset elected to share strategic decision-making authority equally. Wallace recalled, "We functioned like co-CEOs, even though we agreed that I would be CEO and Alex would be COO. She'd focus on production, procurement, and e-commerce. I'd take the lead with marketing, human resources, and finance. We'd share responsibility for product strategy." Wallace went on to explain, "We used the CEO and COO titles to deflect investors' concerns about how two MBAs who were actually co-CEOs would resolve disputes. But we made key decisions together. If we didn't agree, we didn't move forward."

On the surface, this strategy seemed a logical way to avoid co-founder strife. But it turned out to do the opposite. The co-founders, both headstrong, clashed over product strategy and design choices, among other issues. Wallace recounted, "We both wanted to shape the product vision, but we had different aesthetic preferences. Hers were London classic; mine were Brooklyn funky." "There were times," Wallace added, "when one founder made a decision that she thought was wholly in her wheelhouse, and then the other would ask, 'Why wasn't I consulted? I completely disagree!' We had to undo some decisions, which took a lot of energy."

Nelson and Wallace tried to keep their debates discreet—a nearly impossible task in a small, open office. And once Quincy's employees became attuned to these disagreements, they found ways to play the founders off against each other. "We went to a nearby Starbucks to have more private conversations, and that's where we went to fire people, too," Wallace recalled. "Pretty soon, everyone learned that 'Do you want to get a coffee?' meant something bad was happening."

The potential for conflict was amplified by asymmetry in what the founders had at stake with the venture. Nelson had more to lose: Her mother was the company's first investor and her brother worked there as a software engineer. Wallace noted, "When your family also has skin in the game, the stakes and risks can't feel like they are shared fifty-fifty."

It's not unusual for co-founders to share decision-making equally—at least in the initial stages. Co-founders often work together intensively for months before others join the team; they grow accustomed to talking through every choice. Likewise, more than one co-founder may covet the CEO role, so rather than risk a fight over this choice, they often defer the decision—at least until investors press them to define their roles more clearly. Wasserman's research shows that 21 percent of founding teams avoided naming a CEO when they first assigned formal titles. This is a wise decision if the co-founders realize that neither is a good fit for the CEO role and they need to go outside to find one—as Google's founders did with Eric Schmidt. But, if two founders aspire to the CEO job and both view themselves as qualified, deferring the decision for too long can have deadly consequences. As Quincy's experience shows, tension will build and squabbles over strategic direction may slow down the startup just when it needs to be at its most nimble.

In this situation, co-founders have three options.

- **Internal:** The co-founders can agree upon a date by which they will have to come to an agreement, perhaps after a trial period during which they alternate as CEO to see who is better suited.
- **External:** The co-founders can delegate the decision to a neutral third party and agree to abide by that individual's choice. A seasoned investor who joins the startup's board of directors is often well placed to make this call: He will understand the skills and traits required of an early-stage startup CEO, the challenges confronting the venture in question, and the capabilities of the co-founders who seek the CEO title.
- **Draconian:** One co-founder, recognizing he will never be satisfied with a subordinate role, can leave. Not a great option, but sometimes it's a Hobson's choice—the only option available after exploring and rejecting all other alternatives, and thus best for all concerned.

My survey of early-stage startups revealed that issues with founder fit like those described above can contribute to startup mortality. Specifically, compared to their counterparts in more successful ventures, the founder/CEOs of struggling startups or those that shut down had significantly less prior work experience in the industry in which their startup operated. And, consistent with Quincy's experience, co-founders were much more likely to report they lacked clarity over their roles, along with frequent conflict among themselves and with other senior team members.

Team

For Quincy's small team—comprised largely of apparel industry specialists—a lack of flexibility and initiative contributed significantly to the venture's demise.

Lack of Flexibility. As noted above, it took some time for Quincy's founders to understand the many tasks and related roles involved in apparel design and manufacturing. Nelson and Wallace assumed that their first few employees, by virtue of being experienced, would be able to fill multiple functions as needed—a reasonable assumption, given that employees in most early-stage startups are jacks-of-all-trades. However, the industry veterans whom Quincy hired were accustomed to the high levels of specialization found in established apparel companies. As a result, they weren't flexible when asked to tackle tasks outside their area of expertise. It turns out, Quincy had hired individuals who were more comfortable working within a familiar, well-defined process—not with inventing a process from scratch or with taking on multiple roles.

Lack of Initiative. Furthermore, Quincy's industry veterans did not show the initiative required to make a startup successful. In addition to their "not my job" attitude, these employees were reluctant to speak up when their industry know-how should have clued them in to potential problems. For example, no one sounded the alarm that fabric used for the jacket lining was likely to bleed pink. As Wallace put it, "Our production team, which in theory had experience in these matters, should have seen the problem coming." The same was true for the blouse with small wrist openings. These missteps suggest that the employees were 1) following norms learned in established apparel companies that had smoothly functioning production processes, and where they rarely needed to challenge management decisions; and/or 2) did not feel motivated enough to ask questions when something seemed awry. Either possibility points to problems with the approaches the founders used to hire, supervise, and motivate the employees.

In retrospect, Wallace acknowledged her own failure to address her employees' lack of initiative. She said, "I didn't push the team hard enough. Alex became the bad cop, demanding results. I'd try to calm things down after she came down hard on someone. But Alex's authority was undermined once employees learned that they could complain to me." Wallace added, "We hired some people who seemed to think that they were doing us a favor by working for an underfunded startup. We did not find enough people who thought this was the best opportunity of their lives—a way to get in on the ground floor of the next big thing. As a result, I managed in a way that said, 'Thank you so much for doing us this favor.' "

Instead of hiring employees who had relevant skills but lacked flexibility and initiative, Quincy should have sought out a seasoned senior manager with experience in both apparel production *and* with new ventures—granted, easier said than done. This manager would then have been able to recruit specialists with both the necessary skills and the flexibility to adapt to startup rhythms. Without such a person on the team, Quincy's founders faced a challenge familiar to many entrepreneurs: How do you hire the right specialists when you don't know much about their functions and you don't have a professional network rich with candidates?

This hiring challenge is a recurring theme because as ventures mature, most continue to add new types of specialists. In Chapter 8, I'll examine the challenge of recruiting seasoned specialists into crucial senior management roles in late-stage startups. For an early-stage startup like Quincy, the solution to finding employees with the right balance of specialized skill and "can do" attitude is threefold:

- Step one is **finding someone with relevant industry experience** who can 1) leverage their network contacts to fill your recruiting pipeline with skilled candidates, and 2) help you with interviews to assess candidates' skills. Given the challenge of bringing such a person on board as an employee, he could also be an investor or an adviser. This adviser might serve as an informal mentor or could be formally recruited to a board of advisers and compensated with a small slice of equity in exchange for a contractual commitment to spend a specified amount of time per month helping the venture. Any equity grant should vest over time, and both parties—adviser and startup—should be free to terminate the arrangement at will.

- Step two is **interviewing for attitude.** A founder can and should probe candidates' past accomplishments to determine whether they have experience solving novel problems and taking initiative. Likewise, interviews should explore candidates' motivations for considering a job in a nascent company. Are they seeking new challenges and professional growth? Are they attracted to the startup's mission? How well do they understand work patterns in an early-stage startup?

- Step three, whenever possible, is **giving candidates a "tryout"** before committing to hiring them full-time. Hand them a project of modest proportions to complete in a specified period of time—one that requires working with current employees—with an understanding that the candidate and the founder will gauge mutual fit upon the project's completion.

Investors

Quincy's founders had initially planned to raise $1.5 million in venture capital, but managed to secure only $950,000 in seed funding. As a result, at the time of launch, the startup had less than twelve months of runway, instead of the eighteen months that seed-stage ventures typically target. This shortfall left less room for mistakes. If Quincy's founders had met their original fundraising goal, they could have produced enough inventory for a third collection—and might have had enough time to shake out production bugs before running out of funds.

One way to interpret what happened is that Catch-22 at work again, in that potential investors, while impressed with the founders' idea and the evidence for demand supplied by their early MVP tests, were still skeptical of the founders' ability to execute, due to their lack of industry experience. Another possibility is that technology VCs saw Quincy as an apparel manufacturer—a category they usually avoid. Technology VCs *hope* for a 10x return from any given investment, but they *expect* only a small percentage of the companies in their portfolio to earn such returns. By contrast, private equity investors in the fashion/retail sector seek only a 2x to 4x return, but they expect a larger percentage of their investments to yield a solid payoff down the line; thus, they're more patient and less inclined to withhold additional funds from startups that stumble.

To attract venture capital, Nelson and Wallace positioned Quincy as a disruptive online innovator—a tech startup employing the direct-to-consumer model in the apparel space, akin to Warby Parker and Bonobos, both of which had attracted significant funding from technology VCs. Yet, it might have been a mistake for Quincy's founders to take money from technology VCs.

The venture capital investors that Nelson and Wallace managed to attract compounded the startup's troubles in a variety of ways. For one, these investors didn't contribute much in the way of strategic counsel or recruiting contacts. The founders had assumed that their lead VCs would have relevant expertise because they'd previously invested in other direct-to-consumer fashion tech startups, including Bonobos and Warby Parker. But Quincy's VCs hadn't been as directly involved in those ventures as the founders had surmised. As Wallace reflected, "They didn't get board seats with those investments, and that's how an investor really builds domain experience."

In addition, funding from Quincy's lead investors came with strings attached. The capital was doled out every quarter in chunks called "tranches"—but only if Quincy met specified milestones of sales growth. Tranching is an uncommon—but not unheard of—practice for seed-stage VC investments. It allows VCs to limit their exposure if a startup goes off the rails. But it can also exert undo pressure on the venture. While Quincy did meet its investors' targets, Nelson explained, "We felt like we had to continuously sell our investors on Quincy, which made it difficult to be candid about strategic and operational challenges. The investors never seemed like true partners."

Finally, Quincy's lead investors were small and relatively new VC firms that were constrained in their ability to provide bridge financing when the startup began struggling. One of the investors was about to commence raising a new fund and had limited capacity to contribute more capital to Quincy from its current one.

So, how do founders find the most appropriate investors? Before they commit, they should ask two important questions. First, just as founder fit is crucial—having founders with the right skills and industry experience, given the opportunity at hand—so is funder fit. Will the investor add value in the form of skills and experience, beyond the capital they contribute? Second, are their risk/reward preferences consistent with those of the founders?

Gauging **funder fit** requires a review of the investing firm's track record. Do they have a good hit rate? If they do, they'll have credibility and relationships that will help with attracting investors to the next fundraising round after this one. Do entrepreneurs who've worked with them say that they offered good advice and contacts? Do founders—especially founders of failed ventures—say that the investor was supportive and that they'd work with them again? Finally, does the firm have enough capital in its current fund to provide bridge financing, if required?

Many aspiring entrepreneurs fail to consider the full range of financing alternatives available to them. Venture capital is the default, especially for graduates of elite MBA programs, where venture capital investors are lionized. But the pressure that comes with venture capital is not well suited for all businesses, nor is this **risk/return profile** suited for all entrepreneurs' temperaments. For example,

Quincy's VCs pushed the founders to "swing for the fences," sad-
dling the startup with aggressive growth targets. Nelson recounted,
"The investors advised us to keep a lot of inventory. They said stock-
outs were the worst thing that could happen to a retailer. In hindsight, we should have said 'No, we'll be conservative and see how
our new styles sell—and then replenish inventory.' Over-ordering is
a big risk in fashion, because tastes change, and they are hard to
predict."

Looking back, Wallace concluded that instead of raising funds
from VC firms, Quincy could have sought financial backing from a
clothing factory. That would have solved two problems: A factory
with an equity stake in Quincy would have expedited orders and
worked harder to correct production problems, and factory owners
with deep industry experience would have known how to set an
optimal pace for the growth of a new apparel line—in contrast to
Quincy's VCs, who pressured the founders to grow at full tilt.

Whether to persist—as Quincy did—if initial fundraising stalls
far short of the founders' goals is a tricky issue. If investors decline
to back the startup, is it that they perceive problems with the idea,
the team, or both? Assuming that the founders have done their best
to address potential investors' concerns—for example, by pivoting
to a better idea based on market feedback and by bolstering the
team through tactics described above—is the shortfall a reliable signal about the venture's lack of viability? If so, then entrepreneurs
should consider pulling the plug. But fundraising signals can be
noisy: Investors' herd behavior often means that no one invests until
someone else invests—thus, no one invests. And, if this "herd behavior" standoff persists long enough, an otherwise promising venture
risks being perceived as stale, damaged goods.

When Quincy's founders raised much less seed capital than they
had originally targeted, they faced a difficult choice. Prior to May
2012, they'd raised $250,000 from angels, friends, and family; most
of that had been spent or committed to the production of their first
clothing collection. That May, they secured commitments from two
VC firms for another $700,000. This was enough to last through

year-end, funding the design, production, and marketing of a second collection—but that was it.

Having failed to raise enough money to fund a third collection, should they have pulled the plug rather than taking the new VC money? Proceeding with less meant gambling that at year-end they'd have enough traction to raise more substantial funds—but it also meant the venture had no room for strategic or operational errors. However, pulling the plug would require them to inform their early backers that their investment wouldn't deliver returns. Even worse, they'd have to admit they lacked the confidence to proceed even though an additional $700,000 was available. It's not hard to understand why Quincy's founders chose to gamble.

The fundraising dilemmas confronting Quincy's founders are echoed in the results of my survey of early-stage startups. Consistent with Quincy's experience, the startups I surveyed that were struggling or shut down were more likely than their successful counterparts to have missed their targets in their initial round of fundraising. Likewise, the founder/CEOs of these struggling startups were more likely to have been disappointed with the quality of advice they received from their investors and more likely to report frequent, serious, and divisive conflict with investors over strategic priorities.

Partners

Finding the right strategic partners can have a major impact on an early-stage startup's performance. Partners can lend their resources—key technologies, manufacturing capacity, warehouses, call centers, and so forth—to a new venture that lacks the wherewithal and/or time to develop such resources in-house. However, the asymmetry in bargaining power between a big, mature, resource-rich company and a fledgling startup can make it difficult to secure the right resources on reasonable terms.

Quincy, for example, outsourced manufacturing to third-party clothing factories, a common practice for apparel startups. However, due to their lack of industry experience, the founders had no prior relationships with these partners. As a result, the factories sometimes pushed Quincy's orders to the back of the production queue when an established customer needed an order expedited. Wallace recalled, "We'd ask factory managers, 'When will you have this ready?' and they would tell us two weeks. Then we'd show up, and nothing was ready. We'd ask, 'How much will this cost?' and they'd quote 50 percent more than their original bid." These obstacles disrupted operations and led to shipping delays.

In retrospect, it shouldn't have been a surprise that a startup with no reputation, unusual sizing requirements, and small orders would encounter indifferent service from apparel factories. Quincy's struggle to get good service from its factory partners highlights a risk endemic to early-stage startups when they partner with established players. It's easy for a mouse to get trampled by an elephant. Even an elephant with good intentions may be clumsy and too slow moving to avoid squashing the mouse.

Unfortunately, there's not much that an early-stage startup can do to ensure that a larger partner fulfills its commitments. Threatening lawsuits for breach of contract isn't realistic: The startup's managers are too busy to manage a protracted legal battle, and, in any case, spending scarce cash on legal services would be unwise. Nevertheless, an entrepreneur may have a few points of leverage over this partner—and shouldn't hesitate to use them. For example, a founder with a big social media platform might have the megaphone to warn the larger partner about the negative consequences to its reputation if other customers read about the startup's bad experience. Similarly, the startup's investors and advisers may be positioned to lean on the partner.

To level the bargaining playing field, founders might choose to work with a partner that is hungry for more business, perhaps because it's not yet well established or has recently suffered setbacks. Of course, there's risk with this approach—does the partner need more business because it lacks key capabilities? Maybe a history of failing to deliver? In this case, the best course is to conduct careful due diligence on potential partners at the outset by speaking to current customers with a similar "mousy" profile to find out if their partners honored their commitments. Another option is for the founders to give a business partner equity in their startup so that both sides have a stake in its success. Of course, that option means more dilution of equity stakes and a messier divorce if the partnership falls apart.

Starting Small

Quincy's founders identified a promising opportunity, but they failed to attract the resources required to capture it. The missing resources included another co-founder with industry experience, a more committed team, more helpful investors, and more cooperative strategic partners.

Unfortunately, the nature of the opportunity Quincy pursued amplified the challenges involved in mobilizing resources. As we've seen, the design and manufacturing of apparel is a complex process that requires tight coordination among many specialized functions. This type of process puts a premium on the industry experience that the founders sorely lacked. In addition, the complexity posed another problem: There is no way to run a lean experiment to prove, in advance, that a planned production process will work. You must fully develop the process and then run it in order to demonstrate its effectiveness. Producing apparel in sample quantities, which Quincy's founders did successfully after their trunk show tests, is a completely different ball game compared to manufacturing it in volume. So, while Nelson and Wallace could provide potential employees and investors with some assurance that trunk show tests had validated demand, there was no way to offer evidence in advance that the founders could manage operations. Resource providers would have to take a leap of faith.

Another compounding challenge was that before Quincy made any sales, the startup had to build lots of inventory because its sizing scheme required more stock-keeping units for each style than a traditional apparel manufacturer would produce. The venture needed sufficient inventory to support growth, but that required consider-able capital. Inventory buildup carries an additional risk, common to all apparel businesses: They have to forecast fashion trends, and any mistakes meant they'd be left holding inventory that could only be liquidated at a deep discount, if at all.

Finally, apparel like Quincy's is sold in seasonal collections. Be-cause of this timing, the startup's capital requirements were not only large but also lumpy. To offer a new clothing collection, the founders needed enough cash on hand to fund inventory production along with many months of design work. Funding three collections instead of two would have required another big lump of seed capital. And, the third collection was an all-or-nothing proposition—Quincy could not tiptoe into the spring with just a few items offered in lim-ited volumes.

So, startups are more likely to be vulnerable to the Good Idea, Bad Bedfellows failure pattern when they pursue opportunities that involve 1) complex operations requiring the tight coordination of different specialists' work; 2) inventory of physical goods; and 3) large, lumpy capital requirements. By contrast, consider the more modest management demands on a purely software-based startup like Twitter when it launched. A small team of engineers created the site, and it spread virally without a paid marketing push. Capital requirements were modest and there was no physical inventory to manage. As Twitter grew, it eventually added an array of specialists to manage various functions—for example, community relations, server infrastructure, copyright compliance, etc. But it didn't need these specialists at the outset.

What can founders who confront the risk of Bad Bedfellows do to improve their odds of success? In hindsight, Quincy's founders saw many "could have/should have" possibilities. They fall into two big categories: *bolstering resources* and *constraining opportunity*. This chapter has already presented a range of suggestions for entre-preneurs seeking to bolster their resources. Founders who fear that they may not be able to amass the resources required to pursue an attractive opportunity should also consider ways to constrain that opportunity. They can do this by reducing the scope of their effort—at least initially, until proof of concept is established and it becomes easier to mobilize resources. This approach is somewhat counterintuitive because startup dogma holds that growth is the prime goal for a new venture. Instead, with this contrarian approach, a startup should start small in order to get big.

When the capabilities of a founder and his team are limited, when partner support is erratic, and when funding is in short supply, constraining the initial opportunity may make sense. For example, an early-stage startup might be able to constrain its scope by limiting the breadth of its product line, by outsourcing difficult-to-master activities, or by focusing on a single customer segment or a specific geographic area. In Quincy's case, Wallace and Nelson could have reduced the challenges they faced in mobilizing resources by initially limiting the product line to a single garment type—blouses, dresses, or jackets. Bonobos took this path, selling only one style of pant for several years, in different fabrics and colors, before branching out into multiple styles, suiting, and other apparel items.

Limiting Quincy's product line this way would have allowed its team to master production and ensure good fit before tackling the complex operations associated with designing and manufacturing multiple garment types. Asked what she'd do if she could start over, Nelson said, "We could have built a reputation for having the best blouses, for example. We could have perfected fit for that one garment and for one fabric type, using a longer beta testing phase. One garment and one fabric type would have meant one pattern. Variety could come from different color and trim options. Once we got that focused supply chain working, we could have gradually introduced other fabrics and styles."

According to Nelson, Quincy's founders also could have outsourced end-to-end management of their entire production process to a single clothing factory, in order to avoid having to devise a production process from scratch. The downside with this approach: It would have given the startup less control over product quality and fewer opportunities for learning that could influence product design choices. But it also would have helped them avoid many early operational setbacks.

A word of warning: Entrepreneurs who are considering whether to limit the scope of the opportunity they pursue need to weigh the attendant risks against the benefits. First, narrower scope may make their offering less appealing to customers. Second, unless potential investors are confident that the venture can eventually expand in scope, they may be reluctant to fund a "start slower/start smaller" plan, projecting that the payoff from the venture will be too small. Finally, by limiting scope, the startup team risks deferring the "learning by doing" that will eventually be necessary to manage more complex operations. Because the venture will be bigger in the future, any errors that the team makes when they eventually expand the product line or bring outsourced activities in-house will be more costly.

In the next chapter, we'll see how waiting too long to learn about an opportunity's flaws can also be fatal.

CHAPTER 4

False Starts

Sunil Nagaraj founded Triangulate in 2009 while he was still a student at Harvard Business School. He originally planned to build a "matching engine"—software that recommends compatible pairings by using algorithms to analyze data on the attributes and preferences of potential partners on each side of an exchange—say, a date, a job offer, or a real estate transaction. He aimed to start by licensing an engine to established dating sites such as eHarmony and Match.

Nagaraj's software would draw inferences about a user's inclinations and attractiveness to prospective partners by analyzing their digital "footprints": the websites they visited and bookmarked; the apps they used, and for how long; the movies and music they consumed on Netflix and Spotify; and so forth. His premise was that "triangulating" a profile from this computer-generated behavioral data would paint a more accurate picture and thus result in better matches than the self-reported information used by many matching sites, where users could exaggerate their responses or simply lie when creating profiles ("... and I love Russian literature, running marathons, and volunteering at my local animal shelter").

Nagaraj chose online dating as Triangulate's first market in part because he believed it was ripe for disruption. The $1.2 billion industry hadn't seen much innovation since 2000, when eHarmony launched with a sophisticated algorithm that analyzed responses to a long questionnaire. Nagaraj also reasoned that the problem of inaccurate self-reported information was worse in online dating than in the other markets Triangulate might someday serve—for example, corporate recruiting, school admissions, or the matching of individuals with service providers, such as trainers, therapists, interior designers, or investment advisers.

Three critical assumptions drove Nagaraj's Big Idea. First: that objective, computer-generated data could indeed produce better matches than self-reported information. Second: that users of online dating sites would recognize these superior results and be willing to pay a premium for them. Third: that established dating sites would wish to license a product that made better matches. Nagaraj envisioned a model whereby consumers would pay, say, an extra $10 per month (on top of their regular $60 subscription) for access to Triangulate-powered "eHarmony Gold," and that Triangulate would keep half of the premium.

To raise venture capital, Nagaraj knew that he'd have to validate these assumptions. First and foremost, he had to create his matching algorithm, and for that he'd need a dataset made up of happy couples and strangers, so he could compare their online behavior. Practically speaking, this meant he'd have to find people who would trust him to track their computer usage. So, a few months before graduating, Nagaraj recruited one hundred volunteers to download and install RescueTime—a productivity application normally used to track how much time you spend on different applications and websites. Unfortunately, his modifications to RescueTime didn't work properly on most participants' computers, derailing the trial before he could begin to validate his assumptions (though the exercise did show Nagaraj that he'd be better off operating Triangulate entirely "in the cloud," thus avoiding an application download).

Nagaraj's other crucial assumptions—that consumers would recognize and be willing to pay a premium for better matching results and that Triangulate could license its technology to existing dating sites—also went largely untested. Nagaraj admitted, "I didn't spend enough time getting into consumers' heads to understand their needs around online dating." And, while Nagaraj had met the CEO of eHarmony, he hadn't pitched him yet on his concept for Triangulate.

Nagaraj hit another bump in the road when he lost the co-founder who'd developed Triangulate with him. Jack Wilson, a former colleague and close friend who'd previously launched two startups, had agreed to take the lead on fundraising and partnerships with dating sites while Nagaraj, who had an engineering background, focused on product development. But they later squabbled over the CEO role, with Wilson proposing a co-CEO arrangement and Nagaraj insisting on being sole CEO, citing the importance of quick decision-making. Worried about overlap in co-founder skill sets and with other opportunities on the table, Wilson bowed out.

So, Nagaraj moved to Palo Alto after graduation to pursue his vision alone. He recalled, "I had blind faith, but I had no validation for my idea, no investors, no product, and no team. I look back and wonder how I ever did it." Upon arrival, Nagaraj recruited two new co-founders: an engineer and a data scientist. The team finished building the first version of Triangulate's matching engine in October 2009. This version automated the collection of users' digital information from sites like Facebook, Twitter, and Netflix using browser plug-ins and application programming interfaces (APIs). To avoid all the technical jargon, Nagaraj referred to these plug-ins and APIs as "life-stream connectors." For version two, which would use that data to recommend compatible matches, the team would need to "train" algorithms to find compatibility by using historical data from happy couples and strangers. This posed a Catch-22: To get lots of data for training, Nagaraj would need a dating site as a partner; to get a partner, he'd have to demonstrate that version two of the matching engine was fully trained and working well.

By building their matching engine without "getting into customers' heads," Nagaraj and his new team were heading for a *False Start*—a failure pattern common to many early-stage ventures. A false start occurs when a startup rushes to launch its first product before conducting enough customer research—only to find that the opportunities they've identified are rife with problems. By giving short shrift to early and accurate customer feedback and by neglecting to test their assumptions with MVPs, they simply run out of time to fix all the flaws, thus turning Lean Startup's "Fail Fast" mantra into a self-fulfilling prophecy.

Time is an early-stage startup's most precious resource and a false start wastes a feedback cycle. Afterward, the team should still try to pivot toward a more attractive opportunity. But each pivot consumes time and, with it, scarce cash; moreover, it may take more than one pivot to strike gold. In his book *The Lean Startup,* Eric Ries defines a startup's runway not in the conventional way—as the number of months remaining before the startup exhausts all of its capital at its current cash "burn rate"—but rather as the number of *pivots* the startup can complete before its cash reserves are depleted. With the clock ticking, one wasted cycle uses up precious runway, which means the startup has one less chance to pivot to an attractive opportunity.

As Triangulate moved forward, it discovered that the online dating business was a prime example of an opportunity that yielded problem after problem, requiring pivot after pivot.

Pivot #1: Wings. While building the matching engine, Nagaraj was also pitching Triangulate to venture capital firms, but the only response he got was "Call us back when you get the eHarmony deal." By November 2009, this refrain—coupled with a push from an adviser who was an academic expert on online social networks—led Nagaraj to rethink his strategy. In parallel with the plan to license a matching engine to leading dating sites, Triangulate would now launch its own online dating service on the fast-growing Facebook Platform. Doing so would provide the user data needed to fine-tune the matching engine and demonstrate its effectiveness to potential licensees, while also providing a window of opportunity for Triangulate's entry into the intensely competitive online dating market.

Launched two years earlier, Facebook Platform allowed third-party applications and websites to integrate with Facebook's "social graph" and gain access to a treasure trove of data on Facebook users. No fewer than fifty thousand apps and sites had already generated a combined $500 million in revenue this way—among them, Zoosk, a dating site with forty million members that, since its 2007 founding, had raised $10.5 million in venture capital.

Compared to Zoosk, Triangulate's site made far more use of data on Facebook users' behaviors. Triangulate also brought a unique twist to online dating: It would supplement objective data on users' digital behavior with "social proof" in the form of a friend's endorsement. Nagaraj reasoned that this novel concept would help the site grow virally, since daters would be highly motivated to sign up friends who could vouch for them. This would be an online version of the "wingman" that singles had long relied upon when approaching a possible romantic partner in public—which is why Nagaraj dubbed the new site, which launched in January 2010, "Wings." However, once again he had developed his product without conducting extensive consumer interviews—in this case, failing to get feedback on the appeal of the wingman concept.

Anyone with a Facebook account could use Wings, free of charge. Users joined either as a single or, when invited by a single, as a wingman. Users could then edit and augment profiles that were automatically generated using Facebook data, as well as information collected by Triangulate's other life-stream connectors. Users were given badges that signified behaviors and interests gleaned from the data, like "celebrity sunglasses" for being tagged in many photos or headphones for a strong interest in music. Wingmen could highlight aspects of a single friend's profile and add anecdotes about him or her. Singles could peruse each other's profiles and also received five free recommended matches per day. Upon sign-up, users received free digital "coins" that they could use to purchase virtual gifts, additional matches, or the ability to message matches. They could buy more coins with real-world currency or earn coins by adding to their profile—say, by authorizing Triangulate to access their Netflix data, or by inviting friends to join. A similar approach to monetizing an otherwise free dating site was already working well for Zoosk.

The team was able to use early data from Wings to refine the matching engine and assess its ability to predict compatibility. A January 2010 test involved fifty pairs of singles who were heterosexual strangers and fifty wingmen who recruited their long-standing romantic partners to help with the test. The engine predicted which ones were the real-life couples with high accuracy.

This time, Nagaraj got a very different reception from VCs: "The venture capitalists believed that we had a sophisticated matching engine, but they didn't push on the technical details of the algorithm. How we told our story about the engine seemed much more important." The VCs were also intrigued by the prospect of viral growth for Wings, which could allow the site to avoid the massive advertising campaigns that drove leading dating sites' cost of acquiring a new subscriber to over $100. By contrast, Nagaraj projected that Triangulate could acquire a paying Wings user for only $45 and that an average paying user would have a lifetime value of $135, based on $15 in monthly revenue from coin purchases over a nine-month customer life. In March 2010, Triangulate closed a $750,000 seed round led by Trinity Ventures, a well-regarded Silicon Valley VC firm. Cash in hand, the co-founders hired their first employee, a graphic designer.

Pivot #2: Wings Clipped; Engine Stalled. Once Wings went live, the team finally started getting the direct input from consumers that they'd mostly neglected up to this point. They became adept at using this feedback to add new features quickly to Wings—testing and learning, in the mode of a nimble Lean Startup. Nagaraj recalled, "In the beginning, we made users' profile photos very small, because we felt that they should trust our engine rather than defaulting to looks. But users wanted to look at lots of big photos. We tested this by adding a dummy 'Photos' button. When users clicked on it, it said, 'Coming soon.' After the test got a huge number of clicks, we added fully featured photo albums within a few days."

Wings attracted early users through coverage in the technology press and when Facebook added Wings to a dashboard promoting Platform partners. The startup also spent about $5,000 per month on online ads to attract new users. By September, Wings' user base had grown to thirty-five thousand—thirty-two thousand singles and three thousand wingmen. Ten thousand users—70 percent male/30 percent female—were in California, where Triangulate concentrated its marketing efforts to boost the odds of users finding geographically desirable matches.

It cost Triangulate about $5 to sign up each new user through geographically targeted ads on Facebook and other ad networks. Another set of ad networks ran ads that offered incentives to consumers—say, digital coins that they could spend on Farmville or other social games—if they registered with Wings. Triangulate paid only 50 cents per new user acquired through these social gaming–focused networks, but this method posed two problems. First, not all of the incentivized users were truly interested in dating: On average, only 25 percent of them returned to Wings in the week after their initial visit. Second, the users were spread across the United States. Those in California had solid odds of finding a nearby match, but new users in places like North Dakota didn't. Disappointed, they disengaged and, even worse, gave Wings low satisfaction scores in Facebook Platform's app store, which drove up customer acquisition costs.

Managing content that was crowdsourced from users yielded important insights about their preferences, which in turn spawned new features. For example, to counteract a small minority of users who posted inappropriate photos, Nagaraj was personally reviewing all photo submissions: roughly fifteen hundred photos per day from about three hundred new users. To relieve this burden, the team created a "Rate Singles" feature that outsourced the reviewing task to users, who were asked to rate the photos' attractiveness under the auspices of improving their own matches. This proved very popular and, for some, downright addictive: Heavy users of the feature were spending up to forty-five minutes at a single stretch, clicking on a new photo every five seconds or so. The Rate Singles feature soon accounted for 20 percent of Wings' page views.

A user's attractiveness rating provided one input to a quality score that became the primary criterion for recommending daily matches. By October 2010, it became clear that users didn't consider the matching engine's algorithmically generated results to be superior, so Triangulate gave up on using the original engine for that purpose. This was their first false start. Instead, the team now relied on practical metrics to calculate a user quality score, with high marks given to users with completed profiles; photos rated by the community as "attractive"; responsiveness to messages; and heavy usage. Nagaraj reflected on the decision to set aside the matching engine: "What we've learned about consumers—after almost two years—is that they just want a date. They want someone they find interesting to answer them. It's a very practical need. The goal is to find a person, not an algorithm. And consumers like me often make snap judgments based on superficial impressions."

In the fall of 2010, Triangulate also dropped the wingman feature, their second false start. Compared to singles, wingmen were not as engaged and were not delivering hoped-for virality. Furthermore, maintaining these two roles made the site cumbersome to navigate and added to the time required to program new features.

In September 2010, metrics for the site were mixed. The good news: Wings' user base had grown 44 percent, month over month. The bad news: User engagement was underwhelming, with only 27 percent of new users in California returning in week two after they signed up. Also, virality was low. Anticipating a strong network effect and a boost from wingmen, Nagaraj had originally projected that each new user would attract an average of 0.8 additional new users. However, in September, new users in California were each only bringing in a negligible 0.03 additional new users. Finally, coin spending was low, averaging just 177 coins per California user per month. To make matters worse, Triangulate had sold just a tiny fraction of these coins; users acquired the rest from the 200 coins freely awarded upon sign-up and from actions taken on Wings. The selling price of a coin was one U.S. cent, so the site had a long way to go to reach Nagaraj's original projection of $15 in revenue per paying user per month.

The team had a range of plans to improve engagement, virality, and revenue, such as adding a subscription option to Wings. Excited about these plans, in October 2010, Nagaraj was gearing up to raise a Series A round. He'd just recruited a head of marketing and a chief technology officer, but that month he got a shot across the bow. At a board meeting, an investor/adviser who'd founded an online gaming company told Nagaraj, "When virality hits, it happens within a few months, and you've had a few months." The board even discussed rescinding the two recent job offers to slow the depletion of Triangulate's cash reserves.

Pivot #3: DateBuzz. After the board meeting—described by Nagaraj as "the single worst day of my life"—he and his co-founders regrouped. They decided to keep the new hires, but the board's push led them to brainstorm options for a new dating site. Building on the success of "Rate Singles," they came up with other ideas for new features that would make a dating site more social. In December 2010, Triangulate launched DateBuzz, which let users vote on various "bite-sized" elements of other users' profiles—their self-description, lists of favorite movies or songs, badges, and so forth—*before* viewing their photos. Nagaraj elaborated: "Most online dating users are dissatisfied with their level of interaction. So much hinges on reactions to photos. Less attractive individuals get too little attention, and more attractive individuals get too much." Based on the votes a user gave, DateBuzz showed them matches that Triangulate's software suggested they would like. "When users started this way," Nagaraj explained, "many of the less attractive individuals got more attention, and the more attractive individuals still got plenty. We redistributed traffic and attention to encourage a broader cross section of users to interact with each other."

Although DateBuzz had solved a major pain point for online daters, the site did not immediately take off. DateBuzz was seeded with users from Wings, which had been shut down, but only about three thousand Wings users—roughly one-third of its active base—migrated to the new site. The team also purchased online ads and experimented with a range of "guerrilla" marketing tactics, such as handing out flyers at train stations. However, after a few months, the average cost to acquire a new DateBuzz user was still about $5—no lower than it had been for Wings.

In February 2011, when Triangulate still had $200,000 of cash on hand but was spending about $50,000 per month, Nagaraj approached Trinity Ventures about funding Series A. Trinity's partner told him, "We love you as an entrepreneur, but we're not sure what's keeping you going. If you can share what gets you so excited, we'll work something out." This soft touch made Nagaraj think deeply about whether to forge ahead.

On the one hand, Triangulate's team had become what Nagaraj described as "a well-oiled machine." With DateBuzz, they "took the juiciest feature out of Wings—bite-sized voting—and turned it into a product that actually was changing the dynamics of online dating. We only had to crack the code on acquiring users. Virality could improve after a critical mass of users had experienced the product." On the other hand, friends who were entrepreneurs or VCs told Nagaraj, "with varying degrees of diplomacy, that Triangulate was not going to hit the bar for raising Series A." Nagaraj got close to selling Triangulate to a big tech company but never received an offer. In March 2011, he saw the writing on the wall. He shut the company down, paid his employees severance, helped all of them get new jobs, and returned $120,000 of the $750,000 seed round to his investors.

Triangulate's team had completed three big product pivots in two years but never found a market. In that, they are hardly alone: An analysis of startup postmortems by CB Insights shows that "no market need" was the most frequently cited cause of failure. When I took a step back to study other early-stage startups that had targeted opportunities that turned out to be weak or nonexistent, I learned that many, like Triangulate, had rushed their first product to market before conducting enough customer research. Not surprisingly, their product failed to hit the mark. So, they had to head back to the product design drawing board—having burned through scarce cash and wasted precious time.

With these new insights, I returned to Triangulate for a rigorous postmortem. My first question: Was Nagaraj simply a hapless jockey? Far from it, in my view. Nagaraj wisely avoided a co-CEO arrangement with his original co-founder, wary of the potential delays in decision-making. He recruited and led a very able team—one that could rapidly process customer feedback and, in response, crank out novel features with remarkable speed. And, Nagaraj raised funds from a top-flight venture capital firm. Weak founders rarely attract strong teams and smart money.

So, what went wrong? Lean Startup gurus advise founders to "launch early and often," putting a real product into the hands of real customers to secure their feedback as fast as possible. Triangulate's team did that, over and over. With each product iteration, they responded to customer feedback quickly and pivoted in a nimble manner. In doing so, they heeded another Lean Startup mantra: Fail Fast.

But Triangulate's team, like many entrepreneurs, neglected yet another Lean Startup precept: complete "customer discovery"— a thorough round of interviews with prospective customers—*before* designing and developing a minimum viable product. In Nagaraj's postmortem analysis of Triangulate's failure, he acknowledged skipping this crucial early step: "In retrospect, I should have spent a few months talking to as many customers as possible before we started to code. And I completely ignored a question that many friends were asking me, which revealed a lot about their true needs: 'Are there any hot girls or guys on the site?' "

As a result, the opportunity that Triangulate pursued was riddled with flaws. Looking at the four opportunity elements, only Technology & Operations was on track; the other three exhibited serious problems.

Customer Value Proposition. Triangulate's team never identified a differentiated, superior solution to a strong, unmet need. The wingman concept had limited appeal. In his postmortem analysis, Nagaraj acknowledged that individuals might not want their dating ups and downs to be an open book to friends. Furthermore, the pivot to matching based on user attractiveness and engagement measures didn't sufficiently differentiate Wings from existing dating sites, which used similar approaches for matching but offered access to many more potential romantic partners. In short, Wings had evolved into a *Middling Mousetrap*.

DateBuzz was a move in a better direction. Its social features helped boost engagement, and voting on aspects of user profiles other than photos addressed a real consumer pain point. However, Triangulate's cash well was running dry by the time its team identified this promising opportunity.

Triangulate also suffered from poor market timing. Nagaraj saw an opportunity to leverage Facebook Platform, but by the time Wings launched, Zoosk had already captured a dominant share of Facebook daters. Latecomers who fail to offer a superior solution will almost always face an uphill battle, especially if they target a market—like online dating—with strong network effects. Nagaraj reflected, "At first, the industry seems approachable, which is why new online dating startups are launched every week. Most of these entrepreneurs are single, like I was. From personal experience, they see lots of problems with dating sites that make them obvious targets for improvement. But network effects are incredibly strong in dating because people are really picky. It's not just about getting a ton of users. There need to be many compatible pockets of the network—like enough San Francisco–based twenty-eight-year-olds who are athletic, use good grammar, and don't mention God in their profile—or do. And every variation you can imagine."

He continued, "To attract these users, you have to compete in a mature industry with behemoths like Match, who've bid up customer acquisition costs over the past twenty years. They look like tech companies, but they are really huge marketing machines. Match spends something like 70 percent of revenue on ads, which is why everyone knows about it. I made the mistake of thinking of Triangulate as a technology company that could succeed with a great product alone."

The challenge of developing a superior value proposition for

Wings and DateBuzz was compounded by the fact that their services were free—at least until a dater exhausted his initial grant of coins and wished to message a match. Being free removed a barrier to signing up—a good thing, given network effects—but it also meant that Triangulate attracted many casual users who were just "poking around." By contrast, someone who pays $60 for a monthly subscription to eHarmony is much more likely to be a serious dater who spends time on the site and responds to messages.

Furthermore, being free made it difficult for Wings and DateBuzz to cope with a conundrum confronting all dating services that aspire to help users find a committed romantic partner: If they satisfy their customers, their customers go away. With a service like Match or eHarmony, satisfied customers terminate their subscriptions, and then their profiles are removed from the site. But with a free site, the profile of a dater who loses interest—for whatever reason—will remain in view. Users who message these stale profiles will be disappointed—and be more likely to abandon the site.

Marketing. Lacking a critical mass of users—and therefore unable to harness network effects—Wings and DateBuzz found it difficult to attract new users: a Catch-22. Nagaraj also wrongly assumed that word-of-mouth referrals by wingmen would drive viral growth, eliminating the need for big spending on marketing. That plan—*Build It and They Will Come*—didn't pan out. It turned out Wings acquired 60 percent of users through ads; only 30 percent through word of mouth, press coverage, and Facebook's dashboard; and a mere 10 percent through in-app viral actions. A $750,000 seed round simply wasn't big enough to fund the marketing required to capture consumer attention and establish a new brand.

Profit Formula. Lacking virality and suffering from a subscale network, Triangulate had to spend more than originally expected on advertising and promotional incentives to acquire users. These unforeseen expenses wreaked havoc on the company's profit formula because the modest revenue that Triangulate could generate from users sending messages and virtual gifts did not come close to covering the marketing outlay needed to acquire each new user. Simply put, Triangulate could not pass a *Show Me the Money* test. A subscription plan might have improved the profit outlook, but the team ran out of runway before testing this idea.

In summary, these flaws stemmed from a set of erroneous assumptions that repeatedly sent Triangulate's team down the wrong path. When he launched Triangulate, Nagaraj believed that computer-generated matches based on behavioral data would be superior to those based on self-reported information and that users of online dating sites would be willing to pay a premium for these improved results. But by failing to test these assumptions before his team commenced engineering work, he discovered too late that "our matching algorithm based on behavioral analytics ended up being unimportant to Wings and DateBuzz. An algorithm can be useful when people feel insecure about their ability to choose, for example, when they are selecting financial services. But if you show me profiles of seven women, I don't believe I'd need any help picking the one I'd like to meet."

Before launching Wings, in late 2009, Nagaraj did field an online survey, asking 150 consumers if they'd prefer matching based on questionnaire responses or objective, computer-generated data. The problem was that the survey didn't rise to the level of a true MVP, which puts a facsimile of a real product in consumers' hands to gauge their demand. Triangulate could have conducted a landing page test by quickly building a website that presented a compelling and authentic-looking marketing pitch for a new dating service— one that leveraged computer-generated behavioral data for matching—and then by inviting consumers to sign up. Nagaraj could've used a similar landing page test to explore demand for the wingman concept, but, again, he bypassed an MVP and launched Wings as a fully functional product.

Had Nagaraj spoken to prospective customers at the outset or tested a true MVP, his team might have designed Triangulate's first product to conform more closely to market needs—and avoided wasting months on software and features that were eventually shelved. He also might have put more effort into enhancing user profiles through use of the life-stream connectors, which did have consumer appeal. And, the team might have iterated faster to the potentially powerful concept of voting on "bite-sized" profile elements.

Why Are Founders Prone to False Starts?

Reflecting on these missteps, Nagaraj admitted that the reason he didn't spend more time talking to consumers about their dating preferences was that he couldn't wait to start building. His bias for action is typical of entrepreneurs, who often are champing at the bit to get started. And engineers—like Nagaraj and his teammates—love to build. So, when you have entrepreneurs who are also engineers, their impulse is often to build and launch their product as fast as they can.

Founders without engineering backgrounds, including many of the MBAs I advise, fall victim to this mistake, too. Nontechnical founders tend to be insecure about their inability to build the solution they envision, having been told repeatedly that having a great product is a "do or die" requirement. Nontechnical founders tend to be persuasive and good at networking, and frequently can recruit an engineer to fill this gap. However, an engineer's hefty compensation means that the cash flow meter is running faster, so the pressure is on to build and launch a product ASAP. As a result, the engineers often start building before the team has a good understanding of the problem or solution.

At the risk of stereotyping, another reason that some technical founders avoid interviewing prospective customers is that many engineers are simply too introverted to push themselves to query strangers. When they do get out and conduct interviews, both engineers and nontechnical founders often botch them by posing leading questions ("Do you like our idea?") and then hearing what they want to hear. The worst offenders are so arrogant about the solution they've come up with—perhaps due to prior industry experience—that they don't see any value at all in customer input.

How to Avoid False Starts

Entrepreneurs can avoid false starts by undertaking a thorough and thoughtful design process *before* commencing engineering work. Founders with a flawed understanding of Lean Startup logic too often skip early process steps—they jump straight to MVP testing, which allows them to build a first version of their product. However, MVP testing should be the *next-to-last* step of the design process. Starting with an MVP forfeits crucial learning from earlier steps.

The full process can be depicted using the Double-Diamond Design framework developed by the British Design Council. The left-hand diamond represents the first phase of the process, *problem definition,* and the right-hand diamond represents the second phase, *solution development.* During the problem definition phase, you identify unmet needs and the customer segments for whom those needs are most pressing. The goal is to ensure that you've found genuine pain or desire—that is, a problem truly worth solving. Once a real problem is identified, you then enter the solution development phase, which involves exploring different ways to address the problem and selecting the best one.

As shown in the following image, the left side of each diamond has arrows pointing away from each other; arrows on each diamond's right side point toward each other. These arrows represent an initial focus on divergent thinking—generating lots of ideas—followed by an emphasis on convergent thinking—deciding which ideas are best. For the problem definition phase, divergent thinking means exploring the full range of customer segments you might plausibly serve and, for each segment, identifying the full set of unmet needs you could conceivably address. Next, convergent thinking allows you to home in on which customer segments you will target and which needs you will focus on. The same "diverge then converge" rhythm applies to solution development. You generate lots of possible solutions to customers' problems and then select the most promising one. In the pages that follow, I lay out a variety of tasks you can undertake at each stage.

The process is depicted as a left-to-right linear flow, but you'll

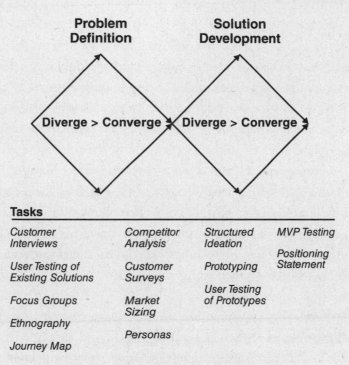

Tasks

Customer Interviews	Competitor Analysis	Structured Ideation	MVP Testing
User Testing of Existing Solutions	Customer Surveys	Prototyping	Positioning Statement
Focus Groups	Market Sizing	User Testing of Prototypes	
Ethnography	Personas		
Journey Map			

The Double-Diamond Design Model

encounter feedback loops at every step. At any point, you might learn something new that sends you back to a prior step to reconsider your earlier work. From there, you commence another left-to-right iterative pass.

Iteration should stop only when you're confident you have formulated a compelling customer value proposition—also known as a positioning statement—that includes answers to all of the blanks listed below:

- **For** [INSERT: target customer segments]
- **dissatisfied with** [INSERT: existing solution]
- **due to** [INSERT: unmet needs],
- [INSERT: venture name] **offers a** [INSERT: product category]
- **that provides** [INSERT: key benefits of your defensible, differentiated solution].

Double-Diamond Design has two core principles. You should not start developing a specific solution until 1) you've defined the problem, that is, you've prioritized a set of strong, unmet needs for distinct customer segments; and 2) you've explored lots of alternatives and you're sure you've identified the one that *best* meets your customers' needs and also allows you to earn a healthy profit over the long term.

Most entrepreneurs have a solution in mind at the outset. That's good, but Double-Diamond Design asks you not to become too emotionally attached to that solution. Rather, you should stay open to possibility: More pressing unmet needs or better solutions might be out there. Entrepreneurs who fall victim to a false start are closed to these possibilities; they jump directly to the end of the design process.

My survey of early-stage founders shows that many are vulnerable to false starts. Specifically, compared to their counterparts in more successful ventures, founder/CEOs of startups that are struggling or have shut down conducted significantly less up-front customer research, were less likely to complete rigorous MVP tests, and were less likely to say they had a very deep understanding of customer needs. Also, compared to their more successful counterparts, these founder/CEOs said they completed too few or too many pivots. These findings are consistent with the False Start failure pattern: Founders who skip up-front research are more likely to need to pivot away from an initially flawed solution. Likewise, as we've seen, a false start consumes capital, reducing the number of pivots that the startup can ultimately complete.

To avoid a false start, it's important to understand the objectives for each step in the Double-Diamond Design process, the tasks you can undertake at each step, and best practices for completing those tasks. These topics can and do fill entire books. Here, I'll share just a few salient points about each of the key tasks and highlight some mistakes that entrepreneurs make in executing them.

Customer Interviews. Customer interviews form the backbone of the problem definition phase. Lean Startup guru Steve Blank exhorts entrepreneurs to "get out of the building" and conduct *customer discovery interviews* before they start building. "Discovery" is the right mindset: Entrepreneurs should be looking for unmet customer needs. If an entrepreneur doesn't conduct enough customer interviews (Nagaraj's misstep), speaks to the wrong individuals, or manages the conversations poorly, she cannot be sure that she's identified a problem worth solving. Common errors with customer interviews include:

- **Assuming you understand customer needs because you *are* the customer.** To some extent, Nagaraj fell into this trap, extrapolating his own preferences when designing dating solutions. But people have very different needs when they date online. It's not necessarily a mistake to create a solution that addresses your own needs—provided you've spoken to enough potential customers to be confident that a sizable number share them.

- **Convenience sampling.** Entrepreneurs often interview friends, family, and co-workers because they're easy to reach and likely to cooperate. Unfortunately, because we tend to surround ourselves with people similar to us, this can be akin to interviewing yourself. Also, friends and family may be inclined to tell an obsessed and stressed entrepreneur what they think she *wants* to hear rather than what they really think.

- **Not interviewing all concerned parties.** It's important to interview everyone who'll have a voice in the purchasing decision. In a business-to-business setting, for example, the end users of a software system are typically not the individuals who select it or authorize its purchase. Likewise, in a family setting, parents may decide what their children are allowed to consume. In these cases, you need to seek feedback both from the end user *and* the decision-maker.

- **Focusing only on early adopters.** The instinct to cater to the needs of one's early adopters is understandable—after all, these are the people you'll rely on to spread the word about your product. But early adopters for a new solution often have stronger—and different—needs than "mainstream" individuals who may purchase later. For example, the earliest adopters of Dropbox were über-geeks who had sophisticated requirements for synchronizing files across devices, sharing files, and backing up their work. By contrast, years after the service launched, a typical new user might struggle to find the "Power" button on her PC. Dropbox wisely designed the product so this user could still navigate it successfully.

Simultaneously meeting the needs of early adopters and mainstream users is a challenge. I'll devote the next chapter to exploring this dilemma, but here, I'll merely emphasize that it's important to understand the differences between the needs of each group. Put simply, you must research both. The distinction between early adopters and mainstream users is relevant not only for customer interviews but for all the research techniques discussed below.

• **Leading questions.** Entrepreneurs must take care not to phrase questions in ways that encourage respondents to say what the interviewer hopes to hear. Instead of "Wouldn't you say it takes too much time to sort through stale Match profiles?" ask a more open-ended question, like "What's been your experience searching through Match profiles?"

• **Asking for predictions.** If you ask someone what they'll do in the future, you'll often get wishful thinking—especially if the behavior is desirable. For example, "How often will you go to the gym next month?" might elicit the response, "Every other day." Instead, ask about past behavior, for example: "How often did you go to the gym last month?" which might yield, "Um, I've been busy, and I haven't been there in three weeks." Despite any caveats they might add about extenuating circumstances, past behavior is likely a good indicator of how they will behave in the future.

• **Pitching your solution.** Entrepreneurs tend to be so excited about their ideas that they can't resist pitching them to see how people react. But this is not a helpful exercise. Whether it's because they don't want to hurt your feelings, or because your intensity scares them a little (or both), many interviewees will say they love your concept, even if they don't. Early in the design process, founders shouldn't waste time pitching. There's a right time and a right way to get feedback on solutions, later on. At this point entrepreneurs should be probing only for unmet needs.

User Testing of Existing Solutions. You can learn a lot about unmet needs by observing how target customers use a rival's existing product. Ask them to talk aloud as they complete typical tasks, saying what they like and dislike, what confuses them, etc. Nagaraj, for example, could have asked consumers to search for a date on eHarmony or fill out their profile upon registering at Match and then noted their reactions.

Focus Groups and Ethnography. These two techniques aren't suited for every venture. Focus groups are best for products that elicit strong emotional reactions; for that reason, they would have worked well for Triangulate. In a focus group, a well-trained facilitator leads a discussion among six or so strangers with similar backgrounds, in a setting that feels psychologically safe. Ideally, one individual's comments will spur reactions, memories, and stories from the others that might not emerge in one-on-one interviews. But it takes a skilled facilitator to get everyone talking, to avoid groupthink, to gently quiet individuals who otherwise would dominate the discussion, and to defuse harsh judgments of others' comments.

Ethnography—going "into the field" to observe individuals directly as they try to solve a problem—is a favorite technique of professional designers. For example, an entrepreneur building an online grocery service might learn a lot by watching shoppers traverse a brick-and-mortar grocery store. Of course, this kind of access isn't always feasible. For instance, you couldn't observe couples deciding which contraceptive method to use. And, as with focus groups, it takes some training to know what to look for in the field.

Journey Mapping. After using these research tools to gain an expanded understanding of the problem space, it's important to synthesize one's learning. *Journey mapping* offers a visual method. On the map's horizontal axis, you plot all the sequential steps in a customer's buying journey: gaining awareness of a problem, researching potential solutions, purchasing one, using the solution, seeking after-sale service, considering repurchase, etc. Then in each vertical column, you add text at each step that briefly describes issues that impact the customer's level of satisfaction or her emotional state—in either positive or negative ways. For example, for Dropbox, "Easy and quick download" would be plotted on the positive end of the vertical axis for the early buying journey step "Installation." You should create separate maps for different types of customers.

Competitor Analysis. Having identified a broad range of unmet customer needs for different customer segments, you now shift into convergent thinking mode. The goal: Decide which unmet needs to address and which customer segments to target. Through customer interviews and user testing of existing solutions, you should have developed hypotheses about unmet needs. Now, it's important to confirm that those needs are truly not being met, which requires a more comprehensive competitor analysis. Is it possible that a rival already offers a superior solution? You may *think* you've encountered every existing solution, but entrepreneurs are startled by rivals all the time. After working on a problem and its solution for weeks, they stumble upon a competitor that seems to have a silver bullet. It's better to be systematic about assessing the competition early rather than risk being surprised later on.

Competitor analysis usually takes the form of a grid, with rows representing the features and performance attributes (e.g., reliability, ease of use) and columns showing existing solutions, as well as your own startup's envisioned product. A version of this chart makes it into almost every entrepreneur's pitch deck, with check marks in every cell for the startup's own product ("We'll do all of that!") and—of course—fewer checks for rivals.

There are two traps to avoid when conducting competitor analysis. The first is ignoring features or performance attributes for which your prospective solution falls short. It's easy to fall prey to wishful thinking—for example, "this feature really doesn't matter"— especially when pitching investors. The second trap: contending that you actually don't have any competitors because your product is the first of its kind. Sometimes, radically new concepts—like Airbnb—

truly inaugurate a new product category. But such category-defining inventions are rare, and most investors will view "we have no rivals" with skepticism. Somehow, humans have been trying to solve the problem that you'll address, and it's crucial to understand what customers like and don't like about those supposedly inferior solutions.

Customer Surveys. Surveys can be a powerful tool when deciding which problems and customer segments to target. They should be used to validate hypotheses about the extent to which an existing solution meets a given need. Surveys can also be used to corroborate assumptions about differences in the needs and preferences of certain customer segments. Finally, surveys can help size the market opportunity by asking how often respondents engage in certain behaviors.

When conducting surveys, entrepreneurs are prone to many of the same errors they make with customer interviews: convenience sampling, posing leading questions, and asking respondents to predict their future behavior. Other mistakes include not pilot testing questions for clarity, excessive survey length, and too-small sample sizes from which it's impossible to draw valid inferences.

Another common pitfall is surveying customers too early in the design process. You can't ask the right survey questions until you have hypotheses to prove or disprove—which means first completing the research described above. It's easy to see why entrepreneurs often jump the gun, when SurveyMonkey and similar online services make surveys so easy to administer. Also, survey results *feel* scientific and can boost a pitch's credibility. For example, when Nagaraj conducted an online survey to gauge the appeal of behavioral matching, he was motivated mostly by a desire to impress investors.

Market Sizing. Estimating the size of the *total addressable market* (TAM) is a crucial step before you're ready to move out of the problem definition phase. Even if your startup offers a compelling solution to a real problem, it can still fail if the initial targeted market is too small and you don't have a clear path to broadening the set of customer segments you'll serve. Sizing the market involves estimating the number of prospects who could conceivably be interested in your offering: both current customers of rival products who might prefer your superior solution and non-customers whose needs aren't being served by any of your existing competitors. Market size estimates typically are based on customer survey results and/or published data. The trap here mirrors the one discussed above for other research tasks: putting your thumb on the scale to impress investors, and then believing your own exaggerated projections. This trap is an easy one to fall into, which explains why most pitch deck estimates of a new venture's TAM reach or exceed $1 billion.

Personas. The best way to synthesize all of this convergent thinking is to develop *personas*—fictional examples of archetypal customers used to focus product designs and craft marketing messages. Personas often have memorable names—say, "Picky Paula," for a hard-to-satisfy dater—along with imagined photos, specific demographic and behavioral attributes (e.g., recent Duke graduate living in Austin who's been dating online for six months and visits OkCupid and Coffee Meets Bagel several times per week), and distinctive functional and psychological needs (e.g., not inclined to discuss online dating habits with friends and family; very concerned about safety when meeting matches in real life). Personas should seem like real people to make it easier for the team to view potential solutions from this person's perspective. After a startup embraces personas, team members will use them as shorthand when discussing product design options and marketing messages (e.g., "Paula wouldn't like that because . . .").

It's generally best to create three to five personas, with one or two being "primary," that is, representative of your target customer segments. Having too many primary personas can result in a product that tries to be all things to all people. Other personas can represent key influencers in the purchase process (e.g., wingmen, for Triangulate) or customer segments that your startup will explicitly *not* target.

Brainstorming. Also known as structured ideation, brainstorming is the first task as a startup shifts from problem definition to solution development. The best brainstorming practices are ones that help a team spawn as many ideas as possible. For example: asking people to generate ideas before anyone speaks, discouraging naysayers from shooting down others' ideas, ensuring that everyone shares, giving people space to build upon one another's concepts, voting on which ideas should be developed further, and corralling "HiPPOs"—the highest paid person's opinions. The brainstorming process should be as inclusive as possible, recognizing that great ideas truly can come from anywhere.

Prototyping. With lots of ideas in hand, your team can turn to prototyping. A prototype is any representation of a design idea, ranging from low to high fidelity. A higher-fidelity prototype is closer to the envisioned final product in terms of its functionality, its "look and feel," or both. A low-fidelity prototype can be as simple as a series of sketches that depict the flow of screens along a software program's navigation path. Jeff Hawkins, inventor of the PalmPilot, famously started designing the device by carving a block of wood into its shape, and then trimming a chopstick that he used as a stylus. To get a feel for whether and how he might use a PalmPilot, he carried the prototype for weeks, pulling it out every time he needed to schedule a meeting or access contact information.

Early in the solution development process, an entrepreneur is likely to create both "works like" and "looks like" prototypes. "Works like" prototypes explore technical feasibility and show how a solution will deliver required functionality. Nagaraj's aborted RescueTime trial was a "works like" prototype, aimed at demonstrating that algorithmic analysis of digital data could predict romantic compatibility. When Hawkins showed his block of wood to someone, he was getting their reactions to a low-fidelity "looks like" prototype.

When creating "looks like" prototypes, it can be tricky to decide how much fidelity is ideal. On the one hand, polished, high-fidelity prototypes make it easier for potential customers to envision the intended solution, so their feedback may be more reliable. High-fidelity prototypes also provide a clear road map for engineers who'll build the product ("Make the screens look exactly like this"). But on the other hand, high fidelity has a number of drawbacks:

• Creating a high-fidelity prototype takes more effort. If a lower-fidelity version will yield useful feedback, this additional effort can be wasteful—especially early in the design process, when lots of potential solutions are likely to be rejected.

• Without proper guidance, reviewers may focus excessively on cosmetic design elements (e.g., "That button is too red"). Choices about such elements aren't relevant at this stage of the process; polish will come later.

• Some reviewers may be reluctant to criticize a prototype if they sense that a great deal of effort has gone into its creation—simply because they don't want to hurt the designers' feelings.

• Finally, some designers and engineers may become emotionally attached to a prototype in which they've invested great effort. As a result, they may be reluctant to abandon it and thus be inclined to ignore negative feedback.

Prototype Testing. The methods for getting feedback on prototypes are similar to those discussed above for User Testing of Existing Solutions. Potential customers can be asked to talk aloud while they use the prototype to complete specified tasks. A great trick is to show someone two prototypes at the same time, then ask which they like better. As just noted, test subjects are often reluctant to criticize a design, but they'll be happy to say which of two options they like better, and why. Throughout, the focus should be on whether the solution delivers value, not on the prototype's usability or attractiveness—again, that will come later. To explore perceptions of value, questions might include:

• What problems would this product solve?
• When would someone really need this? Why?
• Today, what might someone use instead to solve the problem? Why might this new solution be better? Worse?
• What barriers might someone encounter when using this product?
• What's missing? What could be removed?

With the last questions, you are not looking for design advice; test subjects aren't good at that. Instead, you are probing for unmet needs. So, if they say something's missing, your response should be, "Okay, why would you want that?" A question to avoid is "Would you use this?" As with interview and survey questions, the answer from someone eager to please will too often be "yes."

MVP Testing. Prototyping and prototype testing should proceed in iterative loops until a dominant design emerges. Based on test feedback, designers should reject some prototypes and refine others, producing higher-fidelity versions. Once they converge on a single, favored solution, it's time for minimum viable product testing.

An MVP is a prototype—a facsimile of the future product. What distinguishes an MVP from other prototypes is how it is tested. Rather than sitting across a table, getting verbal feedback from a reviewer, you put a prototype that seems like a real product in the hands of real customers in a real-world context. The goal is to quickly but rigorously test assumptions about the demand for your solution—and gain what Eric Ries calls "validated learning"—with as little wasted effort as possible. A good MVP should embody the lowest fidelity possible to get reliable feedback because lower fidelity implies less wasted effort. Put another way, an MVP should provide no more "looks like" polish and "works like" functionality than is strictly necessary to conduct a test. Functionality comes in two flavors. *Front-end* functionality encompasses everything directly experienced by customers; for Wings it was daters' profiles, daily matches, messaging, search, etc. *Back-end* functionality is invisible to the customer but integral to serving them. For Wings, this would include the lifestream connectors, the matching algorithm, the servers, etc.

MVPs come in four basic types, depending on whether they constrain front-end functionality, back-end functionality, or both:

• **Constrained Front-End Functionality.** These MVPs omit peripheral product features and focus only on the solution's core front-end features. If customers don't perceive the core features to be valuable, there's no point in building the rest.

- **Constrained Back-End Functionality.** MVPs can rely on make-shift, temporary methods to perform functions that are not visible to the customer—for example, having humans analyze digital data to suggest matches instead of relying on software algorithms. Again, there's no point in investing in automation until demand is validated. Such MVPs are sometimes called "Wizard of Oz" tests, recalling the admonition in that movie: "Pay no attention to the man behind the curtain."

- **Constrained Front- and Back-End Functionality.** "Concierge" MVPs use humans to provide *all* functionality—both front- and back-end. Doing everything manually is only possible if you are testing your MVP with a small number of customers. And, keeping the test group small ensures that the entrepreneur will interact directly and intensively with those customers—learning a lot in the process.

- **Smoke Tests.** Some MVPs constrain both front- and back-end functionality to the extreme, testing demand for a product that has not yet been built. Well-designed smoke tests describe the planned product in enough detail that a customer can commit in advance to purchasing it, once it's available. Examples include landing page tests, crowdfunding campaigns like Jibo's, and letters of intent signed by business customers.

The biggest mistake entrepreneurs make with MVP tests is not conducting them at all. But you can make other errors, too—for example, failing to specify a threshold for test success. After all, proper hypotheses can be proven true or false only if tests have a measurable outcome. "Our product will spread virally through positive referrals from happy customers" is too vague because observing just one referral would be enough to pass this test. Better to specify that every ten new customers will bring in eight more.

Another common error with MVP tests is revising one's assumptions and pivoting either too quickly or too slowly in response to test results. Before they pivot, entrepreneurs should ask whether the results they've observed might be false negatives or false positives. False negatives—for example, a test result that suggests that demand will be weak, when in truth it would be strong—might be a spurious reaction to a low-fidelity MVP or a poorly executed test, as opposed to a genuine rejection of the venture's value proposition. False positives—for example, observing robust demand when true demand would be weak—are more likely when an entrepreneur recruits subjects who are category enthusiasts and not representative of the customers the venture will actually target. False positives are a recurring risk for early-stage startups and will be the focus of the next chapter.

CHAPTER 5

False Positives

You land a big whale, and they just drag you along.
—Lindsay Hyde, Baroo founder/CEO

Lindsay Hyde founded Baroo, a pet care provider, in mid-2014. Fittingly, the startup's name was pet-inspired: A dog does a "baroo" when he tilts his head inquisitively in response to a human's voice. Hyde's original concept for Baroo was "Bright Horizons for pets," that is, pet daycare in an office setting, but her early customer research revealed low demand. Commercial property managers were lukewarm—they couldn't pass on the added cost of pet daycare to corporate tenants in the form of higher rent because they'd negotiated long-term leases and their turnover was low. Hyde also discovered that demand from office workers was limited. In an MVP test with twenty-five Harvard University employees who owned pets, no one was willing to pay $20 for a day of pet care at work. While in theory owners thought it'd be fun to see their pets during the day, in reality they didn't want the hassle of commuting to work with them. It was easier to leave a dog or cat at home and arrange for a pet care provider to visit during the day.

That last finding triggered a pivot: Baroo would rent out underutilized space in the basements of apartment buildings and offer pet daycare near people's homes. Residential property managers were very interested because one-third of apartments turn over annually and this amenity could make their buildings more appealing to new residents with pets. Plus, buildings often charge such residents "pet rent," an extra monthly fee to cover the wear and tear caused by dogs or cats.

To gauge demand for her revised concept, Hyde surveyed 250 pet owners at a pet festival. She learned that 80 percent were not satisfied with their dog walker and a similar percentage said that they'd use a pet daycare in their apartment building. Hyde later reflected, "That was encouraging, but I should have asked if they would *switch* from their current provider. Switching costs are very high in this business, once someone gets to know your pet and your household's routines."

Hyde recruited a co-founder, Meg Reiss, who'd been chief operating officer at the first startup Hyde had founded. After raising $1.2 million from angel investors in February 2014, the co-founders launched their service at Ink Block, a newly converted, 315-unit luxury apartment building in Boston's trendy South End neighborhood. Hyde's plan was to start small, and once they achieved profitability, use those profits to fund further expansion. That way, she wouldn't need to raise money from VCs and could avoid their typical pressure for hypergrowth. Consistent with that plan, she'd sought out angel investors who would be satisfied with solid returns in exchange for moderate levels of risk over a three- to five-year payback period.

Baroo offered a range of "high-touch" pet care services, including dog walking, grooming, feeding, in-home sitting, and playdates. Pet owners could book Baroo's services using text, email, phone, or an off-the-shelf scheduling app that Hyde had licensed. And, Baroo's care providers communicated directly with pet owners—sending daily reports or photos, responding to special requests, etc.—through those same channels. The providers would pick the pets up from their clients' apartments, letting themselves in with keys left by pet owners in special lockboxes right outside their doors. The team provided care for any type of pet, not just dogs and cats. Fees were on par with those charged by other pet care providers in the neighborhood—for example, $20 for a thirty-minute solo dog walk. Hyde hadn't completely pivoted away from the pet daycare concept, but she put it on the back burner because, at the time, Ink Block and other early part-ners lacked the space; however, they were open to adding pet daycare facilities in the future.

Most pet care services hire their staff as contract workers, but Hyde decided instead to hire pet care providers as regular employ-ees, mostly on a part-time basis. She reasoned that this would lower turnover, making it easier for Baroo to train employees, implement consistent processes, and justify investing more in building employ-ees' skills. Baroo's workforce would be professional: subject to thor-ough background checks, insured, and wearing uniforms. The total cost to screen, equip, and train a new care provider approached $500. However, hiring employees did have one drawback: Unlike rival pet care services Rover and Wag!, which compensated contract workers only for jobs they completed, Baroo had to pay an hourly wage—averaging $13—to any employee who'd started his shift, even if the startup had no bookings for him.

To acquire customers, Baroo did not invest in traditional paid marketing, such as Facebook ads. Instead, the startup relied on the marketing efforts of apartment building partners and on word-of-mouth referrals from existing customers. Buildings would distribute a welcome gift from Baroo—a chew toy or leash—to new residents who owned pets. The team also hosted quarterly events for resi-dents, such as "yappy hours" and pet Halloween. Finally, building concierge staff would recommend Baroo to residents. In exchange, the startup paid buildings a share of the revenue that it earned from their residents, averaging about 6 percent. Such revenue sharing is standard practice for service providers, like cable TV companies, that want access to residents.

When Baroo launched at Ink Block in South Boston, about 60 percent of the residents owned a pet, and an impressive 70 percent of these pet owners used Baroo's services. Hyde was thrilled with this strong adoption rate and took it to mean that high demand would be replicated with other apartment buildings. Unfortunately, she had fallen prey to our third failure pattern: the *False Positive*. In the context of medical testing, a false positive—that is, a test result that shows that you have a disease when you really don't—can result in unnecessary and dangerous treatments, along with lots of anxiety. In the context of startups, a false positive—early success rates that appear more promising than they actually are—can lead to expansion on a level that is not yet warranted. As it turns out, a false positive can be as harmful for startups as it is for patients.

A false positive often stems from circumstances that inflate early adoption rates. In this case, Baroo's initial blockbuster success was misleading due to three factors that were unique to the launch:

- First, because Ink Block was brand-new, 100 percent of its apartments had recently been filled simultaneously. Upon moving in, most residents were new to the neighborhood and lacked a preferred pet care provider, so they didn't incur any switching costs by using Baroo. By contrast, pet owners who've lived in an established building for several years already have a pet care solution and would confront switching costs if they changed providers.
- Second, it turned out that many Ink Block units were occupied by members of a Hollywood production crew shooting a film in Boston. They'd brought their pets, had no time to care for them, and, with generous per diems, had plenty of money to pay for Baroo's services.
- Finally, the month Baroo launched, Mother Nature dumped a record-breaking ninety-four inches of snow on Boston—almost eight feet!—within just thirty days. Hyde recalled, "Nobody wanted to walk their dog, so we were serving many households multiple times per day. We failed to see that this was a false positive signal. Instead, we reasoned that if we could operate through that winter, we could do anything."

Early Success Spurs Expansion

As business boomed for Baroo, word spread fast about Boston's hot new pet concierge service. The leasing team at Ink Block tipped off their counterparts at other buildings and Ink Block residents told their neighbors. Soon, Baroo was flooded with unsolicited requests from other property managers in Boston—and quickly signed up four more buildings. Plans to steer clear of venture capital and aggressive expansion were set aside; Hyde and the three angel investors who comprised Baroo's board of directors now decided to rapidly replicate Baroo's success in a second city, which they reasoned would help attract venture capital. Hyde revealed, "We felt we had great proof points and a path to geographic expansion with building partners who managed properties across the country. In retrospect, I didn't have the discipline to pass up these growth opportunities."

In the summer of 2015, Baroo expanded to Chicago, where it quickly signed up three buildings that had the same corporate parent as one of their Boston partners. The venture eventually served twenty-five buildings in the heart of downtown Chicago. One of these had space for a dog daycare and leased it for free to Baroo, allowing the team to finally test that earlier concept, which was well received.

Finding the right general manager for Chicago was a struggle. The first GM, a seasoned property manager, turned out to be a poor fit with the startup's culture. As Hyde recalled, "Someone with that training is accustomed to doing everything exactly as specified in the manual, but we didn't have a manual."

A year after commencing operations in Chicago, Baroo raised an additional $2.25 million in seed capital from new angel investors and small VC funds and launched in Washington, D.C., where they again signed buildings managed by national real estate companies with whom they'd worked in Boston and Chicago. But Washington held some unpleasant surprises: Customer attrition spiked when the Trump administration took control in January 2017 and many federal employees who'd been appointed by President Obama left town. Also, apartment buildings were more dispersed in D.C. than in Boston or Chicago, which added travel time between jobs for Baroo care providers.

Managing three locations stretched Baroo's small team to the limit. Hyde commented, "My co-founder Meg had done a spectacular job running operations up to this point, but Washington brought overwhelming new challenges." Despite this, in June 2017, Baroo launched service in a fourth location: the New York City metropolitan area. To fund further expansion, the startup raised another $1.0 million from existing investors and a venture capital firm that had expressed interest in later leading Baroo's Series A round.

By that time, however, the team was feeling some serious growing pains. Relationships with some property managers were strained. Many property managers failed to encourage their building concierges to recommend Baroo, and some property managers were unreasonably inflexible about contractual agreements. For example, they insisted that Baroo organize events for residents, something that Baroo had initially promised but that became less practical as the company expanded. Hyde recounted, "When we were small, hosting a dog Halloween party was easy and fun. As we started to do it across a hundred buildings, we ended up lighting money on fire for events that we were not getting paid for. We'd send some college kid to buy snacks. He'd come back with a six-pack of Bud and a cheese plate from Target—not exactly the high-end brand experience we aspired to."

Operations were bumpy, too. With greater scale, it became difficult to deliver the personalized service that had delighted early customers. For instance, pet owners could no longer request their favorite walker or phone the office to squeeze in a last-minute walk when Baroo's booking application showed that all care providers were busy. Baroo also lacked the technology to manage at scale. Its off-the-shelf booking application was clunky, so many customers relied instead on email or texting, creating complexity when scheduling. Care providers had to use multiple mobile applications, including one to check in upon starting and finishing jobs and another to see their daily lineup and information about pet owners' requirements.

Scheduling was further complicated by the behavior of some care providers. Hyde had reasoned that hiring them as employees paid by the hour, rather than as contractors paid by the booking, would make it easier to train providers to follow consistent processes. As it turned out, that wasn't always the case. Hyde came to realize that Baroo's compensation approach could skew incentives: "An employee could spend time on easier, more pleasurable jobs, like playing with a cute puppy, and then run late on other jobs, or maybe miss that last job of the day with an unfriendly dog. Being paid by the hour, this had no impact on the employee's earnings."

While most care providers were conscientious, employee screening wasn't foolproof. Hyde recalled that, while attending a wedding, she'd received a phone call from a police officer who informed her that a Baroo pet sitter was throwing a noisy party in a customer's apartment. The company's rapid growth was stretching employee morale to the limit, too. Hyde reflected, "We were growing so fast that we had trouble hiring enough new providers—a problem made much worse by high rates of provider turnover—one hundred and twenty percent annually. So, our really good walkers sometimes ended up working twelve-hour days. We were shuttling them all over the city and paying them hourly. We were burning out our best walkers and burning through our cash."

Reckoning and Shutdown

At Baroo's August 2017 board meeting, one of the company's original angel investors questioned Hyde's leadership and the startup's financial health. For the first six months of 2017, Baroo had earned revenue of $600,000 but had an operating loss of $800,000. And while management projected a 50 percent increase in revenue for the next six months, it forecast an operating loss of $700,000. The board member was alarmed, and he and Hyde sparred over when and if the venture might reach breakeven. She'd explained that Baroo's penetration rate—the percentage of pet owners in a building that were Baroo customers—depended on how long the startup had served the building. Hyde noted that Baroo's penetration rate was much higher with newly arrived residents than with tenants who already had a dog walker. In other words, Baroo had to wait for tenant turnover to kick in: "If you believed that line of reasoning, then you probably figured that things would be okay in new markets in a year or two. But if you didn't believe that logic, you might see our margins deteriorating with expansion and assume that our strategy was flawed."

In the months that followed, board debate shifted to whether to try to sell the company—the preferred outcome for the disgruntled angel investor—or to seek a Series A round. The VC who'd invested in the prior round and had expressed interest in leading Series A was now spooked by the contentious board dynamics and passed on the opportunity. Hyde pitched a dozen more VC firms, but none were interested. In January 2018, with three months of cash remaining, she approached potential merger partners. Three companies made offers, but all of these deals unraveled and Hyde shut down Baroo in February.

Reset Expectations

In this case, the cause of failure was relatively clear: Baroo had fallen victim to premature scaling. The false positive had led them to expand too rapidly, and the startup simply didn't have adequate resources to operate successfully in four cities. Capital was in short supply, a small management team was stretched too thinly, and they lacked technology for managing complex bookings.

Despite the lack of such resources, the false positive signal at Ink Block gave Hyde the confidence to step on the gas too early. Baroo's ability to serve customers successfully during Boston's wicked winter of 2015 had convinced Hyde that her tiny, scrappy team could, in her words, "do anything."

Hyde had originally planned to bring Baroo's first markets to profitability and then fund expansion from those profits, rather than raising venture capital to fuel hypergrowth. However, the strong start in Boston convinced her to reverse course. This pivot was strictly a matter of choice for Hyde and Baroo's early investors. Unlike some examples we'll encounter in Part II, for Baroo the decision to expand more rapidly than originally planned wasn't a response to competitive pressure—even though VCs were pouring tens of millions of dollars into Baroo's rivals. Hyde recalled, "I saw Rover and Wag! more as proof that we'd found a strong unmet need than as competitors who challenged us in the marketplace. It didn't feel like we were nose-to-nose with them for customers or pet care providers."

Rapid expansion into multiple markets exposed flaws in Baroo's opportunity "diamond." These flaws weren't fatal; Baroo's team probably could have avoided or resolved them, had they focused their efforts on fine-tuning their model in Boston before expanding. Consider how false positive results for each of the diamond elements reset Hyde's expectations:

• Strong sign-ups and heavy repeat usage at Ink Block provided early evidence that Baroo's *Customer Value Proposition* was appealing. And even as Baroo expanded, its value proposition remained solid and demand was strong. However, there are only a few ways to differentiate a pet care service. Customers want providers who 1) can be trusted alone in their home; 2) understand their household's routines and their pet's needs; 3) are reliable; 4) are easy to schedule; and 5) can accommodate special requests. It's difficult for any pet care service to excel on all fronts. A sole proprietor who walks the family's dog every day will get to know the dog and family well, but with a packed schedule, he may not be able to handle a special request ("We're both traveling; can you do another walk before dinner?"). The reverse is true for a service provider like Wag! or Rover that deploys an army of gig economy workers: It can handle special requests, but it doesn't repeatedly send the same worker to any given home, so building customer knowledge and becoming simpatico with Spot can prove challenging.

In its final days, Baroo was addressing this issue by 1) creating teams of care providers who shared responsibility for a single neighborhood, and 2) asking providers to convey tips about families and pets to peers serving the same home. However, these solutions required a disciplined, experienced workforce equipped with slick technology—and the venture's growing pains put that out of reach. Likewise, Baroo's ability to provide high-touch service—for example, filling last-minute requests—was slipping as the startup scaled up. Ultimately, Baroo differentiated itself by offering easy, reliable access to trustworthy care providers, many of whom had prior experience with a family and its pet—attributes valued by customers, but not by a wide enough margin to command a price premium over other pet care services.

• In the early days, Baroo didn't need much by way of *Technology & Operations*. However, it soon became clear that the company's patchwork technology was insufficient for scaling. As Baroo expanded, the small management team had to make lots of diving catches. Operational issues were compounded by difficulties with hiring, training, scheduling, motivating, and retaining employees.

• With respect to *Marketing,* those early unsolicited referrals from property managers suggested that building partners would voluntarily steer residents to Baroo. But while word of mouth from existing customers was good, apartment concierges did less to promote Baroo than Hyde had hoped.

• Despite the early influx of revenue, Baroo's *Profit Formula* was unproven. The startup was still incurring significant losses in late 2017, and low entry barriers in the pet care business translated into lots of small local rivals that had low profit margins, which ultimately put a cap on the venture's upside. However, Baroo's projected LTV/CAC ratio was 5.9, and if the team could improve operational efficiency, the startup had a plausible path to long-term profitability.

False positives are a problem because they give an entrepreneur undue confidence in a particular expansion path. In Part II, we'll see more examples of startups that suffered dire consequences by scaling too rapidly in response to false positives. But, unlike Baroo, these will be late-stage startups with a rich endowment of resources, making it easier to accelerate growth.

False positives unfold in two ways. With both patterns, entrepreneurs mistakenly assume that the behavior of early adopters will be matched by that of mainstream customers.

With the first pattern, an entrepreneur tailors a solution for early adopters, commits resources to this solution, and then learns that the solution doesn't meet the needs of the larger mainstream market. Without mainstream customers, the venture won't earn enough revenue to survive. By the time the entrepreneur recognizes the need to pivot, he's amassed resources of the wrong type, and a cash-constrained startup lacks the wherewithal to replace them. The result: a variation on the Bad Bedfellows theme.

With the second pattern, an entrepreneur assembles resources to capitalize upon an opportunity. While pursuing this opportunity, he is surprised by the level of demand from early adopters and assumes that the demand from mainstream customers will also be strong. In response, he ramps up expansion plans. But as with the first pattern, the venture's original resources aren't suited for this new direction.

Baroo followed the second pattern. The false positive at Ink Block spurred Hyde to accelerate Baroo's entry into new markets, which exacerbated problems with all four elements of Baroo's resource "square":

- **Founders:** Should we blame the jockey for Baroo's failure? As CEO, Hyde made a number of mistakes. But to her credit, when looking back, she recognized her flawed decisions and took responsibility for them; for example, she acknowledged that she had fallen prey to a false positive. Despite her missteps, Hyde stands out among the founders profiled in this book for her vision, passion, and determination—and for how much she learned from failing.

Hyde also acknowledged she'd been too headstrong when dismissing her co-founder's concerns about Baroo's pace of growth. Hyde confessed, "I don't always bring colleagues along with me effectively or hear when they are resistant. Meg would say things to me like, 'Should we really launch that next city? Should we really do it before we have the technology infrastructure in place?' These were all very sensible things to say but, at the time, they infuriated me." She also came to realize that she and her co-founder "had too much history. Because we'd spent ten years together building my first startup and that partnership worked well, we immediately fell back into old patterns. But before launching Baroo, we'd been apart for three years, and both of us had grown a lot." In other words, they were bound to clash this time around.

• **Team:** Hyde had assumed that making care providers employees and paying them an hourly wage would confer loyalty and boost productivity. This expectation proved wrong: The company was investing too much in employees who didn't stay long.

Unlike Quincy, Baroo didn't suffer from a shortage of industry specialists. Hyde started recruiting them in Chicago, hiring an experienced property manager as Baroo's first general manager there. However, it turned out that scrappy generalist managers—like Hyde and her co-founder—were better suited for the challenges that Baroo confronted.

• **Investors:** Like Hyde, Baroo's original angel investors also fell prey to the false positive signal and reconsidered their preferences about the venture's growth rate. Initially, they'd wanted the startup to take modest risks and deliver moderate returns over a three- to five-year time frame. But as Baroo appeared to be taking off, their views about growth shifted. Hyde noted, "When we started to see lots of buildings wanting us in different cities, we all were excited. But no one fully grasped that we'd need $30 or $40 million to scale successfully. By the end, some investors were feeling schizophrenic: They wanted the safe returns they'd initially signed up for, but they were tempted by a big VC-style payoff, too."

One angel investor proved to be highly disruptive, questioning Hyde's competence and leadership ability—and in the process, scaring off new investors and speeding the venture's demise. Hyde had been warned about him but recalled, "We were hungry for capital and I had confidence—misplaced—that I could manage him. I learned that the happiest you'll ever be with an investor is when you sign the term sheet. I now know that if it's not all rosy then, you should just walk away."

Interestingly, when asked what she'd do differently if she had a "do-over," Hyde asserted that she wouldn't revert to her original "get profitable to avoid VCs" plan. On the contrary, she'd build a business that was ready to run at full throttle. She admitted: "What I have learned about myself is that I like to grow things fast. I like the challenge of building something with scale. With Baroo, I think we probably could have gotten there with more time and with a lot more venture capital. We should have brought in VCs who'd pour gas on the fire."

• **Partners:** The buildings that Baroo served provided less marketing support than expected, and some made unreasonable demands. If Baroo had expanded at a more measured pace, its team might have been able to identify the attributes, such as high tenant turnover, that made some buildings better partners than others. Then, they could have checked whether new buildings had these features before signing them up. But breakneck expansion meant forgoing a careful vetting process in favor of working with any building that expressed interest. In her postmortem analysis, Hyde also concluded that the property management companies should have been paying Baroo, rather than the reverse, since they exerted little effort on Baroo's behalf and, by virtue of their affiliation with Baroo, could collect more "pet rent"—which averaged $50 to $150 per pet per month.

Avoiding False Positives

My survey of early-stage founders shows that many are vulnerable to false positives. Compared to their counterparts in more successful ventures, the founder/CEOs of startups that are struggling or have shut down reported larger differences between the needs of their early adopters and mainstream customers. The greater the discrepancy, the greater the exposure to the False Positive failure pattern.

If the root cause of false positives is misinterpreting signals about early adopters, then entrepreneurs should take two steps to obtain more reliable market feedback. First, they should conduct early customer research that exposes any differences between likely early adopters and mainstream customers. Second, when entrepreneurs are pleasantly surprised by the positive responses from early adopters after the venture has launched, they should consider the possibility that the broader market may not respond in the same way.

How to stay alert to this possibility? It's impossible to generalize about the types of early customers that can generate surprisingly high demand, like those Baroo encountered at Ink Block; by their unpredictable nature, they are Black Swans. Similarly, it's difficult to be disciplined enough to carve out the time—just as your startup is taking off—to determine whether you have a false positive. But when a startup team has been taken aback by an unexpectedly strong response to their product's launch, they really should pause and ask, "What might be unusual about these early adopters?" They can use the personas described in the last chapter to highlight how early adopters differ from the types of customers the startup had planned to pursue.

With respect to the first step—conducting early research to expose differences between early adopters and mainstream customers—the key is selecting the right sample. Convenience sampling—testing the waters with friends and family—often leads to false positive results because loved ones tend to adore your idea no matter what. Crowdfunding campaigns—like the one Jibo ran on Indiegogo—pose a similar hazard. Individuals who back such campaigns are often product category enthusiasts looking for bright, shiny new things and are eager to be first to sample them. Crowdfunding campaigns can demonstrate a product's appeal to such zealots, but they don't provide data on mass-market demand.

The gold standard is explicitly testing a concept with *both* early adopters and mainstream customers. Consider the approach employed in 2012 by Lit Motors, a startup that aimed to build an electric-powered, gyroscope-stabilized, two-wheeled, fully enclosed vehicle code-named "C-1." The C-1 would essentially be a safer, easier-to-handle, eco-friendly, covered motorcycle that would keep commuters dry in the rain.

Founder Danny Kim spent $120,000 of his $1 million in seed funding on a full-scale fiberglass "looks like" prototype of the C-1. His team then used the prototype to get feedback from consumers in mainstream segments. These test subjects answered questions for twenty minutes while actually sitting in the prototype. At the end of the session, they were invited to place a $50 deposit for an opportunity to be one of the first to buy the C-1. The fact that 16 percent did so was seen by the team as a very encouraging acceptance rate.

To gauge interest from early adopters, the team next brought the prototype to the e-Grand Prix in Oregon where they could repeat the research with electric motorcycle enthusiasts. Again, the response was strong and positive, which made Kim confident that the same product design would appeal to both early adopters and mainstream customers.

In some cases, early adopters and mainstream customers have the same needs, but those of early adopters are more intense. We'll see this in Chapter 7, which profiles Fab.com, an online retailer of home décor. Fab's early adopters were home design fanatics: They purchased from the site repeatedly and spread word of its offerings. Customers acquired later were interested in interior design, too— just not as much. They bought less frequently and referred fewer friends to Fab. The result was an LTV/CAC squeeze: As Fab grew, new customers were worth less, and—with fewer free word-of-mouth referrals—they cost more to acquire. Fab's founders fell victim to a false positive signal—similar to Baroo's—by assuming that strong demand from early adopters would carry forward to the next wave of customers.

In other cases, early adopters have substantially different needs from mainstream customers. For example, early adopters may be demanding "power users" with advanced feature requirements and an ability to self-service—they'll install or debug a new product that's still rough around the edges, without having to rely on a startup's overstretched team for help. Mainstream customers, by contrast, may want a reliable, easy-to-use, no-frills product—and lots of hand-holding from a vendor's customer service staff. In this scenario, if a venture tailors its offering to the needs of early adopters, it may end up with a product poorly suited for mainstream customers.

There are various options for overcoming this challenge, but for each, it's crucial to know how the needs of early adopters and main-stream customers differ *before* commencing product development. One option is to optimize an offering for early adopters, then mod-ify it over time to accommodate mainstream customers. A second option is to create separate products for mainstream customers and early adopters—say, a "pro" version for the latter. A final option is to tailor the startup's product to meet mainstream requirements but also make it sufficiently superior to existing solutions to appeal to early adopters, despite not meeting all of their needs.

Dropbox took the last approach. During its product develop-ment process, founder Drew Houston explored the needs of early adopters—software developers and other sophisticated computer users—as well as mainstream consumers, and decided to omit ad-vanced features that would appeal mainly to early adopters. Hous-ton designed an easy-to-use product that, according to his successful application to the elite Y Combinator accelerator, takes "concepts that are proven winners from the dev community (version control, changelogs/trac, rsync, etc.) and puts them in a package that my lit-tle sister can figure out." Houston knew that Dropbox was superior to existing file management solutions and correctly bet that early adopters would embrace it, even without the advanced features.

While well-structured research can reveal the needs of early adopters, entrepreneurs can still find it difficult to spot and avoid false positives. Why? Because we are psychologically wired to see what we want and hope to see. This tendency makes it easy to mis-interpret research results and early performance.

That risk is heightened when founders believe their own hype—an occupational hazard when pitching investors. As we saw in Chapter 4, Nagaraj had sold his investors on the virality of his online dating site, Wings. He subsequently realized that his site looked more viral than it was, due to incentivized registrations, like new users who referred fake friends to earn more coins on Wings.

Baroo's experience shows two more ways founders can be made vulnerable to false positives. The first is that unexpected success can be very seductive. Consider the quote from Hyde that opens this chapter: "You land a big whale, and they just drag you along." Hyde had modest goals for Baroo initially, but when her venture exceeded them right from the start, she couldn't resist setting more ambitious objectives. Despite being dragged by a big whale, Hyde wasn't the obsessed Ahab who had been searching for Moby Dick; she came across the whale—success—unexpectedly, only to find she had a taste for expansion. Her trajectory was more like that of Michael Corleone in *The Godfather*. Michael's initial ambitions are modest: to stay out of the family business and implicitly remain moral. But when his father barely survives an assassination attempt, it is, surprisingly, Michael who avenges him—and he does so brilliantly, with a gun he hides in a restaurant bathroom. Michael becomes head of the family and is really good at vanquishing his enemies, becoming the mafia boss of New York City. But this success costs him both his morality and a real, loving family.

The second vulnerability concerns the importance of founders understanding their own goals. We might wonder if, at the outset, Hyde really understood her personal preferences regarding growth and risk. Maybe, despite her stated initial preferences and perhaps without even realizing it, she truly wanted to board the VC rocket ship. If so, she might have been primed to see what she wanted to see at Ink Block: hypergrowth opportunity—just as Michael Corleone saw his early success at vengeance as a sign that he belonged within his mafia family.

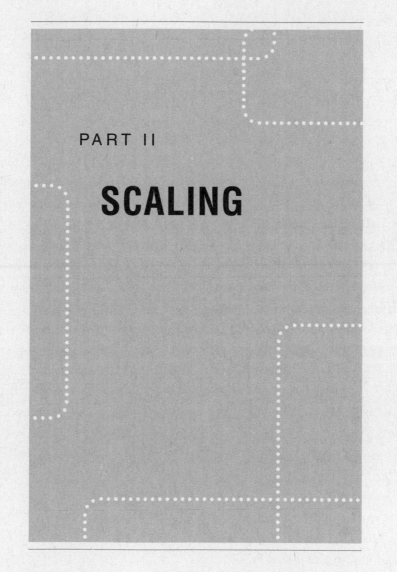

PART II

SCALING

CHAPTER 6

Out of the Frying Pan

It's reasonable to expect that late-stage startups would have much better survival rates than their early-stage counterparts. After all, they've already identified an attractive opportunity and have amassed resources to capitalize on it. Late-stage startups are defined here as ventures that are five years old or more, and at Series C or beyond if they've raised venture capital. Surprisingly, about one-third of them fail to earn positive returns for their investors. When I learned that, I wondered: Why is it so difficult for scaling startups to succeed? After digging deeper, I discovered that as startups move past the early stage, they jump out of the frying pan and into the fire. Early-stage startups falter when their founders cannot identify a good opportunity or fail to mobilize the right resources—or both. Late-stage missteps also revolve around opportunity and resources, but in distinctly different ways.

Opportunity Challenges. Entrepreneurs who lead late-stage startups must maintain balance while pursuing opportunity, which requires them to set goals for speed and scope that are sufficiently ambitious yet achievable. By "speed," I mean the pace of expansion of the venture's core business—that is, its original product offered solely in its home market. "Scope" is a broader concept that encompasses four dimensions. The first three—*geographic reach, product line breadth,* and *innovation*—collectively define the range of the startup's product market: How many additional customer segments will be targeted, and which of their needs will be addressed? The fourth dimension, *vertical integration*, refers to the range of activities that the startup will perform in-house rather than outsourcing to third parties.

1. **Geographic reach.** When Baroo expanded beyond Boston into Chicago and other cities, it broadened the geographic reach of its product market. Other startups extend their geographic reach even farther by launching in other countries.

2. **Product line breadth.** Startups also can expand the scope of their product market by launching more products, as Google did by adding Gmail, YouTube, Maps, Drive, and dozens of other products to its original search business.

3. **Innovation.** For some startups, extraordinary innovation yields products with truly novel features or vastly superior performance. These breakthroughs can broaden the scope of a startup's product market by allowing it to target underserved customers. Some startups make bold business model innovations; that's what Stitch Fix did when it offered a new subscription styling service. Others innovate by exploiting new technology, as Solidia Technologies did with advances in chemical engineering that enabled the venture to cut the carbon footprint of cement production by 70 percent.

4. **Vertical integration.** Vertical integration enlarges the scope of activities that a company performs by bringing functions in-house that formerly were outsourced to third parties. "Upstream" (or "backward") integration involves product development and manufacturing activities, while "downstream" (or "forward") integration encompasses marketing, sales, and the physical distribution of products. Apple, for example, integrated upstream by designing its own semiconductors instead of relying on vendors like Intel. And it integrated downstream when it sold its products through Apple Stores, in addition to third-party retailers like Best Buy.

Speed and scope each generate a Goldilocks dilemma for entrepreneurs, akin to those discussed in Chapter 2: Put simply, too much or too little of either can be fatal to a late-stage startup.

Resource Challenges. As they balance speed and scope, late-stage ventures also face significant challenges when it comes to managing resources. To scale, they typically need to raise a large amount of capital, but the vagaries of financial markets can thwart them. Sometimes, entire sectors go out of favor and investors shun even healthy ventures. If that happens just as a startup is gearing up to raise another round—eager to fund aggressive growth or cutting-edge innovation—the startup can wither and die, a victim of the misfortune of bad timing rather than management mistakes.

Entrepreneurs must also manage a rapidly expanding pool of human resources as their scaling startup goes through two profound organizational transitions. First, many specialists with deep functional expertise—say, in marketing or operations—join a staff previously comprised largely of jack-of-all-trades generalists who, in the venture's early days, ranged flexibly across functions as circumstances required. Second, a fluid approach to managing gradually gives way to formal structure and systems. The venture creates organizational charts and job descriptions, introduces employee performance reviews, refines budgeting and planning processes, and so forth.

These late-stage organizational transitions bring more Goldilocks dilemmas—and require more balancing. Hiring specialists too soon can cause trouble, as can delaying their recruitment. The same holds true for formal structure and systems. Such problems are rarely the main reason for a late-stage startup's failure: The root cause is almost always that goals for speed or scope are out of whack. Nevertheless, organizational problems can act as amplifiers, boosting the odds of failure by distracting management when marketplace challenges require their full attention.

The Six S Framework

To assess the likelihood that a scaling startup will succeed and spot reasons why it might fail, entrepreneurs can use the Six S framework. It depicts three elements within a triangle, all of which are related to the venture's internal organization: its *Staff*; its *Structure*, encompassing both reporting relationships and management systems; and its *Shared Values*, reflected in company culture.

Within a circle enclosing the triangle are three elements that represent the venture's external relationships. Taken together, *Speed*—meaning the pace of expansion of a startup's core business—and *Scope*—with respect to geographic reach, product line breadth, innovation, and vertical integration—define the startup's product-market strategy and, with it, the venture's relationships with its customers, competitors, and suppliers. The last element, *Series X*, denotes the startup's capital market strategy. Venture capital fundraising rounds, called "series," are sequenced alphabetically. Hence, Series X represents relationships with current and future investors.

In the pages that follow, I'll describe these elements in more detail, and discuss how each evolves as a startup matures. Then I'll explore how the elements interact and influence each other. Finally, I'll focus on the challenges of keeping the elements in alignment as a scaling startup follows an ever-shifting path.

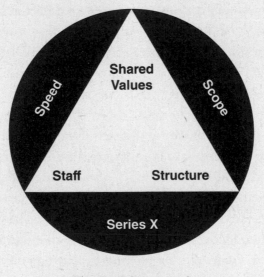

The Six S Framework

Speed

How quickly to expand the core business is probably the most important decision the CEO of a late-stage startup will make. Entrepreneurs—and the investors who back them—*love* rapid growth. It usually leads to a higher valuation for a firm's equity, based on the assumption that a bigger startup will ultimately earn greater profits. Meanwhile, rising equity valuations make it easier to attract talented employees, who are drawn by the prospect of stock option gains. And opportunities for promotion in a rapidly expanding firm are a lure for top talent.

Growth can be self-reinforcing when it bolsters a startup's business model, allowing the firm to acquire customers more efficiently, raise prices, or lower operating expenses. Specifically, three potential benefits of growth stand out:

- Assuming that its customers are satisfied, a startup's **brand recognition** should increase over time and new customers should be more responsive to advertisements and word-of-mouth referrals from existing customers. As a result, the cost of acquiring customers may decline.

- If the business enjoys **network effects,** then a larger user base will attract more new users—again, reducing customer acquisition costs. Also, a bigger network means that customers can interact with a broader set of possible partners. This may allow the growing startup to raise prices, since customers value having access to a bigger network.

- Finally, as transaction volumes increase, **scale economies** should reduce a startup's unit costs, that is, expenses incurred in producing and fulfilling a typical customer order. Scale economies can be achieved in three ways. First, unit costs decline when *fixed overhead expenses*—such as a factory manager's salary—are spread over more units. Second, with the experience that comes from operating at higher volumes, employees will leverage a *learning curve* and discover ways to improve productivity and lower costs. Third, *cost-saving automation* that wasn't affordable at low volumes—say, adding robots to an assembly line—might become economically feasible at high volumes.

That's the good news about speed. But there's bad news, too. Four countervailing forces set a speed limit for a startup, determining the maximum rate at which it can grow without undercutting its potential to earn long-term profits. These forces include:

- **Saturation.** A startup's product is tailored for the needs of buyers in one or more customer segments. Eventually, after a startup has marketed its product intensively, most potential customers in those segments will have been made aware of the product and will have had an opportunity to buy it. At this point, the startup's target market has been saturated, and to keep growing, it must attract buyers from other customer segments. Unless the startup modifies the product, it won't be tailored for the needs of potential customers in those new segments. To persuade them to purchase the product, the startup must lower its price or market more intensively—or both—thus reducing profitability. Alternatively, the startup can modify its product to meet the needs of new customer segments, but that risks alienating existing customers. Or, the startup can avoid saturation by launching a new product that is tailored to the needs of new customer segments—an option explored below under the discussion of Scope.

Most early-stage startups are a long way from saturating their target market. Baroo, for example, could have signed up many more luxury apartment buildings in the cities where it operated. But after years of hypergrowth, scaling startups can hit a saturation point. Facebook is an example: In the United States, its growth slowed after it was adopted in sequence first by a majority of college students, then high school students, and finally adults.

- **Rivalry.** Early-stage startups like Quincy or Triangulate do not typically provoke imitation: They are too small to be noticed and their concepts are not yet proven. The story is different for late-stage startups, whose rapid expansion often attracts competitors. Sometimes these are startup clones; in other instances, they are "sleeping dragons"—established companies who are roused from their slumber by an upstart venture on their turf. We'll see an example of clones in the next chapter with Fab.com, an online retailer of home décor. Fab was copied in Europe by Rocket Internet, a Berlin-based incubator that targets successful U.S. startups.

Intense rivalry can have nasty consequences for profitability. New entrants often launch with low prices to gain a foothold, and incumbents must respond with price cuts to protect their market share. And if they vie for the same resources—like drivers, in the case of Uber and Lyft—rivals will bid up costs.

• **Quality and customer service problems.** Hypergrowth can strain a startup's operations and contribute to quality problems—especially when the company relies on large numbers of employees in production and customer service. It can be difficult to hire enough employees to staff these functions, and then train them to get the job done right. We'll see this in Chapter 8, which profiles Dot & Bo, an online retailer of furniture and home décor that was dealing with a big order backlog and couldn't hire enough customer service reps to answer customers' queries about order status promptly.

• **Impact on morale and company culture.** Rapid growth can be exhilarating, but working at one's limit for months on end in order to achieve it can hurt employee morale: Recall the problems that Baroo had when it couldn't hire enough care providers to meet demand and asked its best walkers to work twelve-hour days. Staff expansion can also undermine a startup's culture (I'll elaborate in the following section on Shared Values). The first employees of an early-stage venture are often motivated by the startup's mission, the opportunity to work side by side with the founders, and their small team's "all for one and one for all" camaraderie. By contrast, in a late-stage startup, hordes of new hires are more likely to view their work as "just a job."

As we'll see in the chapters that follow, growing too fast—exceeding the speed limit—can put a late-stage startup on the path to ruin.

Scope

Entrepreneurs generally make one of two strategic decisions about scope. With the first—the more common of the two—an entrepreneur gradually expands her startup's scope as it matures—starting narrow and then broadening over time.

With the second, an entrepreneur commits to ambitious scope right from the outset—usually with respect to radical innovation, but sometimes planning for ambitious vertical integration and geographic sprawl, too. If these bold commitments turn out to be "a bridge too far," the consequences usually manifest themselves quickly, and the startup becomes an early-stage disaster—it never gets funded or dies within a year or two.

However, in Chapter 9, we'll see that a few founders who commit to audaciously ambitious scope do manage to attract enough resources to scale their ventures for many years. These "big bang" startups are often founded by high-profile, charismatic entrepreneurs who can spin up a reality-distortion field to persuade investors, talented employees, and others to help them pursue their "change the world" vision. Theranos fits squarely into this profile.

Regardless of whether an entrepreneur pursues a gradual path or a big bang, each of the four ways to expand a startup's scope comes with pros and cons:

Geographic Reach. Many startups are tempted to enter new territories. Uber, for example, launched into city after city in the United States, then followed the same playbook overseas. Investors aiming for a bigger opportunity will pressure an entrepreneur to pursue this strategy. There are other reasons for geographic expansion. Entering another market is much easier when you can leverage the know-how you gained in your earlier markets, as Uber did. And, the presence of competitors in other territories may motivate entry. As rivals gain momentum, a startup's window of opportunity to compete successfully in a new territory may close.

The leading online marketplace for secondhand apparel in the United States, thredUP, confronted such pressure. Europe had lagged the United States by a few years in terms of developing marketplaces like thredUP's, but by 2016, clones were gaining traction there. Investors asked if thredUP was willing to forfeit to these clones an entire continent with revenue potential that matched that of the United States. After considering a range of options—for example, acquiring a European rival—thredUP's co-founder/CEO James Reinhart decided to serve European customers in a strictly limited way—at least initially—shipping items to them from the United States rather than building or acquiring a European business with a full array of local marketing and warehousing capabilities. Reinhart reasoned that, given the many remaining challenges and opportunities for thredUP in the United States, simultaneously managing aggressive expansion into Europe would overtax the startup's management team and could deplete capital reserves that served as the startup's buffer against a "rainy day."

Several risks can offset pressures for geographic expansion. Entering new markets is costly and, as Baroo's struggles showed, can stretch a management team too thin. Also, every market brings new competitors, new regulations, and cultural differences that shape customers' needs. If entrepreneurs don't grasp these differences and adapt their offerings to local requirements, they can be in real trouble, as Disney famously learned when it opened a theme park outside Paris. It turned out that Europeans were far less likely than Americans to spend several days at a Disney park, and they also wanted wine with their meals.

Product Line Breadth. Launching more products can be a great way to grow, and a late-stage startup may be well positioned to diversify its product line. Its managers should have a deep understanding of marketplace needs and may spot gaps they can fill. Also, as a known entity, the startup should be credible when marketing new products, especially if it is targeting customers who have already bought the startup's original product; this should reduce customer acquisition costs, compared to those that a newly minted startup would incur. Finally, a scaling startup already has engineers who can build the new products, and they may be able to speed up development by repurposing some technology and components. Likewise, the team may be able to gain operational efficiencies by leveraging slack capacity in operations, say, in warehouses or call centers.

While these benefits from product line expansion may be compelling, the risks can be daunting. Any new product faces all of the liabilities of newness that we reviewed in Part I: Demand may be weaker than expected, rivals may offer a better mousetrap, product development may be delayed, and so forth. Added risk also comes from the internal conflict over scarce resources between the team responsible for a new offering and the team managing the original product. In the subsequent discussion of Structure, I'll propose ways to manage such conflict.

Innovation. Chapter 2 examined the trade-offs that entrepreneurs who lead early-stage ventures need to consider when they ask, "How much should we innovate?" These trade-offs apply equally to late-stage startups. Radical innovation can deliver a superior, differentiated solution to strong, unmet customer needs, but it risks 1) raising the cost of switching from prior solutions, thus deterring adoption if it demands a major change in customer behavior; 2) increasing marketing outlays if customers must be educated about the new, innovative product; and 3) boosting the chances of product development delays if such innovation requires significant scientific or engineering breakthroughs.

Pressure to innovate frequently stems from the simple fact that products tend to age—often rapidly, especially in technology markets—and eventually must be retired or replaced by next-generation products. Entrepreneurs in late-stage startups confront tricky choices on this front. When should they stop making incremental improvements and leapfrog to the next generation? Over time, innovating an existing product yields less profit bang for the engineering buck. One reason is that the features added later in a product's life cycle are usually less valuable to customers; basically, the most important product features are included at the outset and features that get added later are frequently just bells and whistles. The other reason is that, as products mature, each new feature must be technically compatible with every feature previously added, making it more difficult to engineer and thus more time-consuming and costly to develop. The larger the number of existing features, the longer it takes to determine if a new one will hobble any that were added earlier.

At some point, the payoff from innovation becomes negative, and it's time to consider a fresh start. However, entrepreneurs are prone to miscalculating when and how to replace their current product with a next-generation version—especially the first time, when they lack experience. If they wait too long to launch the next generation, a large share of their customers may have already migrated to rivals' state-of-the-art products. And if a startup team tries incorporating too much innovation into their next-generation product, they will need to invest heavily in engineering and run the risk of development delays.

Vertical Integration. Once a startup gains scale, it can consider bringing in-house some activities that previously were outsourced to third parties. An early-stage startup typically lacks the capital, know-how, and sales volume to do this. For example, Quincy, having only raised seed capital, could never have afforded its own apparel factory. But if the company had eventually reached, say, $50 million in annual sales, it might have built one.

By its nature, vertical integration doesn't directly expand a startup's market. Rather, the motivations for vertical integration usually include 1) increasing profit margins by capturing the markup otherwise charged by third parties, and/or 2) ensuring higher and more consistent quality in "mission critical" functions, when the startup's partners might have reliability and commitment issues.

Vertical integration can be risky because it typically requires significant investment and the development of new skills and capabilities, both of which increase a startup's fixed costs—a problem if revenue growth ever reverses. That said, vertical integration is normally less perilous than other ways to expand scope. The exception occurs when the founder of a "big bang" venture, who has grand ambitions and exacting demands, wants to do everything in-house, right from the start. We'll see this behavior in Chapter 9 with the venture Better Place, whose founder/CEO Shai Agassi pushed to develop internally a range of technologies, like charging stations for electric vehicles, that could have been outsourced to third parties.

If, as is more typical, a late-stage startup expands scope gradually, then some activities outsourced to third-party providers will eventually become candidates for vertical integration. In this scenario, managers should have good information about volumes, costs, and investment levels when they ponder "build versus buy" decisions. Consequently, after running the numbers, they usually get these decisions right. As we'll see in the next chapter, online retailer Fab.com vertically integrated upstream by acquiring furniture makers in Europe. Through these acquisitions, Fab.com was positioned to offer profitable private label merchandise. (See the sidebar "Scaling through Acquisitions" for a discussion of the pros and cons of boosting Speed or expanding Scope by acquiring other startups.)

Scaling through Acquisitions

To meet their objectives for Speed or Scope, late-stage ventures can consider acquiring other startups. By merging with direct rivals, they can speed the growth of their core business and remove a competitive threat, as Grab, the leading ride-sharing company in Southeast Asia, did when it acquired Uber's operations in that region. Late-stage startups can also expand their scope through mergers by 1) entering new geographic markets, as with Uber buying Careem, the leading Middle Eastern ride-sharing service; 2) adding more products to their lineup, as with Google buying YouTube; or 3) integrating vertically, as with eBay acquiring PayPal.

For mature corporations, management scholars have observed that the average economic payoff from mergers is negative: Buyers tend to overestimate synergies and consequently overpay. Mergers are more likely to yield a good return when a corporation does a lot of them and has a well-honed process for performing due diligence and for integrating the acquired entities. As rookies in the acquisition game, most startups don't bring such experience to the table, so they probably would be out of their depth.

Even so, an *average* negative payoff means we might still see plenty of successful acquisitions. When they were still scaling startups, some of today's tech titans made brilliant acquisitions that were second-guessed at the time for being too expensive, for example, Google + YouTube, eBay + PayPal, and Facebook + Instagram.

Compared to a "do-it-yourself" approach, the main advantages of scaling through acquisitions are 1) time savings, which can be especially valuable in fast-moving markets; 2) cost savings, if redundant functions can be eliminated (e.g., legal teams, sales teams); and 3) avoidance of early-stage startup risks related to opportunity identification and resource assembly.

However, acquisitions pose three major risks for scaling startups: 1) overpayment, 2) disappearing talent, and 3) rocky post-merger integration that disrupts the organization and distracts management. To prevent talent from leaving, acquirers can try to lock in employees by negotiating new contracts that vest their equity gains from the merger over, say, eighteen months. However, incentivizing an employee to show up at work doesn't guarantee that she will have her head in the game.

Integration risk comes in three forms:

• **Technical incompatibility.** When two newly merged startups' products have different technological roots—for example, one was coded in C++ and the other in Java—their engineering teams face a thorny choice. Should they rebuild one of the products so that both employ the same technologies, or keep things as they are? Sharing a common technology base should save costs when launching new features, but switching can be messy. Similar choices will apply to information systems used for tracking orders and inventory, bookkeeping, payroll, etc.

• **Organizational design.** Managers must make difficult—and often politically charged—choices about who reports to whom after an acquisition. For example, if a U.S. online retailer acquires a similar business in Spain, should the marketing head in Spain report to the country manager there, to the U.S.-based chief marketing officer, or both?

• **Cultural fit.** If two entities have different company cultures, integration may hit snags over an endless series of misunderstandings about the right way to do things. Also, morale in the acquired company may suffer if its employees feel that a new culture is being forced on them or that they are viewed as misfits.

Series X

The key fundraising decisions for late-stage startups echo those discussed in Chapter 2 for early-stage ventures: when to raise capital, how much to raise, and from whom? Beyond these basics, late-stage startups should be aware of additional risks related to fundraising as their ventures mature.

Growth Pressures. In Part I, we saw that VCs are primed to pressure entrepreneurs for aggressive growth because the VC business model requires huge profits on a small percentage of investments to cover losses or ho-hum returns on most others. Investor pressure for growth can be especially acute with late-stage startups because VCs, competing for the right to invest in a venture that has demonstrated strong traction, will aggressively bid up the startup's share price, to the point of overpaying. This phenomenon is known as the "winner's curse" because in an auction setting, winning bids tend to exceed the true value of an auctioned item. This can happen when 1) there is considerable uncertainty about the item's true worth, resulting in a big spread in bidders' estimates of value; and 2) a well-run auction harnesses "animal spirits" that fuel frenzied competition.

A winner's curse may be at play when VCs bid for the right to invest in a rapidly scaling late-stage startup. There's lots of uncertainty about what any startup will be worth, and—believe me—the typical VC exhibits plenty of animal spirits. The downside of this feeding frenzy is that the winning VC has a high bar for earning a positive return, putting even more pressure on the venture to continue to grow rapidly.

VC Fred Wilson has estimated that two-thirds of the startup failures he's familiar with are caused by overfunding an idea that's promising but has unresolved problems. He says, "The investors and boards of these companies (i.e., me) are responsible for failures like this. . . . Most venture backed investments fail because the venture capital is used to scale the business before the correct business plan is discovered."

Down Rounds. In Chapter 2, we saw that startups are exposed to the risk of a "down round"—that is, raising additional capital in a new round at a share price lower than the price paid by the previous round's investors. A down round is a nasty event: It signals that a firm is struggling, which can make it difficult to attract and retain employees who seek upside from equity grants—or who worry about going down with a sinking ship.

The VC bidding frenzies noted above mean that entrepreneurs whose startups have great traction may have the opportunity to raise capital at a huge share price. Before accepting a sky-high offer, however, they should evaluate how realistic it will be to sustain the momentum that led to that high price. It's hard to turn down an exorbitant offer, but if growth stalls, a down round could accelerate their startup's demise. As Fred Wilson advises, "Just because investors are willing to throw gobs of money at you and your company, it doesn't mean it is smart to take it."

Funding Risk. In Chapter 8, we'll see that entire sectors sometimes fall out of favor with investors. When this happens, even healthy firms may not be able to raise capital for months or even years. Consequently, before they commit to ambitious expansion plans, entrepreneurs leading late-stage startups should have a contingency plan in case of a funding drought. Should they keep some capital in reserve? Can they cut back fast enough to survive on internally generated cash flow?

CEO Succession. In an early-stage startup, founders often control a majority share of board of director votes. When a new VC firm leads an additional investment round, it typically receives a newly created seat on the board. After a few such rounds, investors outnumber founders on the enlarged board—and together have enough votes to replace a founder who stumbles. The faster the startup expands, the more capital it will require, accelerating these dynamics. A founder who wants to remain in the CEO seat—and retain control over strategic priorities by keeping her board small—should think carefully before raising lots of capital in quick, successive rounds. Of course, this path not only means slower growth, but it forfeits the guidance and network connections that a larger, well-run board can provide.

Board Priorities. Adding new investors in successive rounds creates another issue for entrepreneurs. The investors who funded the startup's latest round are likely to have different priorities than those who contributed its earliest capital. For late-stage investors to earn an attractive return, the startup must continue expanding aggressively. If the startup has saturated its core market, for example, it might need to enter international markets or launch new products—risky endeavors, as explained above. By contrast, early-stage investors, having acquired equity at a much lower share price, can anticipate a terrific return if the startup just stays on the rails, avoiding risky product line diversification or forays abroad. Consequently, board members who are early-stage investors may be less enthusiastic about aggressive expansion plans than their late-stage counterparts. In this situation, the challenge for a CEO is to prevent the board from gridlocking over strategic decisions.

Staff

The first three S's pertain to the startup's relationships with external parties: customers, competitors, suppliers (*Speed* and *Scope*), and investors (*Series* X). The remaining three S's focus on internal organization: the startup's *Staff,* the *Structure* of its reporting relationships and management processes, and its *Shared Values.* As a startup matures, Staff, Structure, and Shared Values all undergo significant transitions. The pace and nature of these transitions will be determined mostly by the startup's strategy with respect to Speed and Scope. Mistakes with the organizational S's are less likely to be fatal than mistakes with Speed, Scope, and Series X. However, organizational problems can distract management and make it more difficult to sustain strong marketplace and financial performance.

Generalists to Specialists. The composition of the staff of a scaling startup changes dramatically over time as specialists are recruited and early leaders exit. A small team of jack-of-all-trades generalists, who each can fill many roles as circumstances require, gives way to a large group of specialists who have the know-how to improve the efficiency and effectiveness of engineering, marketing, and other operating functions. For example, teams of specialists might be added to run digital ad campaigns, provide after-sale technical support to new customers, and monitor product quality.

A scaling startup also requires specialists in headquarters staff functions. For example, in finance, specialists maintain control over spending and disbursements; in human resources, they manage recruiting processes, promotion reviews, compensation, benefits, and employee training.

Executive Turnover. As specialists proliferate, it may become clear that members of the venture's original management team—possibly including the founder/CEO—now lack the knowledge and skills to lead their units successfully. As Ben Horowitz, co-founder of the venture capital firm Andreessen Horowitz, puts it, "Managing at scale is a learned skill rather than a natural ability. Nobody comes out of the womb knowing how to manage a thousand people." In some cases, senior team members may not have enough experience in their functions to hire and effectively manage the specialists who now report to them. For example, a head of marketing who has never optimized digital ad spending may be out of her depth when managing a team that's about to spend millions of dollars on Facebook and Google ads.

More broadly, the skills and attitudes that make for great early-stage entrepreneurs may not be conducive to leading a larger organization that is formalizing its organizational structure, management systems, and communication flows. For example, a common attitude for founders in early-stage startups is to go with their gut instinct and make fast decisions, which keeps their young ventures nimble. Careful quantitative analysis often isn't an option in early-stage startups because they lack the data that comes with an extended operating history. But in a late-stage startup, where data is available, basing decisions solely on "gut feeling" can lead to costly errors.

For these reasons, executive churn is common as ventures mature. VC Fred Wilson estimates that a typical startup will turn over its management team three times between its inception and when it achieves significant scale. Wilson emphasizes that turning over a team is not the same as firing someone for poor performance. Still, it can be tough to create new roles for senior managers who can't handle the evolving demands of their current positions, and terminating them can be demoralizing for colleagues who've worked with them since the beginning—especially if those individuals are torchbearers for the startup's mission and values. Wilson notes that serial entrepreneurs, having seen these patterns before, are better equipped to manage executive churn. He also advises founders to be open with new hires, letting them know that "they may not make it to the finish line, but they will be handsomely compensated with equity."

Of course, what to do with an incumbent in a particular position is only half the executive turnover equation; the other half is where and how to find her replacement. In Chapter 8, we'll see some echoes of the Good Idea, Bad Bedfellows pattern as late-stage startup Dot & Bo repeatedly fails to find a VP-Operations who can reduce its order backlog and get shipping costs under control. This "Missing Manager" problem can become acute when the talent gap is in a mission-critical function—like operations, in the case of Dot & Bo. Likewise, the odds of selecting the wrong individual rise when a CEO has limited prior experience with that mission-critical function, both because she doesn't know what to look for in a candidate and she lacks a professional network rich with potential hires.

CEO Succession. Some founder/CEOs of late-stage startups are afflicted with what Steve Blank calls the "Peter Pan Syndrome"—they don't want to grow up. Such founders long for the chaotic rhythms, camaraderie, and scrappiness of the venture's early days and seek to relive them by focusing their energy on new initiatives that they can build from scratch—even when their team should be driving hard to improve and expand the existing business instead.

Venture capitalist John Hamm recommends that founders get guidance from a board member or mentor to overcome habits that may have been helpful in an early-stage startup but can hurt performance when scaling. According to Hamm, these impulses include 1) loyalty to colleagues who may lack the skills to fulfill evolving leadership roles, 2) a relentless focus on executing today's "to-do list" at the expense of thinking strategically, and 3) working in isolation instead of with management team members or ecosystem partners, which is especially prevalent among founders who excel at product development.

Founders who successfully led their firms through the scaling phase and beyond come readily to mind—Bill Gates, Jeff Bezos, Mark Zuckerberg, Elon Musk. However, these entrepreneurs are the exception rather than the rule. Despite coaching, most founder/CEOs cannot master the skills required to lead a larger, more complex startup. According to research by Yeshiva University's Noam Wasserman, 61 percent of founders who held the CEO role when their ventures launched were no longer in that role after their firms raised Series D financing. For nearly three-quarters of those CEOs, the venture's board initiated the change; the rest realized on their own that they needed a replacement. Among those who were replaced as CEO (voluntarily or not), about a third left; otherwise, the founder moved into a different executive role.

As we've seen in the highly publicized cases of Uber and WeWork, the board-initiated replacement of a founder/CEO can be a contentious and divisive affair, with battle lines drawn and invective hurled. The ensuing drama distracts senior management and can paralyze decision-making, putting the venture at risk of losing ground to rivals. However, when assessing the performance of startups that have replaced a founder/CEO, drawing conclusions about cause and effect is tricky. On the one hand, firms that are faring poorly (cause) are more likely to conclude that they need new leadership (effect). On the other hand, the organizational disruption engendered by CEO succession (cause) might hurt performance (effect).

Structure

In a late-stage startup, the informal communication and decision-making processes that worked well back when a dozen early employees worked shoulder to shoulder in a small office (or on a single Slack channel) no longer cut it. As a startup matures, it must formalize reporting relationships and introduce management systems to ensure that 1) information flows where it's needed, 2) a more complex range of activities are coordinated, and 3) cross-functional conflict can be resolved quickly and effectively.

A key decision for scaling startups is when to add formal organizational structure and management systems. Most entrepreneurs are disdainful of bureaucracy, so they're inclined to delay. That's not always a bad idea, especially if moving too early leads a firm to introduce structure and systems that are not well suited for its next phase of growth.

Formalizing Reporting Relationships. As a scaling startup acquires more and more employees, its leaders must inevitably formalize the structure of the organization, often in discrete steps. They add middle management layers within functional units, because frontline specialists need bosses who can tell them what to do and because top management wants someone within each function to be accountable for results and to serve as a conduit for top-down direction and bottom-up information flows.

It's tempting to assume that the types of employees found at startups would reject formal management structures, but that isn't always the case. As the late Bill Campbell, a seasoned Silicon Valley executive and coach to many technology industry CEOs, put it, "Technical founders often think that engineering hires don't want to be managed, but that's not true. I once challenged a founder to walk down the hall and ask his engineers if any of them wanted a manager. To his surprise, they all said, 'Yes, we want someone we can learn from and someone who can break ties.' "

Tie-breaking is important not only within but also across functions. Once startups hire specialists, cross-functional conflict is inevitable, given the incompatibility of their priorities. For example, the sales team, in response to customer requests, pushes for new features and product customization. At the same time, manufacturing specialists argue for product standardization to realize economies of scale and achieve better quality. Coping with such trade-offs can be challenging for entrepreneurs encountering them for the first time. Therefore, managing cross-functional conflict usually involves changes in organizational design. For example:

• Adding *product managers* who specify their product's functionality and its "road map" for feature additions after getting input directly from customers and also from colleagues in engineering, marketing, customer service, and other units.

• Adding the position of *chief operating officer,* to whom the heads of all operating functions report, including engineering, product management, marketing, sales, manufacturing, and customer support (but not the heads of finance or human resources). If peers running the operating functions cannot resolve a dispute themselves, the COO makes the final call.

- Creating profit centers, each with a *general manager* who has control over key functions such as product development, marketing, and operations—if the startup's scope has broadened to include multiple product lines or geographic territories.

Adding Management Systems. In parallel with formalizing reporting relationships, scaling startups must introduce a range of management systems and processes that facilitate strategic and operational planning, financial budgeting, performance tracking, employee recruitment and development, and other activities. Scaling startups that ignore this need or introduce inadequate processes run the risk of missing deadlines, losing control of costs and quality, and wasting effort on repetitive manual work that could be automated.

Management systems can seem mundane, and indeed, their shortcomings or absence are rarely the primary cause of a late-stage startup's demise. But some systems are more important than others, and problems with mission-critical systems can compound other difficulties, boosting the odds of failure. As we'll see in Chapter 8, the limitations of the system used by Dot & Bo to track order and inventory status contributed significantly to shipping delays that led to customer complaints. Resolving these problems reduced Dot & Bo's profit margin, causing the company to burn through its capital faster than expected.

Shared Values

Venture capitalist Ben Horowitz defines company culture as how employees make decisions when their boss isn't there. In a company with a strong culture, employees "just know" what to do when confronted with a nonroutine issue. For example, if an important customer asks to have their order expedited—which would make other customers' orders late—employees will know, without consulting their superiors, whether to comply.

In a rapidly scaling startup, the arrival of legions of new employees can make it challenging to sustain a strong, coherent company culture: The new hires simply haven't been around long enough to assimilate company values. Lacking cultural guardrails that would help them "just know" what to do, new employees may do nothing as problems or opportunities arise. Also, compared to early team members who often retain a passionate commitment to the startup's mission, the new hires may view their employment as "just a job," further diminishing their sense of accountability. As executive coach Jerry Colonna puts it, "Some companies' cultures are like rock tumblers. . . . You put dusty, dirty, roughed-up stones into the tumbler and then hours later you end up with polished jewels. The stones banging into each other forces positive transformations. . . . The problem is, though, not everyone wants to work in a rock tumbler."

Cultures in scaling startups can fracture in two ways. First, "old guard versus new guard" conflicts may arise if early team members resent the growing power of specialists or some new employees' lack of initiative and commitment. Recent hires, in turn, may be jealous of early employees who've amassed enormous stock option gains ("That engineer in the next cubicle does the same thing I do, and she just made $5 million"). Second, as specialists are added to the staff and their units expand, functions can develop their own subcultures. Employees may feel a stronger sense of attachment to their functional unit—say, marketing or warehouse operations—than to the venture overall.

Given these dynamics, how can a scaling startup's leadership team sustain a strong company culture? This is a big topic, and entrepreneurs can find more thorough guidance in many other books and blog posts. In brief, some steps to promote a strong culture include:

• **Mission and values statements.** Most startups have a mission statement (Google's: "Organize the world's information and make it universally accessible and useful") and a list of company values (among Google's: "Do no evil" and "Fast is better than slow"). What separates statements that are meaningful from those that are just banal is how they are developed, communicated, and reinforced.

Many startups engage their entire team in the process of formulating mission and values statements and post them in every conference room.

• **Communication.** Entrepreneurs who aim to build a strong company culture communicate their venture's mission and values relentlessly—for example, leading off every all-hands meeting with a reminder of the venture's mission and telling stories about company heroes who embody its values.

• **Operating decisions.** Note that lip service won't suffice, because employees have a flawless radar for hypocrisy. Therefore, the best way to reinforce values is through action. Senior executives must live up to stated values by making decisions about strategy and staff that are consistent with these values ("Would that be evil?").

• **Human resources practices.** Company culture can be reinforced through a range of HR practices. Cultural fit can be explicitly considered when recruiting employees. Employee onboarding can include sessions on the startup's history, mission, and values—ideally taught by senior managers. Firing an employee who is performing well but who is widely known to ignore or violate company values can send a very powerful signal.

• **Measurement.** Best practice involves surveying employees periodically to learn whether they understand the venture's mission and feel encouraged to live up to its values.

A strong culture doesn't guarantee that a venture will succeed; it still needs great products, a sound strategy, and crisp execution. However, in a fluid, fast-moving environment, having employees who can and will take initiative independently speeds decision-making and frees up management time. And a strong culture often helps attract top talent, too.

When a scaling startup seeks to expand its scope, however, a strong culture, normally an asset, can sometimes prove to be a barrier. Dropbox offers a good example. For many years after its founding, the startup had an engineering-driven culture. Its product was a technical marvel, and the challenge of building leading-edge Internet infrastructure had attracted many top-notch software developers. Engineering prowess was celebrated culturally; other business functions at Dropbox, which were smaller than those of other software companies, played second fiddle. For instance, Dropbox had grown rapidly without much marketing, through word-of-mouth referrals and the harnessing of a strong network effect, as individuals collaborated and shared files. Likewise, because the product was engineered so well, users rarely experienced problems, so Dropbox needed few customer support reps.

When management debated whether to create a version of Dropbox for large corporations, cultural concerns surfaced. A version for corporate customers would require a sales force—something new and different for Dropbox. Salespeople are loud and extroverted; in some ways, they are the polar opposite of great software engineers, who hate small talk and don noise-canceling headphones to get into the zone and code. Dropbox successfully pursued the enterprise opportunity, but management wisely took time to consider what diversification might do to the company's culture.

Two Paths for Scaling Startups

The discussion above of the Six S framework suggests that its elements frequently interact and influence each other. My analysis of scaling startups shows that these interactions frequently follow two predictable paths—each with its own catalyst. The first path starts with a drive for Speed—that is, accelerated growth for the startup's core business. With the second path, the catalyst is a vision with ambitious Scope. As we'll see in the chapters that follow, these two paths expose startups to unique risks—and unique modes of failure.

Scaling for Speed

Scaling for Speed starts with rapid early growth, and then the venture goes through the following transitions, in sequence:

1. **SPEED ↑ → SERIES X ↑** Enthusiastic early adopters fuel rapid growth, attracting investors.

2. **SERIES X ↑ → SPEED ↑** Access to capital fuels more growth—consistent with pressure from new investors, who paid a high price for their equity.

3. **SPEED ↑ → STAFF ↑ → STRUCTURE ↑** To manage growth, the startup hires specialists in marketing, operations, and other functions. Specialists require middle managers to supervise them, so hierarchical levels are added to the organizational structure and roles are formalized. Specialists also introduce management systems to coordinate their work and improve efficiency and effectiveness. Management positions (e.g., product manager, chief operating officer) and processes are added to coordinate across functions.

4. **SPEED ↑ + STAFF ↑ + STRUCTURE ↑ → SHARED VALUES ↓** The pace of growth is exhilarating but also exhausting, and morale can suffer as a consequence. As functions expand, subcultures emerge and cross-functional conflict sharpens. As the staff expands, "old guard/new guard" conflict comes up. Company culture can dissipate as early team members—torchbearers for the original vision—leave the venture or are demoted because it no longer requires jack-of-all-trades generalists.

5. **SPEED ↓ → SCOPE ↑** If growth slows due to market saturation or competitive pressures, the startup may try to sustain growth by expanding its scope: entering international markets, launching new products, or reinventing the core business through a next-generation product encompassing radical innovation. Likewise, if operating margins are poor due to either competitive pressure or operational problems induced by hypergrowth, the venture may pursue vertical integration, aiming to boost profits by bringing previously outsourced activities in-house.

6. **SCOPE ↑ → STAFF ↑ → STRUCTURE ↑** The startup must undertake another round of adding specialist staff and adjusting its organizational structure to manage its expanded scope.

With so many transitions for late-stage startups to go through, it's easy to understand why a large percentage of them fail. However, some ventures do make it through this intense "Scaling for Speed" gauntlet and emerge as profitable industry leaders. Google, Amazon, Salesforce, Facebook, Spanx, LinkedIn, Zappos, Dropbox, and Netflix come to mind as examples. Others, however, falter due to mistakes or misfortunes that occur with one or more of the transitions listed above. We'll see examples of that in the next two chapters, which describe, respectively, 1) the *Speed Trap* failure pattern—when demand from enthusiastic early adopters fuels explosive early growth that cannot be profitably sustained in the mainstream market, and 2) the *Help Wanted* failure pattern—when a startup is not able to amass the resources required to meet strong mainstream demand.

Scaling for Scope

Scaling for Scope starts with a bold, innovative vision. The vision captivates investors, who supply enough capital to fund a protracted product development effort. From that point, the startup's organizational transformations in many ways mirror those of ventures that pursue Scaling for Speed.

1. SCOPE ↑ → SERIES X ↑ A bold and innovative vision attracts investors willing to fund a multiyear development effort.

2. SCOPE ↑ → STAFF ↑ → STRUCTURE ↑ To develop its product, the startup hires engineers and other specialists, along with middle managers to supervise them.

3. SCOPE ↑ + STAFF ↑ + STRUCTURE ↑ → SHARED VALUES ↓ The pressure to meet product development deadlines is relentless, and morale can suffer as a consequence. As functions expand, subcultures emerge and cross-functional conflict sharpens. As the staff grows, "old guard/new guard" conflict ensues, and company culture dissipates as early team members leave the company and newcomers lack affinity with its mission.

4. SCOPE ↑ → SCOPE ↑ One way to boost employee morale, gain some technical proof of concept, and possibly generate cash to help fund the lengthy core product development effort is to launch a "base camp" business: an ancillary offering that leverages some (but not all) of the technologies and capabilities that the startup is developing. In this manner, ambitious scope may beget even greater scope. (See the sidebar "Base Camp" for more on "base camp" initiatives and some examples.)

5. SCOPE ↑ → SPEED ↑ → SERIES X ↑ Once they launch their core product, some scope-driven startups must push for rapid customer growth because their business model requires a big customer base to harness network effects or attract partners who must justify committing resources. Rapid customer growth, in turn, necessitates an infusion of fresh capital.

6. SPEED ↑ → STAFF ↑ → STRUCTURE ↑ The startup must undertake another round of adding specialist staff and adjusting its organizational structure as it aims to rapidly expand its customer base.

Note how these two scaling paths converge. Startups that initially pursue Speed may eventually broaden their Scope. Startups that initially embrace ambitious Scope may eventually pursue Speed.

As with speed-driven scaling, the scope-led path is fraught with peril. In Chapter 9, we'll see that when Scaling for Scope, a late-stage startup's success typically hinges on everything going right, which exposes them to the *Cascading Miracles* failure pattern.

Base Camp

With "tough tech" ventures—in which product development demands a vast amount of leading-edge science and engineering work—entrepreneurs often consider creating ancillary businesses *before* launching their primary business. These pared-down versions serve as the first application for the technologies they're developing. Samir Kaul and his partners at Khosla Ventures have likened these ancillary businesses to a base camp, where mountaineers pause to organize their provisions and get acclimated to low oxygen levels before their final push to the summit. Examples of base camp businesses include:

• Lit Motors, discussed in Chapter 4, whose primary business would be the C-1—a fully enclosed, two-wheeled, electric-powered, gyroscope-stabilized vehicle—was simultaneously constructing a low-cost, foldable, electric-powered scooter that could transport large cargo packages, for use in developing countries like India. Founder Danny Kim reasoned that Lit Motors would gain valuable experience manufacturing the much simpler scooter and could plow profits from the scooter back into C-1 development.

• E Ink, whose primary business would be the electronic paper display technology used by the Amazon Kindle and similar devices, tested early versions of electronic ink by launching a business to provide large signs to promote merchandise in department stores. The signs could be updated wirelessly, reducing store labor costs.

Pausing at base camp isn't just a way to gain experience and generate cash—entrepreneurs may also see opportunities to 1) refine their technology step by step, as with E Ink's department store signs, which required lower resolution than handheld device displays; and 2) give their team an early morale boost, since it might otherwise take many years for them to see the fruits of their labor in the form of a product for the primary business.

The potential downside with base camp: It can turn out to be more difficult to launch and run an ancillary business than anticipated, turning base camp into a distraction for management and a cash drain. E Ink learned this lesson when its team members struggled to get its department store signs to work properly. They'd planned to update the signs through a pager network, but it turned out that pager signals couldn't be transmitted through the copper roofs found on many department stores they'd signed as customers. One way to avoid getting stranded at base camp is to license the relevant technology to another venture with its own team that can focus 100 percent of their energy on turning the base camp opportunity into a viable business.

Speed Trap

How fast is too fast when it comes to scaling? Jason Goldberg gained some insight into that question after founding two start-ups, with vastly different results. The first, a venture that helped company recruiters manage employee referrals, expanded too early and lost its investors a lot of money. His second, a service that referred news items based on what a user's Facebook friends and Twitter followers were reading, was sold within a year to a larger player in the industry; Goldberg and his investors netted over 13x their original investment.

Fresh off this success, Goldberg decided to team up with close friend Bradford Shellhammer in 2009 to launch Fabulis, a mashup of Facebook, Yelp, Foursquare, and Groupon, explicitly geared toward gay men. Membership growth for this social network stalled within a year, but one feature of Fabulis continued to hit the mark: the Gay Deal of the Day. Shellhammer, acclaimed for his design eye, sourced a diverse mix of products—from chocolates, to underwear, to Lucky's Hamburgers—and each day selected a different one to offer at a significantly discounted price. Sales were strong, and the co-founders were surprised to learn that half of their customers were women.

In early 2011, after having raised $3 million, Goldberg and Shellhammer decided to shutter Fabulis and launch Fab.com, a flash sale site for the general public. The co-founders offered to give investors their money back, but all decided to back the pivot. A three-month viral marketing campaign ("Convince 10 friends to join, get a $30 credit") attracted 165,000 members before Fab opened for business in June.

Fab offered deep discounts on products selected by Shellhammer for their aesthetic appeal and functional excellence. Big sellers included Eames chairs, umbrellas, antique typewriters, and vibrators. Customers found great appeal in unique items that conveyed a quirky, cheeky attitude—for example, a chandelier made of martini glasses or a rhinestone-encrusted motorcycle helmet. Fab was an instant hit, selling $600,000 in merchandise in its first twelve days. And because manufacturers drop-shipped items directly to customers, Fab didn't need to hold inventory. Featured offers spread like wildfire through social networks, so the startup didn't need to spend any money on advertising, either. Avoiding these expenses meant that cash flow was positive—at least initially. By year-end, the startup had over a million members and had raised another $48 million in venture capital.

To prepare for further expansion, Fab secured an additional $120 million in venture capital in 2012. That year, the venture sold an impressive $115 million of merchandise, up from $18 million in 2011. However, Fab's business model was starting to unravel; despite its strong sales, the startup lost $90 million in 2012, according to press reports. Why? Because to supercharge its growth, Fab had invested $40 million in marketing that year. Unfortunately, the shoppers attracted through ads were less obsessed with design than Fab's early customers and, as a result, were much less likely to purchase multiple times or spread word of its offers. Goldberg recalled:

> By the summer of 2012, our new customers weren't keeping up with the great results we'd seen earlier. Our "golden cohort" was a couple of hundred thousand users who signed up prelaunch; their performance was always great. And those that followed in the second half of 2011 were strong, too. So, we

poured fuel on that fire, with a big boost in online marketing, which had worked really well early on. But when that started to falter, we added TV and other expensive marketing channels, like direct mail.

Compounding the cash drain was the cost of breakneck expansion into Europe, where Fab had been quickly cloned by several start-ups, including Bamarang, launched in January 2012 by the infamous Samwer brothers. The Samwers' Rocket Internet incubator copied successful U.S. ventures—including Pinterest, Airbnb, eBay, and Groupon—and then demanded that the U.S. company acquire the clone to avoid trench warfare. Goldberg was furious and refused to roll over, writing on his blog, "Let me put Bamarang and other copycats on notice. Ripping someone off is not going to work in this space. Knockoffs are just bad design. In design, customers are smart and value authenticity. Do something original or don't do anything at all."

Goldberg recalled that the Samwers "had cloned us, almost literally pixel by pixel. We figured that since our designers were all over the world, we were credible entrants overseas, and we shouldn't cede Europe." He added that the move abroad had strong support from Fab's board: "We had investors who'd also invested in Airbnb, and they were asking, 'Who's going to stop this? Will anyone challenge this aggressor?' "

To jump-start its move into Europe, in 2012 Fab acquired three overseas flash sales startups, committed $12 million for a ten-year warehouse lease, and staffed a European headquarters in Berlin with 150 employees. By August, Fab had 1.4 million registered members in Europe generating 20 percent of company sales. That summer, the Samwers shut down Bamarang but shrewdly transferred their investment focus along with Bamarang's staff to another portfolio company, Westwing, which sold high-end home furnishings and was eventually successful, completing an IPO in 2018. Meanwhile, Fab had at best achieved a pyrrhic victory; its European operations were hemorrhaging cash. By the time they eventually pulled the plug, investments there totaled a reported $60 to $100 million.

In April 2013, Goldberg, worried that flash sales would lose steam, announced a pivot away from that model—and trumpeted his new plan for joining the pantheon of e-commerce giants. According to Goldberg, daily deals were "a good way to draw people in at the beginning. But every time you send another daily email, you burn people out a little. You have to offer them more than just the daily deal."

By that point, only one-third of Fab's sales came from daily deals; the balance came from a broad selection of products listed on the site: eleven thousand in total, the majority of which were furniture and home décor; other categories included jewelry, food, and pet care. With this abundance of items, Fab completed a major site redesign to enhance searchability for its twelve million members. Also, since drop-shipping had generated customer complaints about slow delivery times, the startup shifted to holding more merchandise in inventory and shipping goods from its own warehouse. Finally, Fab stepped up its efforts to design and sell Fab-branded private label products, which promised higher gross margins. To advance this strategy, Fab acquired Massivkonzept, a German company that designed, manufactured, and sold customized wooden furniture, for stock worth about $25 million.

These moves, which consumed considerable capital, were controversial. Some observers argued that flash sales still had momentum, while others had faith in Goldberg's instincts. Online flash sales had taken off in 2008 during the Great Recession, when Groupon and Gilt Groupe found that many desperate manufacturers of luxury goods and services were willing to deeply discount to jump-start stalled sales. By 2013, however, the economy had recovered, so manufacturers felt less pressure to discount. Meanwhile, a crowd of new entrants—including Fab, Zulily, Rue La La, and One Kings Lane—was bidding up product costs.

Then, to make matters worse, Amazon got into the game. "Competition got fierce," Goldberg recalled, adding, "At the start, it took Amazon thirty to forty days to copy our flash sale products. By 2013, they did this within twenty-four hours. They'd call our designers and say, 'Hey, we'd like to feature you.' It was hard to match their price, and our customer satisfaction scores slipped because we couldn't match their shipping speed. How can you compete when they are offering the same product from the same designer, at the same or lower price, and with free and faster shipping?"

Goldberg now acknowledges the risks with the pivot. "It was capital intensive, and holding inventory exposes you to the risk of buying the wrong stuff. We'd seen that with uneven results for the 2012 holiday season. We'd assumed—maybe with arrogance, and certainly with overconfidence—that we were great at picking winning products. But that holiday season, we failed to sell a lot of merchandise." He added, "We started to lose the curation edge."

With the pivot in place, Fab's board considered two growth plans at its April 2013 meeting. Plan A was to retrench and focus only on the U.S. market, aiming for positive cash flow from about $150 million in annual sales. Plan B was to "continue pushing for 100 percent year-over-year growth and world domination." Goldberg noted, "It wasn't much of a debate. Only one board member argued for Plan A. He was worried about the performance of our recent customers and the fact that we hadn't seen a good return from heavy marketing during the holidays. Everyone else, including me, wanted to ride the rocket ship."

In June 2013, Fab raised $165 million in new venture capital at a $1 billion post-money valuation. But, as Goldberg pointed out, "The reality was, we had failed; we needed $300 million to pursue the plan-of-record and support the large investments already underway. I fielded phone calls congratulating me on achieving unicorn status and remember just being sick to my stomach. Not many people know what it's like to raise $165 million at a $1 billion valuation, fully aware that you're sailing into a shit-storm."

Fab's cash burn rate peaked at $14 million per month. To get it under control, Goldberg hit the brakes hard in October 2013. Fab laid off 80 percent of its U.S. staff, terminated most of its top managers, and narrowed its merchandise selection significantly. Goldberg's co-founder Shellhammer departed. As for European operations, the venture shut down everything but its profitable custom furniture business. By mid-2014, Fab was a shell of its former self. Goldberg decided to spin off the private label furniture business in Europe, named Hem, which had been bolstered by two more acquisitions. Shifting his focus entirely to this business, he simultaneously put Fab's U.S. operations up for sale. In October 2014, a prominent custom design manufacturer acquired Fab's U.S. assets in an all-stock transaction worth about $30 million. Hem was subsequently sold to a Swiss furniture company for a reported $20 million.

Speed Trap

Rapid rise; rapid fall. By expanding at an unsustainable pace, Fab, like many other late-stage startups, fell prey to a Speed Trap. Here's how a Speed Trap unfolds:

• **Step 1: Opportunity Spotted.** An entrepreneur identifies a novel solution to a strong unmet need for a specific customer segment. Fab's daily deals met the needs of shoppers who shared Shellhammer's tastes and were looking for distinctive products.

• **Step 2: Strong Early Growth.** Expansion is fueled by word-of-mouth referrals by early adopters within the target customer segment, and sometimes by strong network effects. As detailed below, Fab did enjoy some network effects during this phase of its growth, but they weakened over time.

• **Step 3: Fundraising Success.** Growth attracts enthusiastic investors willing to pay a high price because they expect continued expansion. If a charismatic founder like Goldberg can sell investors on a dazzling vision, the venture's valuation may soar, stoking ambitions for hypergrowth.

• **Step 4: Rivals Enter.** Growth also attracts rivals. Some might be startup clones, like Bamarang, while others could be fast following tech giants, like Amazon, or "sleeping dragons"—established industry incumbents that rouse from their slumber and become aware that an entrepreneur has tapped into a new opportunity in their space.

- **Step 5: Saturation.** As happened with Fab in 2012, the startup saturates the pool of customers most strongly drawn to its value proposition. To attract the next wave of prospects, the venture must advertise heavily and extend generous promotional offers. While the cost to acquire customers (CAC) is rising, their lifetime value (LTV) is declining, because these new buyers are less loyal and less inclined to repurchase. Many are worth less than the marketing investment necessary to attract them. If investors value growth over profitability, they may be willing to pump more money into the company—but not indefinitely.

- **Step 6: Staffing Bottlenecks.** To support expansion, the scaling startup must hire legions of new employees. Finding so many qualified candidates is challenging, and even if the venture does hire enough people, it may prove difficult to train them quickly. Either way, competent workers will be in short supply, and as a result, products won't be inspected before they are sold, shipments will contain the wrong items, customers' emails will go unanswered, and so forth. By cutting corners, the startup may suffer shortfalls in product quality and customer service. Fab largely managed to avoid serious problems on this front.

- **Step 7: Structure Added.** Coordinating a larger, functionally specialized workforce requires 1) senior managers with relevant expertise, and 2) information systems and formalized processes for planning and monitoring performance. Fab, for example, added considerable complexity to its operations when it brought inventory in-house and started manufacturing its own furniture lines. A scaling startup must acquire the management talent, organizational structure, and information systems to coordinate this more complex array of activities. That's a tall order.

- **Step 8: Internal Discord.** Rapid growth in head count and the expansion of specialty units can lead to conflict, morale problems, and the dissipation of the company's culture. For example, Sales complains about the quality of leads Marketing provided while

Marketing complains that Engineering is late with promised new features. Goldberg acknowledged that Fab suffered from antagonistic subcultures: "I allowed silos of teams and thinking, and that seeded an awful cancerous distrust." The resulting finger-pointing elicits "it's not my fault" responses and provokes ire. Then discord deepens as veterans resent the "just a job" attitude of newcomers; meanwhile, newly hired specialists are frustrated that early team members are clueless about their contributions. Senior management tries to tamp down organizational fires and rally the troops. Middle managers start to wonder if senior management really knows what's going on and what needs to be done—especially since the CEO is spending so much time out of the office, trying to raise more capital.

• **Step 9: Ethical Lapses.** Sometimes, the relentless pressure to sustain growth leads entrepreneurs to cut legal, regulatory, or ethical corners. Uber, for example, was accused of encouraging its employees to book and then cancel rides with its rival, Lyft. Zenefits, a licensed health insurance broker, created software that allegedly allowed its new salespeople to cheat on state licensing exams to sustain the startup's rapid growth. At Fab, however, Goldberg avoided this ethical slippery slope.

• **Step 10: Investor Alarm.** As the venture burns through cash, its stock price declines. Their stock options now worthless, employees exit. Investors become reluctant to commit more capital. Moreover, if an existing investor is willing to throw the startup a lifeline, she'll demand a huge number of new equity shares, massively diluting the equity stakes of senior managers and any investors who don't follow suit. Since the board has to approve such a financing, knockdown, drag-out boardroom fights over whether and how to proceed will ensue.

• **Step 11: Endgame.** At this point, the problem is clear: The company is growing at an unsustainable rate and must slow down. The question is, how hard to slam on the brakes? Is it enough to turn down the marketing spigot? Or, does the startup need to cut head count to survive? Does it make sense to try to sell the company? If investors won't provide the capital required to turn the company around, will a corporation with deep pockets see a strategic fit? We'll explore these questions in Chapter 10, which lays out the moves entrepreneurs can make if they think they are on a path toward failure.

Variations on these themes play out over and over among startups that scale too quickly. Some survive by trimming head count, cutting marketing, and refocusing on more loyal and profitable customer segments. Birchbox, Blue Apron, Groupon, Zenefits, and Zynga are examples. However, for Fab and many other startups, such as Beepi, Homejoy, Munchery, and Nasty Gal, the Speed Trap is fatal.

The RAWI Test

How to avoid or safely pass through a Speed Trap? It helps to have a radar detector, and for entrepreneurs, that is the **RAWI test.** The test asks four categories of questions to determine whether a startup is poised to scale successfully:

- **Ready?** Does the startup have a proven business model? Is its target market large enough to keep growing? When it starts scaling, does it have a high enough profit margin to withstand a price/cost squeeze if new customers become harder to attract?
- **Able?** Can the startup access the human and capital resources required to expand rapidly? Can it train large numbers of new workers and coordinate their efforts?
- **Willing?** Are the founders eager to grow their business? Will doing so advance their original vision? Are they willing to incur the equity dilution that comes with raising lots of venture capital; risk getting fired, as investors take control of the startup's board; and suffer the toll that long hours at work take on personal relationships?
- **Impelled?** Does the startup have aggressive rivals? Is it at risk of waking sleeping dragons? Will powerful network effects, high

switching costs, and strong scale economies provoke competitors to pursue a "land grab"?

It's important to emphasize that the RAWI test isn't conducted just once. Taking marketplace dynamics and venture performance into account, entrepreneurs should revisit the RAWI test at regular intervals—say, quarterly.

Ready?

A startup is *ready* to scale if, for a given pace of expansion, its leaders are confident that it can sustain product-market fit—that is, its product will continue to meet the needs of its target customers in ways that will generate healthy long-term profits. These profits, in turn, will be high enough to attract new investors to sustain scaling.

Long-term profitability will be healthy when the startup maintains an LTV/CAC ratio above a threshold level as it grows. That threshold depends on the venture's business model, especially its ability to harness strong network effects and its level of fixed expenses per dollar of revenue. We'll discuss the impact of network effects on target LTV/CAC ratios in the "Impelled?" section, but, for now, let's look at fixed expenses. Recall that LTV reflects the gross margin (revenue minus variable costs) earned from a typical customer over time. The venture must achieve a high enough gross margin from all its customers to cover their acquisition costs along with the firm's fixed expenses, thus generating a profit. Businesses with high fixed expenses, like "Software as a Service" (SaaS) ventures, must surpass a high LTV/CAC threshold: 3.0 is a typical target for such businesses.

So, how fast can a startup grow and keep its LTV/CAC ratio above the relevant threshold? Factors that set a speed limit, outlined in the last chapter, now come into play. They include 1) *saturation risk,* that is, the point at which the startup has offered its product to most prospects in targeted customer segments; 2) *quality exposure,* that is, how quickly the startup can grow without spawning product flaws and customer service errors; and 3) *rivalry,* in particular, the competitive response provoked by rapid expansion. All three of these factors can have a big impact on a startup's LTV/CAC ratio. We'll explore *saturation risk* below, then discuss *quality exposure* in the "Able?" section and *rivalry* in the "Impelled?" section.

As Fab grew, it saturated its initial target market: early adopters who were superfans of the distinctive products Shellhammer curated. Successive waves of customers purchased less frequently, required deeper discounts, and were more likely to be acquired through paid marketing than free word-of-mouth referrals. In other words, lower prices for smaller and fewer orders reduced the new customers' LTV, as compared to early adopters. And, the need for paid marketing boosted their CAC. So, Fab experienced an LTV/CAC squeeze as it grew—a recurring challenge for startups that run into a Speed Trap.

To determine whether a scaling startup is vulnerable to saturation, an entrepreneur needs to understand the size of each customer segment within the venture's total addressable market and how fast those segments are likely to grow. However, estimates of customer segment size can be imprecise because the boundaries of segments are often blurry. For example, there's rarely a sharp divide between early adopters and mainstream customers; more typically, one segment blends into the other.

For this reason, a startup's team should analyze the performance of successive groups of newly acquired customers—known as *cohorts*—to track saturation. Each cohort consists of customers who were acquired during the same time period—say, the same month or quarter. Ideally, they are also members of the same customer segment and were acquired through the same marketing method, since grouping customers from different segments into a single cohort can obscure segment-specific trends. Similarly, grouping customers acquired through different marketing methods into a single cohort can distort analysis because different marketing methods may attract prospects with varying levels of interest in the start-up's product. For example, individuals who take the initiative to search for a product on Google probably have a stronger need for the product—and thus are more likely to become loyal customers—than those who respond to a broadly targeted Facebook ad.

Separate cohort analyses should track trends for all of the key measures of customer satisfaction and engagement with a product—for example: average spending per period; retention and repurchase rates; numbers of new customers referred; and so forth. The relevant metrics will vary by business model. For instance, with "freemium" products like Dropbox, cohort analysis should include conversion rates from the free version to the premium, paid version. The following table shows a sample cohort analysis table for a freemium product.

Each column of a cohort analysis table can reveal, through quick visual inspection, whether performance is improving or deteriorating. The table's top row shows successive time intervals: Month 1 after the cohort was acquired; Month 2; etc. The rows beneath start with the oldest cohort, with cells from left to right showing how that cohort fared with respect to the performance metric in Month 1 after the customers' acquisition, then Month 2, etc. By scanning down a column, you can see whether newer cohorts are doing better or worse than older ones did. If conversion rates are declining for recent cohorts—as they are in this example—that may be a sign that a startup is saturating its target market. For instance, four months after they were acquired, 7.8 percent of the February 2015 cohort—the oldest group—had upgraded to premium, whereas only 5.0 percent of the August 2015 cohort had done so by its fourth month.

Performance declines may be due to other problems besides saturation, such as customer service shortfalls or escalating competition. However, these problems should impact all cohorts, new and old, equally. After taking into account the impact of other problems that affect all cohorts, an entrepreneur should be able to discern whether saturation is contributing to a bigger-than-expected performance decline for recent cohorts.

Cumulative Free-to-Paid Conversion Rate
for Cohorts Acquired through Google AdWords

Month	Month 1	Month 2	Month 3	Month 4	Month 5	Month 6	Month 7	Month 8	Month 9	Month 10
Feb-15	0.1%	5.0%	6.8%	7.8%	8.2%	8.8%	8.9%	8.9%	9.0%	9.0%
Mar-15	0.8%	5.3%	7.1%	8.0%	8.7%	9.6%	9.7%	10.2%	10.4%	
Apr-15	0.9%	5.0%	5.7%	7.4%	8.6%	8.9%	9.7%	9.9%		
May-15	1.1%	3.2%	4.2%	4.9%	5.1%	5.6%	5.9%			
Jun-15	1.4%	3.9%	5.1%	5.7%	6.1%	6.3%				
Jul-15	0.9%	3.5%	4.7%	5.9%	6.0%					
Aug-15	0.7%	3.7%	4.7%	5.0%						
Sep-15	0.2%	2.5%	3.1%							
Oct-15	0.1%	2.0%								
Nov-15	0.0%									

One problem with using cohort analysis to assess saturation risk is that by the time a trend is evident, saturation has already occurred. My HBS colleague Mark Roberge points out that most measures of cohort performance—for example, subscriber retention rates and free-to-paid conversion rates—are *lagging indicators* of customer satisfaction and engagement. If you focus solely on retention rates, you don't know you have a problem until an unhappy customer disappears. One solution is to track Net Promoter Scores. An NPS survey asks, on a scale of 0 to 10, how likely a customer is to refer the product to a friend or colleague. The score is calculated as the percentage of all customers who are "promoters" (scoring 9 or 10), minus the percentage who are "detractors" (scoring 0–6). NPS scores over 50 are considered excellent. A declining NPS can serve as an early warning sign of problems and can allow managers to take corrective actions before severe damage is done.

Roberge recommends that scaling startups go a step further and focus their cohort analysis on early indicators that are both 1) highly predictive of long-term customer satisfaction and 2) observable soon after customers are acquired. As an example, Roberge's former employer HubSpot, a marketing services startup, tracks the percentage of new customers that use at least five of the HubSpot platform's twenty-five features within sixty days of signing up. This measure is strongly correlated with long-term customer retention and spending. When the result exceeds 80 percent, HubSpot management believes a cohort is staying "on the rails."

Beyond giving startups an early warning, indicators linked to product use can provide more focused solutions than a broad measure of satisfaction like NPS. Every function within a startup affects NPS in some way, so any downward trend requires further analysis to figure out which function to address. By contrast, there are far fewer ways to activate feature use by new customers, so managers can decide on corrective action more quickly.

Conducting cohort analysis will help entrepreneurs avoid the temptation to inflate their LTV calculations—say, with overoptimistic estimates of retention rates or average order size. They should also use cohort analysis to track CAC—customer acquisition cost—over time, by customer segment and marketing method. That way, they're sure to keep their LTV/CAC ratios in sharp focus. To continue with the earlier "freemium" example, the table below shows how the cost of acquiring a free user using Google AdWords is rising. CAC for the three most recent cohorts has roughly doubled, compared to CAC for earlier cohorts.

Customer Acquisition Cost for Cohorts of Free Product Users Acquired through Google AdWords

Cohort	Free User CAC
Feb-15	$0.12
Mar-15	$0.12
Apr-15	$0.13
May-15	$0.08
Jun-15	$0.12
Jul-15	$0.12

Cohort	Free User CAC
Aug-15	$0.20
Sep-15	$0.18
Oct-15	$0.36

This increase in CAC might be a sign of saturation, but not necessarily. Most marketing channels have an upper limit on the number of prospects they can deliver during a given period. VC Jeff Bussgang likens this to drilling for oil: Some channels turn out to be gushers—at least for a while—but eventually every well runs dry. With paid search ads, for example, you can only reach prospects who have typed specific keywords into a search engine. Some keywords are more productive than others for attracting customers. If a startup overinvests in paid search, it will be forced to use less productive keywords, which will boost CAC. This higher spending doesn't automatically imply that all the prospects in the startup's target market have been exposed to its marketing messages; instead, the startup's expenditure on paid search ads may have reached its upper limit. If that's the case, then to keep overall CAC at profitable levels, the startup must slow down or employ other marketing channels.

Another explanation for rising CAC for a given marketing channel is that rivals have stepped up their marketing investments. Again, a higher CAC doesn't necessarily signal saturation: There might be plenty of room within a market segment for a startup and its rivals to continue to grow, but CAC may be spiraling upward solely due to a marketing battle.

Goldberg and Fab's management team conducted cohort analysis and had a handle on deteriorating LTV/CAC trends, but they did not act quickly enough on this data. In October 2013, three months after raising the VC round that made Fab a unicorn, Goldberg wrote in a memo to his team, "We spent $200 million and we haven't proven out our business model . . . we haven't proven that we know exactly what our customers want to buy." He added a litany of his own mistakes as CEO, including:

- *I guided us to go too fast.*
- *I didn't insist on homing in on our target customer.*
- *I spent too much on marketing before we got the consumer value proposition right.*
- *I didn't build enough discipline around costs and business metrics into our culture.*
- *I allowed us to over-invest in Europe.*
- *I didn't see the need to course correct fast enough.*

In his postmortem analysis, Goldberg acknowledged that he'd fallen victim to a false positive: "Our original sin—the root cause of Fab's failure—was never truly achieving product-market fit. We thought we had it, due to great results for our early adopters. With them, we really hit a nerve. They were passionate about the products we sold; those products fit the Zeitgeist. But that passion didn't scale into enough repeat purchases beyond our hardcore, early users. Our first customers weren't representative of those who came next. We mistook early data as being representative of subsequent customers and as a result, we expanded too fast."

Put simply, Fab was not *ready* to scale when it did. Goldberg continued, "Our VC told us our first cohorts were the best they'd ever seen. They'd never seen e-commerce growth this fast. We were earning great NPS scores. So, it seemed smart to step on the gas. I'll never put the blame for this on anyone but myself, but our investors were cheerleaders for hypergrowth. They didn't insist on growth, but they were thrilled about our ambitious growth plans."

As Fab's experience shows, conducting cohort analysis and understanding LTV/CAC trends are necessary but not sufficient for successful scaling. Entrepreneurs must interpret trends correctly *and* act on them. When performance is below expectations, they can choose one of two paths. They can slow things down, freeing up management time that would otherwise be spent fighting fires stoked by topsy-turvy growth. Under less pressure, managers are more likely to be able to diagnose problems and formulate sound plans for fixing them.

Or, they can keep their foot on the gas pedal, believing that 1) they fully understand the problems at hand and know how to fix them; 2) if they slow down they may have trouble regaining momentum, with competitors hot on their heels; and 3) investors might grow wary if they deliberately throttle back growth. This last argument may have influenced Goldberg. According to press accounts, in early 2013, senior team members had recommended cutting Fab's European operations in half, but Goldberg was reluctant to do so until he'd closed the big June 2013 fundraising round. Bottom line: When an entrepreneur is choosing between "slow down" and "go fast," her overconfidence and human tendency to see what she wants to see can often tip the balance.

Able?

A startup is *able* to scale if its leaders are confident they can access and effectively manage the resources they'll need to expand at a given pace. They should be asking themselves three questions:

1. Can we raise the capital required to fund accelerated growth?
2. Can we hire enough competent employees in frontline functions and train them to do their job well?
3. Will we have the right senior leaders, organizational structure, and management systems to efficiently and effectively coordinate the efforts of those frontline employees?

If the answer to *all* three questions is "yes," then their startup will be *able* to scale.

Capital. Fab had raised $165 million in June 2013, but that fell short of the $300 million Goldberg had targeted to fund its aggressive global growth plans—that is, "Plan B."

Frontline Employees. Due to rapid expansion, Fab was indeed at risk of not being able to hire competent employees fast enough, which would have strained operations and hurt customer service. Fortunately, the startup had enough talented staff to weather the storm. While Fab had some issues with delayed shipments, the company largely managed to avoid serious customer service problems. Success on this front also meant the answer to the third question was a "yes": Fab had senior executives who were able to oversee a rapidly growing workforce.

Other rapidly scaling startups are not so lucky. For instance, during the dot-com boom, as consumers embraced online stock trading, Internet brokerages like E*Trade and Ameritrade couldn't recruit and train customer service reps quickly enough to keep up with exploding transaction volumes. Call center reps had to be trained to respond to customers' questions about a wide variety of complex transactions, including "stop loss" instructions, options trades, and margin calls. As a result of staffing and training shortfalls, irate customers with service problems and queries watched trading gains slip away while they waited for a response.

What can a startup do if it cannot hire enough competent employees to handle rapidly expanding demand? Of course, putting the brakes on growth is always an option—but one that is rarely considered, for the reasons described above. Instead, management often chooses to 1) fill the ranks with any "warm body"; 2) pressure current employees to work faster; and 3) scrimp on training, pushing new hires straight into the fray. Under these conditions it's no surprise that errors keep piling up. Sometimes, to conserve manpower, a startup will simply let the backlog of unanswered queries grow unchecked, frustrating customers. As Reid Hoffman says, "For many blitzscaling companies, the key rule is 'Provide whatever customer service you can as long as it doesn't slow you down . . . and that may mean no service!' " Problems can also play out in other operational areas that are short of staff. For example, mistakes may be made in the final inspection at the end of a production line, or in packing orders at a warehouse.

Leadership and Management. If staff shortages threaten to constrain growth, an entrepreneur should make sure managers in charge of the relevant functions know what they are doing—ideally, by virtue of past experience with a scaling startup. As the next chapter will show, recruiting the right function head is easier said than done, especially if the startup's CEO lacks experience in the field. Also, once seasoned functional leaders are in place, the CEO should listen to them. If they say they can't hire and train frontline workers fast enough to keep the train on the tracks, the CEO should push to understand why.

Finally, an entrepreneur should monitor the inputs and outputs of key operating functions in the same way they track customer cohort performance. How has the size of the recruiting pipeline in key functions changed over time? How has the percentage of candidates who receive and accept job offers changed? What's the trend in error rates in production and customer service, and how do those rates correlate with employee experience levels? As with cohort performance, a goal should be to identify early indicators that are strongly correlated with the risk of more serious problems down the road.

Willing?

It may seem odd to ask if entrepreneurs are *willing* to scale their venture rapidly. Isn't the drive for scale a hallmark of entrepreneurship? As Paul Graham, the founder of Y Combinator, asserts, "A startup is a company designed to grow fast." Graham explains that an entrepreneur at the helm of a rapidly growing startup will feel strong pressure to raise more money in order to fuel more growth:

> Money to grow faster is always at the command of the most successful startups, because the VCs need them more than they need the VCs. A profitable startup could, if it wanted, just grow on its own revenues. . . . Whereas VCs need to invest in startups, and in particular the most successful startups, or they'll be out of business. Which means that any sufficiently promising startup will be offered money on terms they'd be crazy to refuse.

As Graham notes, many entrepreneurs who lead successful startups have the option to avoid raising more venture capital and could instead fund slower growth through internally generated cash flow. However, passing up more venture capital "on terms they'd be crazy to refuse" might forfeit the entrepreneur's opportunity to become *really* rich. So, if a startup could scale rapidly but is not impelled to do so by competitors (more on this below), what might hold them back?

First, an entrepreneur faces a radically different risk-reward scenario than a venture capital investor. Assume that scaling rapidly— "swinging for the fences"—has a 1 in 20 chance of earning a huge payoff. With a few dozen companies in its portfolio—that is, with dozens of "at bats"—a venture capital firm can reasonably expect at least one home run, along with a few singles and doubles. Averaging across all of these outcomes, the VC should earn a good return on its investments, even with plenty of strikeouts. By contrast, entrepreneurs don't deal with averages; they get just one turn at bat, and if swinging for the fences significantly boosts their odds of striking out, too, they might prefer a safer strategy.

As an example, if you, as a founder/CEO had one shot, would you rather have 1) a 10 percent equity stake in a startup that has a 5 percent chance of being worth $1 billion; or 2) a 25 percent equity stake in a startup that raised much less capital, grew more slowly, and has a 10 percent chance of being worth $200 million? In terms of personal wealth creation for the founder, both options have the same expected value: $5 million. But with the hypergrowth option, the founder has half the chance (5 percent vs. 10 percent) to earn twice as much ($100 million vs. $50 million).

Second, scaling at high speed puts tremendous personal pressure on a CEO. The hours can be brutal and filled with a constant stream of calamities. Everything happens faster: hiring mistakes, firings, service problems, customer defections. Of course, if things are going well, achievements come faster, too. Some leaders thrive under such pressure and derive great satisfaction from taming the chaos. Others, after skipping yet another child's recital or one more friend's wedding, may ask, "Is this really worth it?"

Finally, if a founder still holds the CEO role and chooses to scale her venture at a faster rate, she must accept the higher odds that she'll be replaced. Faster growth means raising more rounds of venture capital, and each round typically adds a new investor to the board of directors. Investors will eventually control a majority of board votes and can dismiss the CEO if she's struggling. A founder who relishes the power that comes with the CEO role, or who'd be distraught at being separated from a venture to which she's passionately attached, should weigh this risk.

This final concern points to an underlying issue with being *Willing* to scale. "Fast or slow" isn't solely up to the founder—it's a board-level decision. In an early-stage startup, when two founders might outnumber a single investor on a three-person board, those founders can indeed dictate strategy—assuming they are in sync. But as noted above, investors eventually outnumber founders on most late-stage boards. In this setting, if the investor/board members want to expand rapidly, while the founder/CEO has serious reservations, the investors will have to decide whether the CEO is indispensable or should be replaced with someone who'll do their bidding.

And what if the investor/board members can't agree among themselves about the venture's growth plans? As noted in the last chapter, investors in early rounds sometimes prefer more conservative strategies than their late-stage counterparts, because early-round investors, having purchased their equity for a low price, are guaranteed a good return as long as the startup doesn't derail. By contrast, for late-round investors to realize a good return, the startup must sustain its high growth rate—and that might require risky moves, like Fab's foray into Europe. Along these lines, recall that only one of Fab's board members voted for Plan A, slower growth in the United States, while Goldberg and all of the other board members voted for Plan B: "world domination." The majority rules in a situation like this, but board debates can be bruising.

Impelled?

The RAWI test's last question asks if competition—current or expected—impels a venture to scale rapidly. "Impelled?" isn't like the other three RAWI test questions. For each of the other questions—Ready? Able? Willing?—the response *must* be "yes" to give a green light to fast growth. By contrast, if the response to "Impelled?" is "no," an entrepreneur might still attempt fast growth, provided that her answer is "yes" for all of the other three questions. Crucially, this assumes that "Ready?" gets a "yes" because the entrepreneur is confident that overheated rivalry will not trigger an LTV/ CAC squeeze. In this scenario, rapid growth is still a reasonable option—but the startup is by no means *impelled* to expand aggressively.

Of course, if the answer to all *four* questions is "yes," then things are straightforward: Step on the gas, now! But things get tricky if the response to "Impelled?" is "yes," but one or more of *Ready, Able,* or *Willing* gets a "no." When that happens, the venture's leaders will feel competitive pressure to grow while constraints simultaneously hold them back. In its strongest form, however, "Impelled" implies an existential competitive threat. When that's true, even if an entrepreneur doesn't yet *feel Ready, Able,* or *Willing,* she must do her best to address the relevant constraints and then try to grow.

Three structural attributes of certain business models—powerful network effects, high customer switching costs, and strong economies of scale—impel a startup, along with rivals who share these attributes, to accelerate growth.

Network Effects. A product that facilitates interactions between its users has network effects if adding users makes the product more valuable to every user, by providing more potential partners for interactions. For example, the first Skype user couldn't do anything with the product until a second user came on board. The subsequent arrival of each new Skype user made the product a little bit more valuable for every existing user, by offering yet another potential conversation partner. For the same reason, Skype's growing user base made the service more attractive to nonusers, by boosting the odds that someone with whom they wanted to speak already had Skype. With network effects, users beget more users. And the stronger the preference for additional interaction partners, the stronger the network effect.

Networks come in two flavors—one-sided and two-sided—depending on the number of distinct user groups they encompass. *Two-sided networks* have two groups of users who each consistently play a distinct role in transactions. For example, credit card companies serve cardholders and merchants, recruiting websites match job seekers and corporate employers, and videogame consoles connect gamers with game developers. By contrast, *one-sided networks* have just one type of user. Although every Skype call has a sender and a receiver, these roles are transient: Most Skype users make and receive calls at different times.

In a two-sided network, members on each side generally prefer having access to more users on the other side; these are positive *cross-side* network effects. For example, signing up more merchants makes a credit card more attractive to consumers—and vice versa. Sometimes, however, cross-side network effects are negative: Adding users to the other side makes the product *less* valuable. For example, consumers may get frustrated with websites that serve up too many spammy ads. In two-sided networks, each group's members may also have preferences about the number of users on *their own side*. For example, gamers may prefer to have the same type of console owned by many fellow gamers, so that they can swap games and play each other online: That's a positive *same-side* network effect. Conversely, bidders in an eBay auction will wish to see fewer rival bidders on their side of the network.

Entrepreneurs have powerful economic incentives to accelerate the growth of products that harness strong positive network effects. Since a product that offers access to a bigger network is more valuable to existing users, it can command a higher price—although price hikes might be deferred, to supercharge expansion. And, because access to a bigger network is also more valuable to *potential* users, a startup exploiting network effects should see declining customer acquisition costs. We see this magic at work with companies like

Airbnb, American Express, Expedia, Facebook, LinkedIn, Microsoft Windows, Nasdaq, Slack, Sony PlayStation, Tinder, and Zillow.

It's important for entrepreneurs to gauge the strength of network effects for their product, because the stronger network effects are, the faster a startup should attempt to grow. Fortunately, it's possible to measure network effects quantitatively using a market research technique called *conjoint analysis*. Conjoint analysis asks respondents—dozens of times—which of two products they prefer, each time varying some of the products' attributes (e.g., for consumers considering a credit card, the network effect—number of merchants accepting the card—would be considered along with attributes such as the card's spending limit, emergency assistance features, loyalty program, interest rate, annual fee, etc.). An algorithm then estimates respondents' strength of preference for each attribute.

Using conjoint analysis, an entrepreneur could measure the strength of customers' preferences regarding network size, in terms of how much more they'd be willing to pay for access to a bigger network. However, it takes some training to use conjoint analysis, and respondents might require compensation for their time, so not many startups employ this technique. An alternative is to assess the strength of network effects for a new product in qualitative terms—low/medium/high—by comparing the product's attributes and customers' needs to those of other similar products known to have network effects.

What types of products enjoy strong network effects? Foremost among them would be marketplaces that connect parties with very specific requirements (the "demand side") with partners who have highly differentiated offerings (the "supply side"). Dating and job recruiting sites fit this profile, as do online auctions like eBay and sites that display real estate listings. If all of the potential home buyers and sellers in a community participate in a single network, then buyers will maximize their odds of finding their dream house, and sellers will maximize their odds of finding the buyer willing to pay the highest price.

Network effects are similarly strong when they facilitate any of the following: 1) *variety,* by providing a series of unique experiences— as with streaming movies or playing videogames; 2) *mobility,* as with credit cards or ridesharing services, because customers want to be able to use such products wherever they go; and 3) *connectivity,* or the ability to communicate with many friends or business acquaintances, as is the case with Skype or WhatsApp, or with social networks like Facebook or Twitter.

Early on, Fab leveraged network effects, but they were not as strong as those in the examples cited above—and the effects weakened as the startup grew. Its first cohort of users enjoyed sharing Fab's distinctive offers with friends: a same-side network effect. But this faded as waves of less enthusiastic customers were recruited. Fab also harnessed a cross-side network effect, at least initially. Vendors who made their unique products available were attracted by the venture's growing base of design-obsessed customers, who in turn were drawn by the site's quirky offerings. However, Fab's commitment to curation naturally limited this enticement: Too broad an assortment would have weakened the site's appeal to its early fans. This cross-side network effect also dissipated as Fab acquired customers who weren't on a quest for one-of-a-kind items.

After its pivot away from flash sales, did Fab harness another cross-side network effect by offering a vastly expanded selection of merchandise? No. It's true that some consumers are attracted to retailers with a broad selection: That's the whole idea behind Amazon, whose tagline is "From A to Z," and Fab's rival Wayfair, whose tagline is "A Zillion Things Home." But a cross-side network effect requires an active decision by users on *both* sides to join the network. This happens with flash sales sites but not with broad-line retailers (who sell many categories of merchandise) like Amazon or Wayfair.

Typically, items sold by a flash sales site are available exclusively from that site, at least for a short period of time. So, vendors who made their wares available for Fab's flash sales had to make an active decision to join Fab's network instead of another flash sales site's—at least for a while. By contrast, a broad-line retailer offers thousands of products that can be purchased through many other retail outlets; these products are sourced from vendors who'll sell to pretty much anyone and everyone. These vendors don't make an active decision to affiliate with the broad-line retailer. They are not attracted by the size of the retailer's customer base—that is, by a cross-side network effect—but rather by the retailer's willingness to place an order and write them a check.

So, as Fab broadened its merchandise selection, it didn't need a big base of demand side users to lure the supply side. Rather, Fab simply needed to write checks and build inventory. But nose-to-nose with Amazon and Wayfair, this was a difficult game for Fab to win.

If entrepreneurs should aim for fast growth when their products have strong network effects, how do they determine how fast is fast enough, or too fast? Above, I proposed using a threshold LTV/CAC ratio to pace growth. This also works for businesses with network effects—with two twists. The first: The target LTV/CAC ratio for a startup with strong network effects should be 1.0—at least for the first few years, as it mobilizes its network. Yet, in the "Ready?" section above, I recommended an LTV/CAC ratio greater than 1.0, to ensure that a startup can cover its fixed costs and earn a profit. When strong network effects impel a startup to Get Big Fast, however, fixed costs and profits can wait for a while. Eventually, the LTV/CAC threshold should be boosted above 1.0, but only after the network has achieved critical mass.

The second twist recognizes that with network effects, customers beget customers. LTV calculations can take this into account by factoring in their product's projected viral coefficient ($"v"$)—that is, the number of additional new customers attracted by each new customer. Specifically, entrepreneurs should calculate LTV by multiplying the gross margin earned, over time, from a single customer by $1 + v$. If the discounted present value of the gross margin from a single customer is $100, and if each new customer attracts, on average, 0.5 additional new customers, then customer lifetime value (LTV) equals $100 x $(1 + v)$, that is, $100 x 1.5, or $150. So, if the target LTV/CAC ratio is 1.0, then this startup can afford to spend up to $150 per new customer on paid marketing. Contrast that to the maximum CAC for a software-as-a-service (SaaS) startup without network effects that happens also to earn $100 in gross margin from each customer. With a 3.0 target LTV/CAC ratio, as proposed in the "Ready?" section, that SaaS startup could spend only $33 to acquire each new customer. That's a huge difference in the maximum affordable CAC and shows how network effects can motivate aggressive marketing.

A caveat about this approach: In projecting a product's viral coefficient, an entrepreneur should assume that her startup has already put its network effects flywheel into motion. At the outset, when a product has very few users, its actual viral coefficient may be abysmally low. The fledgling startup must somehow seed its network—perhaps through paid marketing—with enough users to start attracting more users. Recall the performance of Triangulate's dating app, Wings: Sunil Nagaraj had projected a viral coefficient of 0.8, but his dating site lacked the marketing budget to get the flywheel turning, so Wings's actual viral coefficient was only a paltry 0.03.

Once a startup has successfully harnessed network effects, it should then switch from projected to actual viral coefficients to calculate LTV. But if an entrepreneur forgoes projections and uses actual figures at the outset, her venture may underinvest in growth and stall. One way to guard against overconfidence in making these viral coefficient projections is by basing them on historical figures for similar startups.

Switching Costs. As with strong network effects, when potential customers face high switching costs, entrepreneurs are motivated to race for growth. As discussed in previous chapters, customers incur these switching costs when they change from one otherwise similar supplier to another. These costs include expenditures of time or money, risks and inconveniences, and psychological discomfort. They fall into two broad categories:

• **Up-front Costs.** Finding and vetting a new supplier takes time, as does starting the new relationship. Terminating an existing account can be a nuisance, and configuring a new one—entering billing information, setting preferences, and so forth—can be tiresome. For example, to switch online stockbrokers, users must transfer funds and securities between accounts. Switching some products requires customers to invest in new equipment or software, and then either write off what's been replaced or, if possible, salvage some value by selling the unwanted items. A consumer who switches from Google Home to Amazon Echo, for example, must acquire new devices for every room where a smart speaker is used, since Home and Echo devices don't communicate with each other.

Often, when a business acquires a new information system, its engineers must integrate the new system with existing databases and software, such as linking a new payroll service to the company's bank account and its accounting ledger. Switching may also incur penalties for ending a contract early—as with mobile phone services—or may forfeit benefits earned over time. For this reason, some travelers accept a slew of inconveniences to rack up frequent flyer miles with a single airline. Finally, new products often require a learning period for consumers or training for employees before they can be used effectively.

• **Disruption Risks.** With mission-critical activities, switching suppliers may involve considerable risk. Recall how Baroo found it difficult to sign up customers who already had a trustworthy dog walker: These people weren't eager to give their apartment keys to a stranger. Likewise, businesses can encounter problems when they change suppliers or software systems. For example, replacing one "cloud" service with another exposes a company to the risk of serious disruption if files are lost or corrupted during the transfer.

Strong brand loyalty can also engender switching costs, in the form of psychological discomfort. If a hair coloring product works, why risk a change? And if a brand creates strong emotional associations ("I'm the kind of person who drives a Tesla"), switching brands may provoke a mini-identity crisis.

For Fab's customers, switching costs were low: They invested a little time entering shipping and billing information and learning how to navigate Fab's website, but that's about it. Among the start-ups profiled in earlier chapters, switching costs were also low for Triangulate's daters and Quincy Apparel's shoppers. By contrast, switching costs for Jibo's customers were quite high. Not only would they need to buy a new social robot, but they'd also have to reacquire and configure any third-party applications and would need to spend lots of time "socializing" their new companion.

So, why do high switching costs motivate startups to grow fast? To poach another company's customers, a startup must compensate those customers for the switching costs they will incur. This compensation can take the form of, say, a discount ("buy one, get one free") or a promotional incentive ("get a free iPhone if you sign up for a two-year plan"). Such subsidies raise customer acquisition costs (CAC). In theory, at least, an incumbent can raise the price it charges its customers—boosting the incumbent's profits and its LTV—right up to the point where the customers are indifferent between sticking with the incumbent's product or switching to a rival's subsidized alternative.

Given these dynamics, high switching costs can spur a race in which *first-time customers* are the prize. First-time customers are new to a product category and they don't yet have an affiliation with any provider. Consequently, compared to stealing a rival's customers, first-time buyers will be much cheaper to acquire. They won't incur any switching costs upon purchasing, so they don't require a subsidy. Lower CAC means that first-time customers are more profitable to serve, and they also broaden the startup's total addressable market. Specifically, with lower CAC, the startup can afford to acquire first-time buyers who have lower LTV, while still keeping their LTV/CAC ratio within an acceptable range.

That's the good news: High switching costs, like network effects, can confer powerful economic benefits. And, the best way to realize these benefits is to sign up first-time customers *before* your rival does. But there's some bad news, too. Many startups tend to enter rapidly growing new markets that feature lots of first-time buyers. Your rivals see the same opportunity, so they'll race to acquire first-time buyers before you do. Competition can get intense and rivals may bid up the cost of acquiring first-time buyers. Everyone can afford to bid aggressively, because once a first-time customer is on board—locked in by high switching costs—the winning bidder can charge them a hefty price.

For this reason, *first-mover advantages* can be especially strong in new markets where customers face high switching costs. The first mover in a new product category has a chance to acquire first-time buyers *before* any rivals enter the market. But this advantage disappears once the second entrant arrives; then, the race is on. Since Jibo was the pioneer in the social robotics category—a category with high switching costs—had Jibo survived, it would have enjoyed first-mover advantages, at least for a while.

Scale Economies. Scale economies reduce a startup's unit costs as its transaction volumes increase. Some startups benefit from scale economies to a much greater extent than others; in these businesses, entrepreneurs will feel impelled to grow fast. Potential scale economies will be large when a business has 1) high fixed overhead expenses in relation to its current sales volume, and 2) lots of "learning-by-doing" opportunities.

Unit costs decline when fixed overhead expenses are spread over more units. At low volumes, scale economies can reduce unit costs substantially. However, these reductions wane in importance as output expands. For example, with $30 million in annual fixed costs, a company's fixed cost per unit declines by $15 (from $30 to $15) as annual volume doubles from one million to two million units. By comparison, the same company's fixed cost per unit declines by only $1.50 (from $3 to $1.50) as its annual volume expands from ten million to twenty million units. If that startup's total addressable market is only big enough to support one company selling twenty million units, then the first competitor to reach that level may achieve an unassailable cost advantage over rivals. If, by contrast, the total market can accommodate many companies selling twenty million units, then a startup won't realize a cost advantage over rivals due to scale economies. But that startup had better keep pace with its rivals, or it will be forced to sell its wares at a loss due to excessively high unit costs.

A company can also reduce its unit costs by constantly refining its production approach, for example, by assigning certain activities to specialists or eliminating bottlenecks. Through a phenomenon known as the *learning curve,* companies with greater production volume (i.e., more "doing") are likely to identify more cost-reduction opportunities (through more "learning"). Learning-by-doing tends to be most productive with:

• **High Value-Added Production Processes.** A learning curve— measured as the percentage unit cost reduction realized with each doubling of cumulative production volume—is typically steepest when labor and machinery add significant value in the production process, as with aircraft assembly or semiconductor manufacturing. *Value-added* refers to the difference between a product's final cost and the cost of raw material inputs; this difference consists mostly of labor and equipment costs. Learning-by-doing—for example, finding a way to cut setup times for a new production run—often yields labor and equipment cost savings. By contrast, many raw materials—for example, aluminum or electricity—are sourced in commodity markets, where greater procurement volume does not deliver much unit cost savings.

• **Stable Technologies.** Learning-by-doing is most likely to confer a competitive advantage when production technologies are stable. If a smaller rival surprises the market with a radically new—and significantly more efficient—production process, that rival can leapfrog a larger incumbent, extinguishing the incumbent's hard-earned learning-based cost advantages.

• **Proprietary Learning.** If a company cannot keep its learning proprietary by enforcing patents, nondisclosure contracts, or strict secrecy procedures, it may forfeit its cost advantage as rivals copy its production process improvements.

Like most businesses, Fab benefited from some scale economies, but they weren't large enough to impel rapid growth. Early on, the venture kept its fixed costs low by relying on vendors to drop-ship items; in this way, Fab avoided the fixed expense of managing a warehouse. Likewise, value-added elements—labor and machinery for transforming raw materials into finished goods—represented a small percentage of Fab's total costs. With the exception of private label custom furniture that it manufactured in-house, Fab procured finished goods from vendors. Consequently, Fab did not enjoy big learning curve benefits.

(Fool's) Gold Rush?

Powerful network effects, high customer switching costs, and strong scale economies all impel startups to grow rapidly. Sometimes, however, startups aim to accelerate their growth even if they don't benefit from one or more of these attributes. This is okay, provided the startup is *Ready, Able,* and *Willing*—and competition in its market hasn't overheated to the point where it costs more to acquire customers than they are worth.

Fab competed in an overheated market, even though it didn't have the ability to leverage strong network effects, scale economies, or switching costs. Still, Goldberg pushed the accelerator to the floor. And he wasn't alone: His main online rivals—Wayfair and One Kings Lane—did the same. Wayfair, for example, spent $113 million on marketing in 2012 to generate $601 million in sales. Flash sales sites Gilt Groupe and Rue La La also invested aggressively to boost sales of home décor, and Amazon eventually turned its big guns on the market. Rivals cut their prices and stepped up their advertising, trying to outshout one another to capture buyers' attention. During 2012 and 2013, the category turned into a land grab. Why? Did *everyone* expect to strike gold?

There are at least three reasons why entrepreneurs might overinvest in growth. First, they simply may not understand that they are spending too much on customer acquisition. That's unlikely in the case of online home goods: It's uncommon—but not unheard of—to reach $100 million in sales and not have someone on staff who can scrutinize cohort performance and trends in CAC. Second, they may know that their marketing spending is excessive but, due to over-confidence and wishful thinking, they assume that better outcomes are just around the corner.

The third reason for overinvesting in growth is more sinister: the hope that a greater fool will pick up the tab. If an entrepreneur knows that her sector is locked into land grab logic, and, despite this, investors still overvalue her company, she may perceive an opportunity to exploit a speculative bubble. She can sell equity at high prices to naïve new investors who, notwithstanding the sector's mounting losses, are captivated by its explosive revenue growth. Existing investors in the company may encourage this, reasoning that if the company can be sold or go public before this game of musical chairs ends, they could see a huge payoff.

So, if you are an entrepreneur who's caught in a gold rush, but you fear that your startup is digging its own grave rather than a gold mine, what—if anything—can you do? Slow down. Really! And make sure you have some money in the bank. It could prove difficult to raise capital for a while, but reality should eventually catch up with rivals who are overinvesting in growth. At some point, they'll hit the skids, and investors will abandon them. If you have enough capital in reserve to weather the shakeout, your startup will survive.

Is de-escalation—that is, persuading rivals to slow down—an option? In a new market with many closely matched competitors—like online retailing of home goods—it may well be possible for an entrepreneur to convince rivals that de-escalation would be a win-win outcome. For example, an entrepreneur could slow her spending and then—through statements to the business press, industry analysts, suppliers, regulators, investors, and channel partners—explain the rationale for the slowdown and, in the process, aim to persuade rivals that they, too, are spending too much on growth. Of course, collusion on pricing is illegal, so we're not talking about promises and pacts made in smoke-filled rooms. Rather, the goal here is to lead by example and hope your competitors follow suit.

Scholars who study game theory have learned that mutually beneficial de-escalation is more likely to occur with:

1. *A small number of players.* With a bigger group, someone is more likely to break ranks, boosting spending to steal share as others ease off.

2. *Players who have a long history of interaction.* They have had more experience interpreting one another's signals and moves, and more opportunity to build trust.

3. *Players who expect to continue to interact.* They'll attach more weight to the reputational consequences of defections from implicit agreements to slow down.

4. *Shared beliefs about market opportunities.* The risk of racing too hard increases if competitors have different beliefs about the market's size and growth and about the relative strength of rivals.

5. *Moves that are transparent.* Transparency reduces the ability to "cheat" (e.g., through secret price cuts to key customers) after implicitly agreeing to de-escalate.

6. *Short lags between decisions and observable moves.* This reduces the risk that a firm will escalate, unaware that a rival has made a peaceful gesture.

The only criterion above that definitely doesn't hold for startups is #2: By their nature, new ventures won't have much history of interaction. The other criteria could apply, but there are two risks with signaling rivals to try to get them to spend more sensibly. First, rivals may perceive this as a desperate ploy by a weakened competitor unable to weather head-to-head competition, which may actually strengthen their resolve. Second, it's possible that investors will overreact to this distress call and drive down sector valuations.

. . .

To recap: Fab couldn't pass the RAWI test. The venture was *Able* to scale rapidly, in terms of having adequate human resources on hand and an ability to deploy its workforce effectively. But Fab wasn't *Able* to raise enough capital to fund its aggressive expansion plans. Goldberg was certainly *Willing* to see Fab grow, as were his investors. Fab was not *Impelled* to grow by strong network effects, switching costs, or scale economies. But this wasn't a knockout; it simply meant that expansion was an option, not an imperative.

The startup's fundamental shortcoming was that it just wasn't *Ready* to scale. Fab lost product-market fit as it expanded beyond its first "golden" cohorts to the mainstream market. Attempting to grow into that market resulted in a severe LTV/CAC squeeze—especially as rivals escalated their efforts to acquire customers. Fab's expansion into Europe delivered the coup de grâce.

In the next chapter, we'll meet a startup in the same sector as Fab that also failed the RAWI test, but in a different way. Like Fab, Dot & Bo's CEO and its board members were *Willing* to grow, and, like Fab, this online retailer of home goods was not *Impelled* to expand. Unlike Fab, however, Dot & Bo was *Ready* to scale—the startup sustained product-market fit as it grew—but the venture failed because it was not *Able* to access certain crucial resources.

CHAPTER 8

Help Wanted

Dot & Bo was founded by Anthony Soohoo, a serial entrepreneur who, in 2007, sold a celebrity news website to CBS Interactive, the broadcast giant's digital content network, where he became a senior executive. After a few years there, he saw an opportunity to adapt TV storytelling techniques to drive e-commerce sales in lifestyle categories such as food, travel, and home décor. When CBS wouldn't fund the concept internally, he left to build the business himself. In 2011, Soohoo became an entrepreneur-in-residence at the venture capital firm Trinity Ventures, where he began to explore the opportunity he'd identified.

Before he'd even identified which lifestyle segment to pursue, Soohoo raised $4.5 million at a $9 million pre-money valuation in a Series A round led by Trinity. After six months, he settled on home furnishings: a huge market that was not well served by brick-and-mortar incumbents, which often disappointed consumers with a limited selection of products; pushy, poorly trained salespeople; and lengthy delivery times. Two months later, in February 2013, Soohoo and a small team launched Dot & Bo.

Dot & Bo's key point of differentiation lay in its carefully curated collections of décor and furniture. Individual pieces were presented as components of a cohesive room design. Each collection was conceived as an episode of an imaginary television show (e.g.,

"Einstein's Office," "Modern Outlaw"), with the products as "characters." Soohoo explained, "Typically, when people try to sell a chair, they focus 99 percent of their effort on the chair's attributes. Our idea was, let's focus 50 percent on the chair, and 50 percent on everything else in the room. We would pull everything together and sell the overall concept—the same way a great interior designer might." The company's products were affordable: priced at just a 10 percent premium over IKEA's, with better quality and designs.

This approach resonated with shoppers who wanted design inspiration and guidance. Monthly sales grew rapidly, from $10,000 in February 2013 to $750,000 in December 2013. Dot & Bo's promotional emails—a key marketing channel—were opened at 2x to 3x the industry average. Trinity partner and board member Gus Tai said, "It was one of the strongest launches of an online retailer I'd ever seen."

To fund further growth, Soohoo decided to raise a Series B round. He received two term sheets within two weeks—along with an unsolicited offer from a large brick-and-mortar retailer to buy Dot & Bo for $40 million. Seeing even greater upside, Dot & Bo's board pressed Soohoo to decline the acquisition offer—which he did, closing a $15 million Series B round in March 2014 at a pre-money valuation of $50 million.

Over the course of 2014, it was clear that Dot & Bo was managing to sustain product-market fit as it rapidly expanded its customer base. Repeat purchase rates remained strong, as did word-of-mouth referrals. The lifetime value (LTV) of customers acquired that year was projected to be about $200, and each customer cost, on average, $40 to acquire—a far better LTV/CAC ratio than Dot & Bo's leading rivals in online home furnishings. In some cases, Soohoo remarked, "They might spend $400 to acquire a customer who made only one $50 purchase." Revenue for 2014 was $15 million, an almost sevenfold increase over 2013. While revenue growth was strong and each month's customer cohort met performance targets, rapid growth came at a price: Dot & Bo spent 42 percent of revenue on marketing, and with a gross margin of only 25 percent due to operating problems (described below), the startup had an $8 million operating loss in 2014.

Exploding growth was straining Dot & Bo's supply chain. The startup sourced product in a variety of ways. Some suppliers shipped in volume to Dot & Bo's warehouse in advance of Dot & Bo receiving orders; others sent a series of smaller shipments to the warehouse after successive batches of orders were placed; still others drop-shipped individual items directly to Dot & Bo's customers. This complexity resulted in highly variable and often unreliable delivery times, which in turn led to an alarming gap between Dot & Bo's *post-purchase* Net Promoter Score ("On a scale of 0–10, how likely would you be to recommend Dot & Bo to a friend?") of 41 and its *post-delivery* NPS of –17. Furthermore, the startup's surging growth took suppliers by surprise, leading to inventory shortages that forced Dot & Bo to cancel many orders. Dot & Bo's investors were unperturbed, reasoning that "too much demand is a good thing." It wasn't.

In 2013, Dot & Bo had relied on young, energetic employees to manage its warehouse and shipping. Despite their lack of prior experience with these functions, these employees got the job done—at least initially. As the problems compounded, however, Soohoo realized that he needed a seasoned manager to lead operations. He hired a VP-Operations who had been a general manager of divisions within two large tech companies and had also been a CEO of two startups. However, in none of these roles had he been responsible for e-commerce operations akin to Dot & Bo's.

One of the new VP's first tasks was to select an enterprise resource planning (ERP) system to manage procurement, inventory, orders, and other operational matters. But the team's collective lack of industry experience led to a poor choice. The system they purchased couldn't handle the complex mix of sourcing methods that Dot & Bo employed. As a result, the team couldn't accurately track products' inventory status, which meant that Dot & Bo's website often listed in-stock items as out of stock and vice versa. Potential sales were lost, and many orders were delayed for months, resulting in a flurry of customer service queries. The company was unable to hire and train customer service reps fast enough, so email response times could stretch to as long as eleven days. Rushed shipping to expedite delayed orders cut into Dot & Bo's gross margin.

Soohoo recalled that, due to the faulty ERP system, "We could not answer simple customer questions like, 'Where's my stuff?' We could not accurately calculate shipping costs. The system didn't enable demand forecasting, communication with vendors, or tracking customer feedback to identify problems." He added, "Once you implement an ERP system, it's very difficult to replace—especially if your IT team is small and overburdened, like ours was."

In the second half of 2014, Soohoo focused his team on getting control over the company's logistics and operations. They reduced marketing spending to slow growth in demand—which proved challenging, given the social media buzz that Dot & Bo had generated. At the same time, Soohoo recruited a new VP-Operations with deep logistics experience, most notably at Netflix. Among other initiatives, the new VP renegotiated Dot & Bo's freight contracts, more tightly managed vendor accountability for delivery commitments, and formulated plans for switching to a new ERP system. By the end of 2014, only 15 percent of orders were delayed, down from 40 percent in the spring. Also, the gap between post-purchase and post-delivery NPS closed, with those scores improving markedly to 54 and 55, respectively.

In May 2015, with operations on track and revenue for the year projected to reach $40 million, up from $15 million in 2014, Soohoo set out to raise Series C—hoping to raise $30 million at a $200 million pre-money valuation. In the prior year, however, potential investors had grown leery of e-commerce companies, having seen consumer Internet stock prices decline by an average of 40 percent with Zulily, a flash sales site for moms, leading the pack; its share price plummeted from $70 in February 2014 to just $11 in May 2015.

After four months of futile fundraising, Dot & Bo's board decided to try to sell the company instead. They received a few bids, including one from a major U.S. online retailer who offered $50 million. However, as negotiations dragged on, Dot & Bo's capital reserves were rapidly shrinking. To stem the cash drain, Soohoo reduced head count to seventy-one in late 2015, down from a June peak of ninety-one.

By the spring of 2016, Dot & Bo had yet to finalize a merger. Meanwhile, the news broke that One Kings Lane, an online furnishings rival that had raised $225 million in venture capital, had sold to Bed Bath & Beyond for less than $30 million. According to Soohoo, "That announcement completely froze the market for e-commerce companies." All acquisition offers for Dot & Bo were withdrawn. In September 2016, Dot & Bo's bank called its loan, and the startup's only recourse was to shut down. Proceeds from liquidating inventory were used to repay the loan and to give two weeks of severance to employees, and the company's remaining assets were sold off to Alibaba for less than $1 million.

Financing Risk

In the previous chapter, I introduced the RAWI test for determining whether a startup is *Ready, Able, Willing,* and *Impelled* to grow rapidly. The test's *"Able?"* portion asks if a startup can attract the resources required to scale and can manage those resources effectively. Dot & Bo stumbled on this portion of the RAWI test and fell victim to a failure pattern I call "Help Wanted." Unlike ventures that are caught in a Speed Trap, with the Help Wanted pattern, a startup sustains product-market fit as it grows but cannot mobilize the resources needed to continue expanding. Specifically, Dot & Bo was hampered by its failure to recruit the right senior specialists and couldn't raise capital due to a sector-wide shutdown of new investment in e-commerce startups. Consequently, Dot & Bo failed, due to both *mistakes* (with hiring) and *misfortunes* (with capital market conditions).

Every scaling startup is exposed to some degree to financing risk: the possibility that capital market conditions will impede an otherwise healthy venture's ability to raise needed funds. Sometimes, as with Dot & Bo, the inability to obtain capital is the result of investors suddenly shunning the company's entire sector. When a sector falls out of favor, the decline in investor interest can be severe and can last for years, so a rapidly scaling startup that needs more capital just as a downturn commences may not be able to survive until investor sentiment rebounds. As Trinity Ventures partner and Dot & Bo board member Gus Tai recalled, "In 2015, it became impossible to raise outside capital for an e-commerce startup. Most categories are periodically exposed to funding risk, and e-commerce was no exception. But I was caught off guard by the collapse in investor sentiment."

Reflecting on Dot & Bo's failure, Soohoo said, "Had investor interest in our sector stayed strong, I think we could have been sold for $300 million to a major retailer eager to get into the digital home space. Or, we could have steered the company to profitability. If we'd built out the team more, maybe we could have gone public." Trinity's Tai agreed, "To succeed in e-commerce, you have to execute really well. Dot & Bo did that on the demand side. I believe we could have solved our problems on the supply side, too, with more time and more cash."

Venture capital is prone to boom-bust cycles. Notable examples include personal computer hardware and software in the early 1980s; biotechnology in the early 1990s; clean tech in the late 2000s; and—the mother of all bubbles—Internet companies in the late 1990s. In each instance, VCs poured huge amounts of capital into scores of ventures in some hot new sector. Then, the flow of capital suddenly stopped, and startups, starved for capital, struggled to survive.

Boom-bust investment cycles do not always impact entire industry sectors. Sometimes they are limited to certain segments, like meal delivery services, virtual reality, pet care, bitcoin/blockchain, direct-to-consumer brands, robo-investing, autonomous vehicles, and so forth.

Investment bubbles typically start when entrepreneurs and investors recognize a big, new opportunity, often triggered by technology breakthroughs, like machine learning, gene editing, or voice recognition software (e.g., Jibo). Or, entrepreneurs might see many different ways to leverage novel business models, as with flash sales (e.g., Fab), "gig economy" labor (e.g., Baroo), or "direct-to-consumer" retailing (e.g., Quincy). Or, the rapid proliferation of a new distribution channel—say, mobile phones or Facebook's application platform (e.g., Triangulate)—might spawn opportunity. Early movers gain momentum and attract clones. VCs who missed the first wave of opportunity paddle hard to catch the next one. As "irrational exuberance" grips entrepreneurs and investors alike, they can overshoot the mark, collectively bringing too many new ventures to market. Industry segments then get crowded and startups must spend heavily to gain advantage. A shakeout ensues. No one is surprised when thinly conceived and poorly capitalized players fall by the wayside, but when category leaders succumb, alarms go off and investors pull back en masse. The bubble bursts. That's what happened to Dot & Bo—the startup got caught in a funding dry spell after the struggles of its larger rivals, Fab.com and One Kings Lane, became evident.

What types of startups are most vulnerable to financing risk? Early-stage ventures are by no means immune, but they have an advantage: They need far less fresh capital to survive. With a bridge loan of, say, $750,000, a team of six can soldier on for two more years. Existing investors might be able and willing to extend such a loan.

By contrast, even after they trim their sails, late-stage ventures usually require far more capital. While existing investors might have $10 million on hand to fund a bridge loan, given the magnitude of this investment, they will nevertheless pause and ask whether they might be "throwing good money after bad." And, as Soohoo learned, if existing investors are wary, it's harder to attract new ones. The fundraising dance drags on, and meanwhile, the venture is burning through rapidly diminishing capital reserves. For startups that are growing at an unsustainable pace and headed for a Speed Trap, financing risk represents a big driving hazard. They have to hit the brakes fast enough to avoid a head-on collision with insolvency.

Ben Parsa, Dot & Bo's head of merchandising, concluded that the startup exposed itself to financing risk by emulating the Get Big Fast strategy implemented by Zulily, another e-commerce company in Trinity Ventures' portfolio:

> Trinity earned a huge return when Zulily went public. Zulily had built a strong e-commerce brand really fast. There are a lot of incumbents out there who'll buy a startup because they can't build an online brand themselves. We were following that playbook from the start. To make Dot & Bo a good acquisition target, we needed meaningful scale. We didn't need to be profitable; we just needed enough capital to fuel growth. . . . At the outset, money seemed to be available and Anthony was great at fundraising. So, we built a monster growth engine. Our content and curation strategy really worked. There was lots of pent-up demand that our online rivals weren't satisfying. We built a freight train and got it rolling at high speed. When capital markets shut down, it was hard to put on the brakes to get to cash flow breakeven.

What can an entrepreneur do to avoid financing risk—or at least mitigate its impact?

First, he can be on the alert for boom-bust dynamics. Not that an entrepreneur should necessarily avoid a booming sector altogether or abandon his plans just because his startup will be a late mover in such a sector. After all, Google was a late mover in search, as was Dropbox in file management software. But Google and Dropbox each had a superior product that could capture share from incumbents. So, at the outset, an entrepreneur should ask: What will my venture's competitive edge be when it faces well-entrenched rivals? And, will my early investors be able and willing to provide bridge funding if capital markets dry up?

Entrepreneurs leading later-stage startups can take some precautions if they have a premonition that financing risk might be on the horizon. First, they can try to **raise more capital than financial projections show they will need** to reach their next major milestones. A cushion of extra cash can tip the balance from failure to survival. Amazon, for example, raised $2 billion of debt soon after it completed its IPO—enough to fund its considerable losses for the next few years, when capital markets were frozen after the dot-com bubble burst. By contrast, eToys—previously seen as a peer of Amazon—completed its IPO just before dot-com valuations crashed. eToys was unable to raise more capital and went bankrupt.

Deciding whether to raise a cash cushion can be tricky because it forces an entrepreneur to choose between fear and greed. Fear of a funding shortfall argues for raising more capital, but doing so means greater dilution of the entrepreneur's personal equity stake. If the money won't be needed soon, why not wait until it is required, say, eighteen months from now? If the startup stays on track, by then it will have met key milestones and—assuming capital markets are still open for business—will be able to raise a new round at a higher share price, resulting in less dilution for management and past investors.

However, even if the entrepreneur wants to raise more money than needed, potential investors may not be so ready to agree. They, too, will be torn between fear and greed. The greed: If the company stays on the rails, $40 million invested all at once in a big Series B round will yield a bigger equity stake for the VC firm than $15 million invested in Series B now, and then later, another $25 million invested in Series C at a higher share price. The fear: If the startup goes off the rails after the VC firm has invested the entire $40 million all at once, then the VC firm could lose much more than if it had invested just $15 million.

As a second precaution against financing risk, entrepreneurs can try to **raise capital from VCs who are more likely to be able and willing to provide bridge financing,** should a lifeline be needed. Assuming they earn healthy returns, VCs raise a new fund every three years or so, as they draw down the capital in their current fund. VCs do not normally make follow-on investments in a startup from different funds. So, if a VC has exhausted the capital balance of the fund from which it originally invested in a startup, then that startup should not expect the VC to invest more. The VC might have raised a new fund in the meantime, but investing in the startup from the new fund could pose conflicts of interest from the perspective of limited partners in the new and old funds.

To see why, assume that a VC would like to make a follow-on investment in a startup from Fund IV, having previously invested in the same startup from Fund III. Setting an unreasonably high valuation for the startup in the new funding round would result in excessive dilution for Fund IV's LPs—to the benefit of the Fund III's LPs. To avoid such conflicts, VCs earmark a percentage of each fund for first-time investments in startups that are new to their portfolio, and then reserve the balance for follow-on investments in those startups. But this is an imprecise science; sometimes the VC invests faster than expected and a fund runs out of capital. Accordingly, entrepreneurs should check on the balance in a potential investor's current fund before signing a term sheet.

In the same vein, a VC firm with mediocre returns to date on its current fund may be skittish about doubling down on a portfolio company that could go south, since the VC firm needs to improve returns to gain limited partners' support for a new fund.

As a third precaution against financing risk, entrepreneurs can try to **preserve flexibility to cut costs** should the need arise, despite the trade-offs that might be involved. For example, a startup could forgo the savings available with a long-term real estate lease and pay higher rent to preserve the option to terminate a short-term lease.

Missing Managers

Beyond financing risk, other resource shortages can have a big impact on the odds of a scaling startup's survival. Specifically, *missing managers*—the absence of competent senior specialists in key functions—can hurt a scaling startup's operating performance, causing the venture to burn through capital at a faster-than-expected rate.

Dot & Bo struggled with hiring its first senior specialists. When the startup needed an operations leader, Soohoo recruited a senior generalist instead of a specialist, with poor results. Soohoo's intent had been to groom this individual for a chief operating officer role; he reckoned, reasonably, that a COO would require generalist skills. But unfortunately, this meant he lacked the experience needed to deal with the serious problems at hand. The VP's successor, who did have relevant functional experience, managed to stabilize Dot & Bo's operations. Nevertheless, Soohoo was not happy with the second VP's performance and eventually replaced him, too. Soohoo explained, "He was a big company guy who fixed what you told him to fix. The relevant metrics—say, average fulfillment cost—would improve, but not necessarily in ways that were healthy for the business overall. He didn't think like an owner." Dot & Bo co-founder and head of merchandising Ben Parsa agreed, adding, "Like a lot of big company managers, he was a master at obfuscation; he could massage numbers to make things look like they were working."

Echoing these points, venture capitalist Ben Horowitz warns that a management style honed in big organizations may be perceived as "too political" by a startup's leaders. Horowitz also notes that many corporate executives will have difficulty adjusting to the fact that in a startup, it falls on them to initiate action or nothing will happen, whereas big company managers are deluged with inbound requests for input and decisions.

If the Dot & Bo management team had found the right VP-Operations earlier, they might have conserved enough cash to survive the deep freeze in e-commerce investing. Soohoo made another specialist hiring mistake when he brought onboard a senior marketing professional to replace a young generalist who'd been leading Dot & Bo's marketing efforts up to that point. The generalist had been doing a good job but lacked prior experience managing a team. Soohoo commented, "I thought the outsider could teach us something. But he was a disaster and lasted only four months. He was too methodical, which slowed down our learning and growth. We put the young generalist back in charge, and he got things on track again. The lesson for me: Think twice about bringing in outsiders when insiders are figuring it out."

So, Dot & Bo hired a specialist leader too soon in one function and too late in another, underscoring the challenges that a scaling startup faces in hiring its senior specialists. In part, the reason is that a founder who has previously worked in one function—say, engineering—will typically be ill-equipped to recruit specialists into other functions. The founder simply won't understand key factors for success in the role. What skills are needed? How important is technical knowledge, compared to strong problem-solving abilities? And, in the absence of data for rigorous analysis—a common problem for early-stage startups—when is following prior experience a reliable guide to action?

Rand Fishkin, founder and former CEO of the search engine optimization software provider Moz, offered insight on the challenge of recruiting specialists when he noted that the reason Moz had "struggled, since its inception, to create high-quality software" was due to his own lack of advanced technical skills, which made it difficult to attract outstanding engineers. Fishkin added that "without deep knowledge of a function you are less likely to have connections, so you are less likely to identify great hires in that field."

So, how to proceed? Sometimes, as with Dot & Bo's marketing function, the right approach is to stick with generalists who can "figure it out" and grow into the role. But when a specialist is indeed required, a founder has three options.

A low-risk approach is to leverage referrals or headhunters to **bring a junior specialist on board.** This approach has advantages: The new employee can do necessary frontline work; his pay won't be high, so a hiring mistake won't be expensive; and the startup's leadership team will gain some recruiting experience. The downside risk: Once a junior specialist is hired, no one will have the expertise needed to effectively manage him, so he may drift off course.

Alternatively, the founder can, at the outset, **hire a senior special-**

ist to build out the function, relying on this individual to hire frontline employees and put in place key systems and processes. Founders may balk at a well-qualified candidate's compensation demands. Soohoo, for example, passed on an opportunity to hire a COO who had experience with furniture shipping logistics because his salary would be twice the budget for the role. Even assuming the founder can identify and afford senior specialists, there are risks with hiring them. If the candidate has only worked in big companies, cultural fit may be a problem, as the new hire may struggle to adapt to a startup's rhythms. Also, the senior specialist may prove to be too attached to solutions that worked for prior employers but might not be suited for the startup.

A final solution splits the difference between the first two options: A startup can **hire a scrappy, hungry, mid-level specialist** who is able and willing to do frontline work but who aspires to rise rapidly into management ranks.

The CEO of a scaling startup should seek lots of guidance when making these crucial hiring decisions. Board members should source candidates and also interview them. VCs have helped many other portfolio companies fill their executive ranks, so they may have valuable insights about requirements for a position—especially when a CEO lacks experience with the function.

A top-notch head of human resources can also have an enormous impact on the quality of executive recruiting efforts. As a startup scales, priorities for the human resources function change, and it's important to have an HR head who can manage these transitions. A good model for how HR can evolve comes from Kristi Riordan, chief operating officer of Flatiron School, a fast-growing coding bootcamp. In the first phase, their top priority was recruiting. "Startups can get by for a long time by relying on employee referrals," Riordan says, "but eventually it makes sense to bring a full-time recruiter onboard. This can be a difficult hire, because the market is full of recruiters who have a transactional orientation. You need someone who embraces your mission and culture and will reflect your values when attracting talent."

In the second phase, Flatiron's top priority was people operations, or "creating processes for onboarding and offboarding employees, developing benefit programs and cascading goal setting through the organization."

Flatiron's third phase focused on talent development: training and career progression opportunities for middle managers. At this phase in scaling startups, the head of HR also plays a crucial role in 1) organizational design, which includes reconfiguring reporting relationships as new positions are created; 2) advising the CEO on how to preserve and strengthen the company's culture; and 3) counseling the CEO and other senior executives, to help them augment their skills and adapt their management style to meet new challenges. A head of HR who is adept at these tasks will have valuable insights about how to hire missing managers.

Missing Systems

In an early-stage startup, its small team can share information via hallway conversations and make key strategic decisions over a pizza. As head count grows, however, relying only on ad hoc exchanges is not adequate; every function will require new systems and processes to facilitate information sharing and decision-making. For example, Sales will need processes for prioritizing leads, monitoring account profitability, compensating reps, etc. Product and Engineering will need processes for tracking teams' productivity, a road map that prioritizes new features, and so forth.

The effectiveness of certain systems may have a big impact on a scaling startup's performance. At Dot & Bo, for example, a faulty ERP system made it difficult to track inventory and order status, leading to lost sales and poor customer service. By contrast, Dot & Bo's managers had a good handle on the profitability of different marketing channels—a crucial capability for a company spending over 40 percent of revenue on customer acquisition.

In contrast to early-stage startups, where decisions are often made through informal processes, in a scaling startup, decisions may require a formal review followed by approval from a senior executive. For recurring key decisions, senior managers should clarify who has the right to propose an initiative, who should provide input, and who makes the decision. Formalizing decision-making processes can feel bureaucratic, particularly to early employees who are accustomed to more autonomy and transparency. But without the clarity that comes from formalizing processes, decision-making can grind to a halt, accountability for results can blur, and strategy can drift. The challenge is finding the right balance between bureaucracy and chaos.

Due to the investment required and entrepreneurs' dislike of bureaucracy, few scaling startups adopt management systems ahead of their needs. They're more likely to add systems in reaction to the errors, confusion, inconsistencies, and excessive workloads that can result from a lack of automated and standardized processes. Some startups do invest early and heavily in management systems, especially when their top managers have experience using systems in big companies or, in the case of serial entrepreneurs, in past startups. However, it can be a mistake to invest too far in advance or to simply clone big company systems without careful analysis of whether they meet a scaling startup's unique needs. Those needs evolve rapidly, and building systems too early runs the risk of omitting important features and wasting effort on features that turn out to be unnecessary.

The good news is that the solution to the missing-systems problem is simply to solve the missing-manager problem: Bring on board senior specialists who have experience with scaling startups that faced challenges similar to those now at hand—and who can make smart choices about when and how to add management systems. Passing the "Able?" portion of the RAWI test hinges on having the right kind of specialist leaders at the helm.

CHAPTER 9

Moonshots and Miracles

We wanted flying cars, instead we got 140 characters.
—Peter Thiel, entrepreneur and investor

We might not have flying cars, but Shai Agassi dreamt of a world where the roads were filled with electric ones. He founded the startup Better Place in 2007—before Tesla or Nissan had launched any all-electric models—with a bold vision: He would create a massive network of charging stations for electric vehicles. Agassi and his father, both graduates of Technion, Israel's elite Institute of Technology, had previously co-founded a venture that they sold for $400 million to SAP, Germany's enterprise software giant. Agassi joined SAP's executive board, became president of its Product & Technology Group, and was a candidate to eventually succeed the CEO. In 2005, he attended the Forum of Young Global Leaders in Davos, where he had an epiphany: To reduce the geopolitical instability and environmental damage caused by our dependence on oil, every gasoline-powered automobile, worldwide, would have to be replaced with an electric car running on power from renewable sources.

The following year, at a Brookings Institution conference, Agassi shared his idea with former Israeli prime minister Shimon Peres. Impressed by Agassi's ambition, Peres offered to help by connecting Agassi with the relevant government and business leaders—but only if he'd step away from his role at SAP. "This is a better job," he told Agassi, "because you can save the world."

In March 2007, Agassi resigned from SAP. With help from Peres, he persuaded Israel's government to levy a tax of only 8 percent on electric cars: a key concession, since Israel's import tax on gasoline-powered automobiles was then 78 percent. Early meetings with auto manufacturers yielded another prize: Carlos Ghosn, CEO of Renault-Nissan, agreed to build an electric car compatible with battery swapping stations (described below) that were a key element of Better Place's charging network—in exchange for the startup's commitment to buy one hundred thousand vehicles. The car would be a modified version of the gasoline-powered Renault Fluence, an affordable midsize family sedan.

Next, Agassi turned to fundraising. In June 2007, Idan Ofer, the billionaire CEO of Israel's largest oil company, led a $110 million Series A round—at the time, one of the largest Series A financings in venture capital history. Morgan Stanley, VantagePoint Capital (a Silicon Valley VC firm), and some prominent angels joined the round, which later grew by $50 million thanks to investments from a Danish energy company and an Australian VC firm.

His funding secured, Agassi got to work recruiting a team. Siblings and former SAP colleagues would play key roles. His brother became head of global infrastructure, and his sister was head of marketing in Israel. SAP alumni were appointed as the head of global operations, the head of auto alliances, and CFO. For the key role of CEO of Israeli operations, Agassi hired a former major general of the Israeli Defense Forces. At the outset, no one on the senior team had prior experience with physical products like charging stations or with the automotive industry.

Agassi selected his native Israel as Better Place's launch market. Israel's compact footprint—and the fact that few Israelis travel to the hostile neighbors beyond its borders—made it well suited for deploying a charging network for electric cars, which at the time were expected to have a range of about one hundred miles before their batteries needed to be recharged. Denmark, another small country with many citizens committed to a "green" lifestyle, would be Better Place's second market.

In 2008, Agassi's team concluded that for the venture to achieve scale, they would have to deploy a minimum of two charge spots for every vehicle that Better Place served. These would be located in parking lots, on street curbs, and in customers' garages; they would be able to recharge a fully depleted battery in four to six hours. The charge spots were projected to cost $200 to $300 apiece, including installation. The team was evaluating scenarios in which Better Place eventually served 10 percent of the two million cars in Israel. This would require deployment of four hundred thousand charge spots at a cost of over $80 million.

For trips longer than 100 miles—Israel spanned about 260 miles, north to south—Better Place would need to deploy battery exchange stations, where robots would swap a depleted battery for a fully re-charged one in about five minutes, or roughly the time it took to refuel a gasoline-powered car. In 2008, the team concluded that at scale, one exchange station would be required for every two thou-sand Better Place vehicles. The stations were projected to cost $300,000 to $500,000 apiece, so if Better Place captured 10 percent of the Israeli market, it would need to deploy one hundred stations at a cost of over $30 million.

Israel offered another advantage as a launch market: 70 percent of family sedans in Israel were actually corporate fleet cars, provided to employees as perks. Persuading fleet operators to push Better Place's vehicles, Agassi and his team reasoned, could speed adop-tion. He and his team eventually convinced four hundred Israeli cor-porations to sign letters of intent—not legally binding—to convert their fleets to Better Place vehicles once its charging network became available.

In 2008, the data on consumer demand for all-electric cars were pretty slim: The only such vehicle on the market was Tesla's two-seat Roadster, which had just launched and cost a whopping $110,000. So, Better Place commissioned market research, the re-sults of which indicated that 20 percent of Israeli households would consider acquiring a Better Place electric car and would be willing to pay 10 percent more than for a comparable gasoline-powered car.

But the survey also indicated that respondents wanted more options than a single midsize Renault sedan, and they preferred to pay for it through monthly subscription fees rather than an all-out, up-front purchase.

Although Agassi had promised that his electric cars would be significantly less expensive to own and operate than gasoline-powered vehicles, as it became clear that both the vehicle and the charging network infrastructure would cost substantially more than originally projected, Better Place managers decided to charge Israeli consumers $35,000 for the Fluence—a price comparable to that of its gasoline-powered counterpart. This price did not include a battery; instead, drivers would lease their batteries from Better Place through an annual subscription plan, which would also include access to Better Place's charging network and the cost of the electricity needed to charge the batteries. Subscription fees varied by mileage: A twelve-thousand-mile annual plan cost $3,600. By comparison, an Israeli consumer would spend $3,000 on gas (based on the prices at the time) to drive twelve thousand miles in a gasoline-powered car that got thirty miles per gallon. So much for an electric car being cheaper to operate!

Better Place would pay Renault-Nissan $31,000 (including the 8 percent import tax and value added tax of 16 percent) for a Fluence that did not include a battery. The battery would initially cost $15,000—significantly more than the $8,000 to $11,000 the team had estimated in 2008. In addition to vehicle and battery costs, Better Place had originally projected expenses of about $1,000 per car per year to provide network access; this included electricity, maintenance, and an allocation for the depreciation of charging spots and exchange stations (based on 2008 estimates for deployment cost). With this business model, Better Place Israel could expect to recover the cost of the vehicle and battery after four years and earn modest profits after that. Profitability might improve over time if battery costs declined or if Better Place could negotiate lower vehicle costs—perhaps by striking deals with other automakers.

Before launching in Israel, the team expanded rapidly and spread across the world. Better Place's corporate headquarters was located in Palo Alto; the startup also had offices in Israel, Denmark, France, Spain, Austria, and Australia. Plans for either pilot projects or full network deployment had been announced with partners in Australia, Hawaii, Ontario, California, the Netherlands, China, and Japan. In parallel, Better Place managers began working with a range of vendors to develop various system components. Charge spots were custom designed to be sturdy and to be able to track subscriber usage via wireless modems. Creating the vehicle's software—dubbed OSCAR (Operating System for the CAR)—was particularly challenging. Among other functions, OSCAR had to monitor power use and battery health, alert drivers and guide them to the nearest charging station when recharging was required, manage the rate of recharging to minimize battery damage, and—to avoid electric grid blackouts—selectively and temporarily restrict nighttime recharging on some vehicles if Better Place customers were collectively drawing too much power.

According to tech journalist Brian Blum, whose book *Totaled* (a key source for this chapter) recounts the story of Better Place, the company spent a total of $60 million on OSCAR. Building customer relationship management (CRM) software for tracking usage and managing billing was likewise complex and expensive, given that the CRM software was, like other system components, designed to handle millions of customers. As Better Place's cash burn rate climbed, it was clear that the startup would require more capital. Agassi handily raised a $350 million Series B round in January 2010 at a $1.1 billion valuation.

Despite great uncertainty about demand and costs, Agassi was successful with this fundraising round in large part due to his charisma and ability to spin an inspiring, spellbinding vision of a better tomorrow. It didn't hurt that he'd become something of a business celebrity; in 2009 Agassi was named one of *Time* magazine's "100 Most Influential People," and his TED Talk, in which he asserted that the transition to electric cars was "the moral equivalent of abolishing slavery," garnered 1.3 million views.

As Joe Paluska, who served as Better Place's head of communications and policy, remarked of the founder, "The confidence he has in what he's telling you is incredible." Nimish Mehta, a senior executive at SAP, commented, "I've never seen someone as skilled as Shai at selling abstract concepts," and *New York Times* tech columnist Clive Thompson described Agassi as having "the born salesman's ability to read people and connect with them." But Thompson sensed a dark side, too, adding, "He also has the obdurate quality I've seen in so many people who are drawn to computer programming and logical thinking. Once Agassi has convinced himself of the optimal solution to a problem, he develops a nearly pathological monomania about it."

The team planned to sign up other automakers besides Renault-Nissan as partners. Each would have to design a vehicle with a swappable battery compatible with Better Place's exchange stations. But while many automakers considered Agassi's proposal, none signed up; even worse, he managed to alienate a few. For example, in a 2008 meeting, General Motors executives suggested contracting with Better Place to build charging stations for the Chevy Volt, their planned plug-in hybrid. Agassi dismissed the vehicle: "It has a tailpipe; it's a stupid car. We don't do things halfway. We don't work with tailpipe cars, period." Agassi later confidently asserted to a colleague, "The next meeting we have, it'll be at our headquarters and we'll have a bigger market cap than they do."

Meanwhile, Better Place's relationship with Renault-Nissan soured when their champion at the company departed and was replaced by a Better Place skeptic. The new manager of Renault-Nissan's electric car operations believed that fast charging technology, which could fill a depleted battery to 80 percent of capacity in about thirty to forty minutes, was a superior solution for "range anxiety"—consumers' fear that they might deplete their vehicle's battery before they could reach a recharging station—because the cost to deploy a network of fast charging spots would be a small fraction of Better Place's investment in battery exchange stations. The new manager—who never met with Agassi—also was a strong proponent of the

Nissan Leaf, an all-electric compact car that lacked a swappable battery. The Leaf was launched in late 2010 at a price of $33,000 before tax incentives.

Aiming to avoid a loss on the Fluence, Renault managers battled with their Better Place counterparts over design choices. According to Blum, one involved whether to include "smart screws" in the car that would, on command, release the battery at an exchange station and drop it onto a retractable metal plate. But Renault preferred an alternative that was less expensive, from their perspective: having the station's robot arm remove regular screws. Better Place conceded, even though the design change added to its cost of exchange station hardware and would make the stations incompatible with other electric cars that did not have swappable batteries with an identical configuration of screws.

As the venture geared up to start selling cars in Israel, it became clear that key network components would cost much more than originally projected. Charge spots would ultimately cost about $2,500 apiece, roughly *ten times* more than the 2008 projection of $200 to $300. However, $2,500 apiece was actually in line with current industry practice: In 2011, General Electric started selling a home charge spot for $1,000, with parts and labor for a typical installation adding another $1,000 or so to the consumer's bill. At $2,500 apiece, the total cost of deploying four hundred thousand charge spots in Israel would have been $1 billion, as opposed to the 2008 projection of $80 million.

Similarly, the twenty-one exchange stations that Better Place eventually installed in Israel cost more than $2 million apiece, rather than the projected $300,000 to $500,000. A consultant hired early in the development process had actually estimated that due to construction complexities, exchange stations would cost even more—as much as $3 million apiece. However, Better Place managers had rejected his estimate, arguing that their $500,000 projection was supported by data from European engineering giants Siemens and ABB.

With equipment costs this high, Better Place could not possibly earn a profit in Israel over the near term. Achieving scale economies in the future—*if* they could boost sales in Israel, Denmark, and other markets—might lower those costs, but this was by no means assured. Nevertheless, Agassi forged ahead.

As pressure to meet launch commitments mounted, so did tensions inside the company. At a June 2010 meeting, the board confronted Agassi about the company's profligate spending. When Agassi protested, Ofer, the board chairman, threatened to fire him, but eventually backed down. Agassi's relationships with senior managers frayed, too. He berated employees for poor performance, and according to *Fast Company* magazine, he forced out his head of global operations for allegedly speaking to a board member without consulting him.

Meanwhile, Renault-Nissan was late in delivering the Fluence, and Israel's bureaucratic approval processes had slowed the deployment of charge spots and exchange stations. According to Blum, construction permits in many locations were difficult to secure because they required confirmation that no archaeological artifacts would be disturbed by digging. Installation of charge spots on street curbs—necessary to serve car owners without a garage or driveway—was forbidden. Also, while existing gas stations would have been ideal sites for charge spots and exchange stations, regulations allowed only two hundred square meters of gas station property to be allocated to facilities other than gas pumps. Most station operators were already using this allocation for their profitable convenience stores, so Better Place was forced to scramble to find new charging sites in remote locations. And, Renault's distributor in Israel, understandably skeptical of Agassi's ambitious sales projections for the Fluence, refused to stock the electric vehicle. So Better Place had to spend more of its cash reserves to set up a unit to import and sell the cars itself.

Given these setbacks, it's not surprising that the company missed its early 2011 target for launching service in Israel. Later that year, the startup required more capital, and Agassi raised a $250 million Series C round—mostly from existing investors—at a $2.25 billion valuation. However, the goal had been to raise $350 million, so financial pressure was acute.

When Better Place finally began delivering cars in Israel in January 2012, it was burning through cash at a rate of about $500,000 per day, and sales were slow. Corporate employees were not eager to receive a Better Place vehicle because they'd have to recharge frequently and worried about how far they could drive before running out of power. Since their employer would cover the cost of leasing and operating a company car—including either gasoline or Better Place's subscription fees—the employees' only out-of-pocket cost would be a usage tax they paid on the value of the perquisite they'd received from their employer, in lieu of income. Since the cost of owning and operating a Better Place vehicle was roughly comparable to that of a gasoline-powered car, switching to Better Place wouldn't reduce the usage tax. In other words, employees would be saddled with additional inconvenience, without saving any money: hardly an attractive proposition.

Further, given Better Place's pricing, companies wouldn't save nearly enough to warrant forcing their employees to switch to Better Place vehicles—regardless of their previously stated intent to do so. Moreover, leasing companies, uncertain about the after-market potential for Better Place vehicles, were not inclined to push corporate fleets to adopt them. To gain support from leasing companies, Better Place had to guarantee their resale value by promising to buy the cars back if the after-market price wasn't high enough—a commitment that only added to the startup's financial exposure.

Following this tepid launch, tensions inside the startup boiled over. According to Blum, at a meeting with nine members of his senior management team in early 2012, Agassi told them, "Trust is the most important thing in a company. But trust is gained, and trust is earned. And there are only two people in this room that I trust." In response, Andrey Zarur, Agassi's friend and board member, elicited an admission from most of the team members that the feeling was mutual. And when Zarur, who'd helped Agassi come up with the original vision for Better Place at Davos, warned that the startup would run out of cash by October, Agassi was furious with him and tweeted, "Friends are either true or not friends."

Normally, a CFO would be the one sounding alarms about cash flow problems, but that position had been vacant since the departure of the venture's original CFO the previous year. It was a difficult position to fill, not least because Agassi, dismayed that the board was demanding that the new CFO report to them as well as Agassi, was resisting hiring a replacement.

In late August, Agassi tried and failed to raise additional equity capital from new investors. He did manage to secure a $50 million loan from the European Investment Bank, the government-owned lending arm of the European Union—but that wasn't enough. So, in September, as Better Place was running out of cash, he requested a bridge loan from existing equity investors, who'd already ponied up $750 million. Finally fed up, Ofer denied the request and suggested that Agassi step down as CEO and become chairman. Agassi refused and resigned. Ofer led a final $100 million funding round and recruited two CEOs in quick succession. The first, who'd led Better Place's Australian operations, lasted only four months before losing Ofer's confidence—long enough to lay off five hundred employees and persuade Renault executives to pause their plans to immediately stop manufacturing the Fluence. The second CEO estimated that the startup would require an additional $500 million to reach breakeven—a sum that seemed too far out of reach. So, in May 2013, Better Place declared bankruptcy, having sold fewer than fifteen hundred cars in Israel and Denmark combined.

Cascading Miracles

Was Better Place simply a bad idea—a $900 million misjudgment—fated to fail, right from the start? Not necessarily, but it was a moonshot: a venture so ambitious that Better Place would have had to meet a number of requirements, or it would come crashing down. And with so many challenges, it would be remarkable if each and every one of them worked out.

In short, Better Place fell victim to a late-stage failure pattern I call *Cascading Miracles*. With this pattern, a startup pursuing bold innovation faces many big challenges—and a shortfall with any one of them will be sufficient to kill the venture. Consequently, the startup needs a cascade of miracles to succeed. Consider the challenges confronting Agassi's ambitious plan:

1. **Strong Consumer Demand for Electric Cars.** To fulfill Agassi's vision, large numbers of consumers would have to embrace all-electric vehicles, despite their range limitations and recharging hassles. Although an environmentally minded, modest-sized segment was willing to pay a premium for a green solution, the mainstream market would only drive an electric vehicle if the cost of owning and operating one was lower than that of an otherwise equivalent gasoline-powered model. In regions where gasoline was heavily taxed—for example, Israel and Europe—electricity for charging batteries would indeed cost far less than the gasoline consumed when traveling a given distance. However, these savings would be offset by higher up-front vehicle purchase prices.

When Better Place launched, an electric car with a battery cost about 50 percent more—before any tax incentives—than a comparable gasoline-powered model. So, keeping the cost of an electric car affordable would depend in large part on the availability of significant government subsidies.

2. **Strong Consumer Demand for Swappable Batteries.** What if consumers who might otherwise buy electric cars—despite the higher price tag—were unsatisfied with Better Place's solution to the problem of an electric vehicle's limited range? In theory, they could simply restrict their travel to short distances and use electric cars only for a predictable daily commute or errands around town. But what would happen with longer trips? Practically speaking, only affluent families could afford a second gasoline-powered vehicle for this purpose, limiting demand for electric cars with short range and without swappable batteries.

Direct current (DC) fast charging technology was another alternative. Frequent fast charging can damage batteries, but proponents expected that most consumers would only use fast charging a few times per year, when traveling long distances. During those trips, they might be willing to take a thirty- to forty-minute break to recharge every couple of hours. For everyday use, they could recharge their vehicles overnight at slower AC charge spots that didn't do as much damage to batteries. Contrary to the predictions of fast charging proponents, however, the early adopters of Better Place vehicles *did* make frequent long trips; on average, they used battery exchange stations once a week. Given this uncertainty about consumer behavior and preferences, the superiority of fast charging was by no means obvious when Better Place launched.

Tesla, unlike Better Place, experimented with all of these options. Its Model S sedan, introduced in 2012 and targeted at affluent consumers, was priced at $57,400 for a 160-mile range or $77,400 for a 300-mile range. A larger car like this could have a bigger battery, increasing its range. The Model S also had a swappable battery, like Better Place's Fluence. Tesla opened a battery exchange station between San Francisco and Los Angeles in 2015, but it got little use; consumers instead preferred to use Tesla's "Superchargers": fast charging stations, first introduced in 2012 at strategic points between cities.

3. **Multiple Auto Manufacturer Partnerships.** Better Place could afford only dense deployment of charging spots and battery exchange stations if it achieved a threshold market share. Otherwise they would have to deploy fewer spots and stations, making a Better Place car less convenient and boosting the risk of depleting a battery while driving.

To achieve that threshold market share, Better Place would need to partner with many auto manufacturers. However, those manufacturers would have to adopt Better Place's swappable battery design in order to use their exchange stations. This was a big ask from carmakers, who obsessed over vehicle designs to differentiate their products and to keep costs in line. Manufacturers would also be concerned about demand for vehicles compatible with Better Place's network—and that, in turn, would depend on the startup's simultaneous penetration of multiple markets (see Assumption #4).

As Better Place approached its endgame, its managers did pursue the idea of making its charge spots available to manufacturers whose vehicles did *not* have swappable batteries: an option GM executives had proposed way back in 2008. But by July 2012, when GM Australia announced that Better Place would become its preferred provider of home and dealership charge spots for the Chevy Volt, it was already too late.

4. **Simultaneous Penetration of Multiple Markets.** Given the enormous cost of designing a new car and the huge volumes required to run factories at efficient scale, carmakers need access to very large markets. Therefore, auto manufacturers were unlikely to partner with Better Place unless the startup could promise that vehicles compatible with its charging network could be sold in many countries, within a reasonable time frame. Meeting this expectation would pose huge operational challenges and require vast amounts of capital.

5. **Solid Investor Support.** Better Place's business model required enormous up-front capital infusions, which meant they were in effect asking investors to make a leap of faith long before it was clear whether the model would work as planned. The startup had to deploy a critical mass of charge spots and exchange stations before selling any cars, and it had to shell out the full cost of a car and battery up front, while relying on subscription payments to bring in cash over time. And, it had to do all of this in multiple markets simultaneously.

6. **Effective Execution.** Even if every assumption listed above went their way, Better Place's managers still had to execute effectively across all functions: engineering, marketing, customer service, and so forth. And once again, they had to do so in several countries at the same time. This would prove a tall order: Better Place management had formulated what must have been one of the most complex and operationally demanding launch plans in startup history.

In short, for his plan to work, Agassi was counting on a cascade of miracles. Some of them came to pass. For example, mainstream consumers did begin to embrace all-electric vehicles around 2012 (Assumption #1). Better Place managed to launch simultaneously in Israel and Denmark and had deals in the works in many other markets (Assumption #4). Finally, Better Place raised $900 million in capital (Assumption #5)—thanks in large part to Agassi's riveting salesmanship.

But that's where the miracles stopped. The startup had entered into a partnership with Renault-Nissan—one that soured over time—but hadn't managed to sign up other carmakers (Assumption #3). Execution was erratic (Assumption #6): The team encountered many barriers in Israel that they might have anticipated with better planning; they missed deadlines; and cost control was a serious issue—exacerbated by the absence of a CFO during 2012. However, the biggest problem was a lack of consumer demand for electric cars with swappable batteries (Assumption #2). With charge spots and exchange stations costing far more than originally projected, Better Place simply could not afford to set car prices low enough to be attractive. And ultimately, battery swapping was not the best solution for the problem of range anxiety; Tesla's solution, bigger cars with extended range, coupled with occasional fast charging, eventually prevailed. At its core, Better Place was a big, risky bet on the superiority of swappable batteries over fast charging. That outcome, in turn, hinged on consumer behavior: How often would they make long trips and how important was it to be able finish charging in five minutes instead of thirty to forty minutes?

Once Better Place management committed to swappable batteries, was the venture doomed? Probably not; startups can usually pivot away from a flawed model, and there were plenty of voices inside and outside Better Place advising management to consider different strategies. For example, the startup could have become the preferred provider of charge spots and fast charging stations for GM and other carmakers. Or, when it became clear that demand from Israeli consumers and corporations would be lukewarm, and that local regulations would boost construction costs, Better Place could have pulled the plug on Israeli operations and focused instead on more promising markets.

But a moonshot, once launched, has a lot of momentum and can be difficult to steer in a new direction. Sunk costs loom large after the startup spends hundreds of millions of dollars. And when a charismatic leader has been selling a vision for years—especially one like Agassi with monomaniacal convictions—ego-defensive behavior can lead to what sociologist Barry Staw calls "escalation of commitment" to a strategy, despite mounting evidence that the strategy is flawed.

Moonshots like this one are also highly vulnerable to the Cascading Miracles failure pattern. That's because a moonshot entails audaciously bold innovation with respect to cutting-edge technology, business model novelty, or both. Bold innovation, in turn, implies great uncertainty about customer demand, along with a protracted product development phase. Many moonshot business models harness powerful network effects, high customer switching costs, and/or strong scale economies—attributes that impel rapid scaling after the product is launched. Long development cycles and rapid scaling require enormous amounts of capital. To top off the challenges, moonshots often seek strategic partnerships with established corporations whose priorities may not be fully aligned with those of the startup. They may also need government support for a solution with ambiguous legal standing. To make all of these miracles happen, it helps to have a charismatic founder who walks on water—one with a monomaniacal focus on her bold vision.

The following figure shows how these requirements interact and how a Cascading Miracles failure unfolds. The proximate cause of failure is usually a one-two punch: Customer demand for the venture's product turns out to be weak, and investors—after contributing huge amounts of capital—will not commit more. But the fight typically lasts for many rounds before these knock-out blows are delivered.

The figure's complexity conveys how much has to go right for a

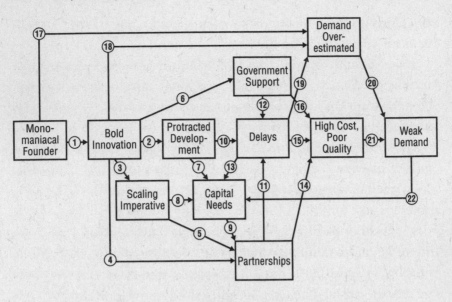

Cascading Miracles

moonshot to succeed, and how many things can—and often do—go wrong. Working from left to right, the bold vision that launches a moonshot often comes from a monomaniacal founder, like Agassi (Line #1 in the figure). The sheer magnitude of the innovation necessitates a protracted product development phase (Line #2), and the envisioned business model often has structural attributes—in particular, network effects and strong scale economies, as with Better Place's charging network—that impel rapid scaling, once the product is launched (Line #3).

Innovation may require strategic partnerships (Line #4) to secure key technologies or crucial system components (e.g., Renault's Fluence); partners may also provide distribution outlets that facilitate scaling (Line #5). If the innovation blazes new legal and regulatory trails, the venture may also need to secure government permission or navigate its bureaucracies, as with Better Place Israel (Line #6). With a lengthy product development phase and a scaling imperative, the venture must raise vast amounts of capital (Lines #7 and #8). As a result, the venture has an incentive to outsource activities to partners, since bringing functions in-house would require even more investment (Line #9).

Several factors may contribute to launch delays. Engineering a cutting-edge product may prove more difficult than expected (Line #10). Partners may be slow to fulfill commitments (Line #11), and negotiations with regulators may drag on (Line #12). The resulting delays boost capital requirements (Line #13), and existing and prospective investors start to doubt the venture's prospects.

As the launch date looms, several factors conspire to boost the product's cost and reduce its quality relative to original plans. Partners may disappoint, as with Renault's Fluence, which was more expensive and had a more limited range than expected (Line #14). Setbacks and surprises in product development also result in higher-than-expected costs for some components, as with Better Place's exchange stations. Similarly, the pressure to meet deadlines forces the team to omit some planned product features, like the "smart screws" for releasing the Fluence's battery (Line #15). Government edicts may also raise costs, as with the need for Better Place to secure archaeological "dig safe" approvals before commencing exchange station construction in Israel (Line #16).

Meanwhile, it's likely that management has overestimated demand. The founder's obsessive enthusiasm for her vision may make her overconfident about customers' interest and blind to barriers the venture may encounter, as with Agassi's conviction that Better Place could meet aggressive sales and cost targets (Line #17). The sheer magnitude of the innovation also leads to great uncertainty about customer demand; no one has done this before, so the team can't base projections on other ventures' experiences (Line #18). And delays in launching mean that customer demand will be a moving target, especially if rivals are aggressively pursuing alternative solutions. Rivals' progress will raise customers' expectations for what a solution should offer and make it more difficult for the venture to achieve its original sales estimates (Line #19).

The combination of unrealistically high expectations for customer demand (Line #20) and a product that costs a lot more and performs more poorly than anticipated (Line #21) results in weak sales when the product is finally launched. As the venture runs low on cash, investors conclude that the cause is lost, and they refuse to provide more capital (Line #22).

In prior chapters, I've examined some of the challenges that entrepreneurs who pursue moonshots encounter. For example, bold, ambitious ventures often display the business model attributes that impel a startup to scale rapidly (Chapter 6) and, as such, face the challenges outlined in Chapter 7 when pursuing an accelerated growth strategy. Moreover, financing risk, discussed in Chapter 8, is particularly acute for moonshots, because they take so long to launch. As a result, they're more exposed to sector-wide shifts in investor sentiment. For example, Better Place, on top of everything else, had the misfortune of being caught in a strong downdraft in clean tech venture investing that started in 2010.

In the following section, I'll examine three additional challenges on the Cascading Miracles path and consider how entrepreneurs can navigate them successfully. They include 1) estimating demand, 2) dealing with launch delays, and 3) harnessing a monomaniacal founder.

Estimating Demand

One big risk that entrepreneurs with a world-altering solution face is that the radical change they promise will turn out to be *too* vast—and scare customers away. The challenge is figuring out how much innovation is too much. Market research in this context is tricky for several reasons. First, due to the protracted development time for many moonshots, it's impossible to get customer feedback on working versions of the product early in the design process. Instead, many entrepreneurs conduct customer surveys and later regret the choice. Recall how Better Place's 2008 survey of one thousand Israeli car owners indicated that 20 percent would consider buying a Better Place vehicle, implying an addressable market of four hundred thousand. Actual sales when Better Place shut down: one thousand.

Iridium is another example of a moonshot that suffered from a gross miscalculation of demand. Founded in 1998 with the mission of providing satellite phone service anywhere on the planet, the venture built upon years of R&D work within Motorola, its lead backer. Before Iridium launched sixty-six satellites into space, Motorola hired several consulting firms to study the market for satellite phone service. Their surveys identified a potential market of forty-two million "wireless addicted" traveling professionals, many of whom were supposedly eager to own a satellite phone. Based on this data, quickly signing up the one million customers required to reach breakeven was expected to be a breeze. However, by the time the startup went bankrupt in 1999, it had raised $6.4 billion in equity and debt—at the time, the most capital ever raised by a startup—but it had attracted only twenty thousand customers: nowhere near the millions envisioned.

Market research professionals routinely assume that survey respondents will overstate their purchase intent relative to their true plans, and researchers have elaborate ways to adjust projections downward to compensate for this bias. But these methods are much less effective with radical new products, since respondents find it difficult to express preferences regarding products with which they've had no direct experience. A quote attributed to Henry Ford makes the risk clear: "If I had asked people what they want, they would have said faster horses."

So, if simply asking customers whether they'll buy a radical new product doesn't yield reliable results, what can entrepreneurs do? They can use tactics described in Chapter 4, like a smoke test that asks customers to commit to pre-purchasing a not-yet-available product, based on a detailed, accurate description of it. Tesla, for example, obtains customer input by requiring a refundable deposit—$1,000 for the Model 3—to reserve a vehicle. Jibo used its Indiegogo campaign, although crowdsourcing, by its nature, reveals more about demand from early adopters than mainstream customers. Also, as discussed in Chapter 4, entrepreneurs can supplement smoke testing by getting customer feedback on a "looks like" prototype, as Jibo's team did when they built a "Wizard of Oz" prototype that could be puppeteered by a hidden human operator to see how consumers would interact with a social robot.

Another barrier to gauging customer demand can be an entrepreneur's paranoia. Some founders insist on staying in stealth mode as long as possible to keep rivals from stealing their ideas. Steve Jobs was famous for insisting on strict secrecy and then introducing new products with a flourish. Dean Kamen, the inventor of the Segway—the two-wheel, self-balancing (via gyroscope stabilization) "personal transporter" unveiled in late 2001—and the startup's founder, was worried about Honda or Sony copying his concept; for years, Kamen refused to let his marketing team get direct customer input. Segway did hire Arthur D. Little (ADL) to estimate demand, but the consultants were not allowed to describe the Segway concept to any customers. ADL estimated that thirty-one million Segways would be sold in the first ten to fifteen years, mostly outside the United States, since cars were costly to operate and not permitted in large areas of many European and Asian cities. In late 2000, when Segway's marketers were finally allowed to give some test subjects a ride on a Segway prototype, they learned that fewer than one-quarter were interested in buying one. This result was a disconcertingly accurate harbinger of weak demand from mainstream consumers; the company sold just thirty thousand Segways in the first six years, and early investors took a big loss on the $90 million they'd contributed. After selling Segways for use in niche markets—like mail delivery, warehouses, and the one featured in the film *Paul Blart: Mall Cop*—the company ceased production of its flagship product in June 2020.

A final problem with customer research was also mentioned in Chapter 4: It is often used to sell investors on a concept. Given the vast amounts of capital required for moonshots, an entrepreneur can be sorely tempted to inflate demand estimates.

Dealing with Delays

All the startups mentioned in the previous section experienced significant delays in developing their products. So did GO Corp, which in 1987 set out to design and build a pen-based tablet computer, complete with operating system (OS). The problems began when the venture's engineers discovered that many hardware and software components would have to be custom designed. Off-the-shelf flat panel displays couldn't handle the pressure of writing with a pen, and existing OS software for managing input and output was too slow, resulting in excessive lag time between using a pen (input) and results appearing on a screen (output).

Meanwhile, as industry interest in pen-based computing heated up, Microsoft, Apple, IBM, and AT&T were all circling the space. So, despite all of the engineering time they'd already invested, GO Corp's leaders eventually spun off its hardware unit, reasoning that tablets would become low-margin commodities like PCs. Meanwhile, the team developing GO's OS, dubbed PenPoint, switched midstream to a different microprocessor—a mobile-friendly chip that used less power—scrambled to perfect PenPoint's glitchy handwriting recognition software, and struggled to reduce PenPoint's memory requirements to avoid boosting tablet costs. Resolving these engineering issues set the launch back by over a year. When GO finally unveiled its PenPoint operating system in 1992, the response was indifferent. After burning through $75 million in venture capital, GO was sold to AT&T, which shut down the project in 1994.

GO's travails point to a recurring challenge with bold innovations that involve a protracted development phase: An engineering team is shooting at a receding target. The longer it takes to develop a product, the further away the target moves, exacerbating delays for two reasons. First, new technologies will likely become available during the development process (as with low-power chips for GO or cloud services allowing off-device processing in the case of Jibo)—and teams must decide whether to take the extra time to incorporate them or to forgo their benefits.

Second, rivals working on similar solutions will announce their plans, forcing teams to decide whether to take the extra time to match them, or risk a feature gap. Iridium's satellite phones, for example, were originally conceived in the late 1980s, when terrestrial cellphone service was expensive and had limited geographic reach. But by the time Iridium launched in 1998, terrestrial cellular services were far more widely deployed, and the customers Iridium targeted were rarely out of their cellphone's roaming range. Another drawback was that Iridium's phones required a clear line of sight to an orbiting satellite to send and receive signals. This meant that—unlike cellphones—they didn't work inside buildings and weren't reliable on the streets of urban "canyons" enclosed by tall buildings. To address this disadvantage, Iridium's team redesigned their phones to switch to terrestrial cellular frequencies whenever possible. The redesign was time-consuming and added to the cost of Iridium's already expensive offering.

What can an entrepreneur who's aiming for bold innovation do when product development is behind schedule? She has four options:

1. **Accept the delays and persevere.** If a startup has a solid head start—as with Better Place and Segway—and has determined that the risk of preemption by rivals is low, then this strategy is reasonable.

2. **Throw bodies at the problem.** Even if a startup can afford it, recruiting many more engineers is probably not a good idea. Brooks's law holds that adding manpower to a late engineering project makes it later. The reasons: New engineers have to come up to speed on what's been done, it takes more time to coordinate the efforts of a bigger team, and many engineering tasks are not divisible. To illustrate the last point, Fred Brooks notes in his classic book on the management of software development projects, *The Mythical Man Month,* that nine women can't make a baby in one month.

3. **Freeze functionality.** Engineers love to polish a product—for example, by devising solutions for all conceivable "edge cases," that is, problems that occur only in extreme circumstances. In an engineering-driven company, it can prove difficult to tell the development team to stop adding functionality. But according to Doug

Field, Segway's engineering lead, "There comes a time in every project when you've got to shoot the engineers and start production."

4. **Cut corners.** If time to market is a priority—either for competitive reasons or because cash is running out—then trimming some features or launching before product bugs have all been ironed out may be the right answer. Jibo's team, which had to deal with cranky Indiegogo backers whose promised robots were nearly two years late, took this approach; as CEO Chambers acknowledged, the robot's set of applications at launch was "shockingly thin." Iridium, too, launched before its software was ready, and for the first few weeks its users reported rampant problems with signal interference, dropped calls, and no dial tone.

However, when weighing whether to sacrifice the initial version's performance for a faster time to market, entrepreneurs should consider the impact of making a weak first impression on early adopters. Ventures with world-changing aspirations often generate enormous hype, so journalists and social media users can be savage when a much-anticipated offering disappoints. Jibo took this kind of beating, with critics calling it a "$900 party trick," as did Segway ("riders look dorky; more Flintstones than Jetsons"), Iridium ("phone bigger than a brick"), and Better Place ("broken promises: not cheaper than a gas-powered car").

Harnessing a Monomaniacal Founder

A monomaniacal founder—that is, one with a fervent belief in her audacious vision and a relentless drive to bring it to life—can be a moonshot's greatest asset during its launch phase. But later—if miracles fail to materialize—such a founder can become the venture's biggest liability.

When a founder's obsessive zeal is coupled with *charisma,* it can give the company a big edge in mobilizing resources. Monomania and charisma don't necessarily go hand in hand, but a leader with both can move mountains.

The term "reality distortion field" was coined for a 1960s *Star Trek* episode, but later was co-opted to describe Steve Jobs's uncanny ability to mesmerize the engineers developing the original Macintosh computer, inspiring them to work eighty-hour weeks for months on end. Jobs exhorted: "We're here to put a dent in the universe. Otherwise, why else even be here?" Under the spell of a reality distortion field, potential employees, investors, and strategic partners perceive a reality in which their commitment to the venture can—despite enormous obstacles—help make the founder's dream come true.

Shai Agassi rivaled Jobs in his ability to spin up a reality distortion field. So did Dean Kamen, Segway's charismatic founder. Like Agassi, Kamen believed he could save the planet, once electric-powered Segways replaced automobiles in cities around the world. And much like Agassi, who predicted that his company would soon overtake GM in market capitalization, Kamen insisted Segway would become the fastest-growing company in the world, because it would "do to the car what the PC did to the mainframe." His pitch, described as "entertaining and irresistible," struck gold: Talented engineers were not only drawn to Kamen's venture, they cheerfully accepted below-market salaries for the opportunity to work with the prolific inventor. Investors, too, were like moths to Kamen's flame: Superstar VC John Doerr of Kleiner Perkins, along with Credit Suisse First Boston and a bevy of CEO angels, all jumped at the opportunity to give him money.

However, the charisma that powers a reality distortion field is often—though not always—one of the many manifestations of *narcissism*. First impressions of narcissists are generally quite positive because they're frequently charming, skilled orators gifted at reading people and knowing how to engage them. But narcissism comes with a dark side.

Narcissists have an inflated sense of their self-worth and are preoccupied with having that viewpoint reinforced. They crave control, power, and fame; have a strong sense of entitlement that stems from their conviction in their beliefs and superior abilities; and are hypersensitive to criticism—often simply ignoring information that runs counter to their worldview. To defend their inflated yet fragile egos, they refuse to admit they've made mistakes and they double down on flawed strategies. For these reasons, narcissists are not only perceived as arrogant and unduly grandiose, they're also especially vulnerable to the *escalation of commitment* blunder mentioned earlier in the chapter.

At the extreme, narcissists may lack empathy and feel no compunction about taking undeserved credit for others' accomplishments and/or casting blame elsewhere for their own mistakes. They demand unconditional loyalty but meanwhile manipulate people to advance their own ends and cast them aside when they're no longer useful.

Narcissism is a personality trait that everyone displays to some extent; we all lie somewhere on a spectrum that runs from "less" to "more" narcissistic. Published accounts of Better Place and Segway that I draw upon in this chapter put Agassi and Kamen on the high end of the spectrum.

If Agassi and Kamen are narcissists, then they're in good company: In his seminal *Harvard Business Review* article, "Narcissistic Leaders: The Incredible Pros, the Inevitable Cons," psychoanalyst Michael Maccoby puts Bill Gates, Steve Jobs, Larry Ellison, and Andy Grove in the same camp. Research has shown that, on average, entrepreneurs exhibit greater degrees of narcissism than the general public. But Maccoby draws a distinction between "productive narcissists"—leaders who leverage their vision, drive, and charisma to achieve breakthrough change—and those who stumble, after silencing dissenting voices and surrounding themselves with yes-men who'll follow their direction uncritically.

While startups of all types are subject to both the productive and unproductive implications of a founder's narcissism, moonshots amplify these effects. By their nature, moonshots require massive resource commitments in the face of great uncertainty, and an entrepreneur with charisma and relentless drive is ideally suited to inspire investors, employees, and strategic partners to take a leap of faith. But moonshots also require a Cascade of Miracles over a long period of time. Many things can go wrong, and when something inevitably does, a founder/CEO may need to reconsider her venture's strategy. Thoughtful recalibration is unlikely to happen if that founder/CEO is thin-skinned or egocentric, reluctant to admit a mistake, and unwilling to accept advice or counsel from anyone other than her own reflection in the mirror.

If a moonshot startup is being led by a narcissist who's already in Maccoby's "unproductive" zone—or headed that way—two things can be done. First, persuade the founder to work with an executive coach. Second, follow best practices for structuring and managing the startup's board of directors.

Executive Coach. With help from a professional coach, a founder may be able to build awareness of her management style and its dysfunctions and take corrective action. The problem is that a narcissistic leader typically doesn't *want* feedback. Convinced she's on the right track, she sees no need for change. So, when the leader won't seek help, others must seize the initiative. A push from a trusted adviser might work, but narcissists tend not to have strong relationships with mentors. A board member may be able to plant the seed, but confrontation is likely to provoke defensiveness and denial. In such cases, protecting the founder's ego and stoking her ambition may soften resistance.

For maximum impact, a coach should also work with any cofounders still at the company, as well as the venture's other senior managers and its board members to help them understand what triggers dysfunctional behavior in their narcissistic founder/CEO—and how to respond. As marriage counselors well know, people may not be aware of destructive relationship patterns that are plainly evident to a professional. Of course, the coach must build a high level of trust with the founder before embarking on this path.

Board Best Practices. A well-structured and well-run board of directors can have a big impact on any startup's performance, but the board's role is especially important in a moonshot venture led by a narcissistic founder. When a founder/CEO strays into the unproductive zone, she tends to drive out the independent thinkers on her senior management team; as a result, no one remains to have constructive debates over strategic options. Elizabeth Holmes is an example: She regularly fired Theranos managers who challenged her. When a depleted management team suffers from groupthink, the board is the last line of defense.

Recruiting the right board members is crucial. Since new investors who lead a fundraising round will typically negotiate for a board seat as a condition for contributing capital, there isn't a lot of room for choice on this front. The good news, though, is that most venture capital partners are effective as board members—it's the primary way they add value to their portfolio companies. VC partners often sit on as many as ten boards at a time and will have served on many others in the past, so they are likely to have deep experience with the strategy issues confronting scaling startups, the leadership styles of different founders, and best practices for startup board management. Segway had one venture capital partner on its board; Better Place had two—one was a Better Place investor, the other was Agassi's friend and Davos co-conspirator Andrey Zarur, who was not an investor in Better Place but brought experience as a venture capitalist and as the co-founder, CEO, and/or board member of three biotech startups.

Selection criteria are more relevant with independent directors like Zarur—that is, board members who aren't investors in the startup or full-time members of its management team. It's good practice to seek an independent director who's been CEO of a scaling startup herself, ideally one who also has insight into how to manage a narcissist founder/CEO—either because she's dealt with one in the past or because she herself has been down that path and gained personal insight. Zarur was a plausible candidate to play this role for Better Place. As Agassi's friend, he had unique insights into Agassi's strengths and weaknesses and at least initially had his trust. Segway, tellingly, didn't have any independent directors on its board, which, in addition to two professional investors, included two angel investors who, as former CEOs of large corporations, lacked extensive experience with scaling startups.

Following best practices for board management can help address the challenges confronting a scaling startup with outsize ambitions—especially one led by a monomaniacal, charismatic narcissist. One key practice is making a *closed session* (one with outside directors only, the CEO and any other senior managers on the board having left the room) a regular agenda item for each board meeting. Agassi's reaction to a closed session nearly led to his dismissal in June 2010. If Better Place had established a norm that made closed sessions a routine part of every board meeting, his paranoia might have been contained.

Two more governance best practices are important. First, the board's annual review of the founder/CEO's performance is a critical forum for a constructive dialogue about the need for change and how to achieve it. Second, the board should have a process for reviewing its own effectiveness as a deliberative body—again, probably annually. Directors need to be on the same page not only with respect to how to coach a troublesome founder/CEO but also with respect to how much risk the startup should take on. Given a moonshot's long product development cycle and its repeated funding rounds, some early investors will own equity shares with a very low price relative to the price paid by more recent investors. As a result, when weighing risks and potential payoffs of strategic moves, each investor may be tempted to focus on her own venture capital firm's narrow interests rather than her fiduciary duty as a board member to balance the interests of all stakeholders. If narrow interests dominate, the board may not be able to reach consensus on strategic direction. To confront this problem head-on, Return Path founder/CEO Matt Blumberg gave each of his board directors two baseball hats—one black and one white—representing their dual roles as investor and fiduciary. When debating strategic options, Blumberg asked the directors to switch hats at intervals to voice concerns from the other point of view.

This chapter has emphasized the risks involved in scaling a company that has moonshot goals, along with some strategies to mitigate them. But I don't wish to leave the impression that the odds of failure for such ventures are so high that entrepreneurs should avoid pursuing bold innovation altogether. It's true that Cascading Miracles are in short supply, which means that many moonshots do fall back to earth. Examples of failed moonshots come easily to mind, because we are so often dazzled by these visionary ventures on their way up and riveted by the huge, steaming craters they leave in the landscape after they crash.

But other moonshots do succeed in reaching their destination. Federal Express did; when Fred Smith founded the company in the early 1970s, it was the biggest venture capital bet in history. More recently, we have Elon Musk's Tesla and SpaceX, both of which have soaring valuations as I write this.

So, expect more moonshots; indeed, we need them to address grand societal challenges like climate change. Visionary entrepreneurs around the world are working on hyperloops, autonomous vehicles, gene editing, and quantum computing. One day, you'll surely be able to chat with Jibo's grandchildren. We may even get flying cars.

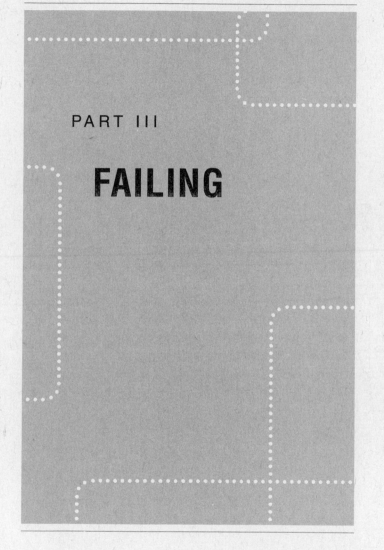

PART III

FAILING

CHAPTER 10

Running on Empty

Failure is not the worst thing; the worst thing is
working on something for years with no end in sight.
—Andrew Lee, Esper co-founder

When they founded Quincy Apparel, Nelson and Wallace prom- ised not to let conflict over how to run the venture threaten their close friendship. They hadn't always seen eye to eye in making decisions about Quincy's strategy; in fact, they'd butted heads re- peatedly. But the co-founders managed to work through their dis- agreements, and their friendship remained intact. That is, until they clashed over whether to shut down their startup. After that quarrel, they were no longer on speaking terms.

Over the years, dozens of founders have sought my advice on the same question that bedeviled Nelson and Wallace: Should I shut down my startup? While I could help them list pros and cons, I could never really say with confidence how those pros and cons netted out. Why was this decision so difficult, and how should a founder approach it?

When I spoke to more founders of failed startups about how and why they decided to shut down, I heard two sentiments repeatedly. First, that the decision was fraught with strong emotions—just as I'd observed with Quincy's co-founders. This is not surprising: Since a founder's identity is wrapped up with his venture's, terminating his startup is akin to negating part of himself—and admitting that a big part of his life is irredeemably flawed. Second, many felt they had waited too long and wished that they had confronted this difficult decision sooner.

It turns out that these two responses are related: The time spent wrestling with the intense emotions engendered by a struggling startup—or avoiding these emotions—leads some entrepreneurs to delay shutting down longer than they should. They are *Running on Empty*—to the detriment of all concerned. The longer this goes on, the longer employees are wasting time on a lost cause, when they could be moving on to their next act. And the longer a founder hopes in vain that new investors or an attractive acquisition will save the day, the longer he is burning through capital that could be returned to investors.

This chapter is the first of two that shift the book's perspective from *why* startups fail to the mechanics of *how* they fail, and to failure's aftermath. Here, I'll focus on how to handle the shutdown itself: how entrepreneurs decide to call it quits; tactical choices they'll confront, once they do; and best practices for winding down. In the next chapter, I'll address how entrepreneurs can manage the resulting emotional fallout.

Prelude to a Fall

Failure rarely sneaks up on a founder; it's usually preceded by a series of choices that don't pan out—some of which seem like Hail Mary passes that fall short of their target. Think of these choices as the prelude to a fall. En route to the exit, founders are likely to try at least some of the following:

- pivoting to a new business model
- raising a funding round from new investors
- selling the company
- raising a bridge round from existing investors
- reducing head count

Sometimes founders succeed in their last-ditch efforts, at least enough to turn their struggling startups around. But more often than not, they don't. Even worse, when one of these initiatives doesn't work out, the next one is all the more likely to falter. For example, if a founder shops the company and then fails to secure an acceptable acquisition offer, existing investors become nervous about committing more capital.

Of course, having the opportunity to pursue these choices assumes that the founder is still in the CEO's driver seat. As noted previously, the board of a late-stage, struggling startup—dominated by investors after several funding rounds—will often conclude that the founder lacks the skill to turn the venture around and will hire a new CEO. But whoever takes on the CEO role must consider the options listed above.

Pivoting. If a startup is not on track, those leading it should ask regularly whether pivoting to a new business model makes sense. Pivoting, in and of itself, is not a harbinger of failure. In fact, many prominent ventures were products of a pivot. For example, PayPal began as a way to beam funds between PalmPilots. When this market proved too narrow, the team introduced fund transfers via email—just as eBay was taking off. Likewise, YouTube started as a service that allowed online daters to upload video profiles.

Successful pivots like these often have one thing in common, however: *They happen early in the venture's development.* Several of the failed startups profiled in this book also completed early pivots. For example, Triangulate originally aimed to license a matching engine to established dating services; Baroo began as daycare for dogs on corporate premises; and Fab.com was spun out of Fabulis, a social network for gay men. Unfortunately, in these cases, even after the ventures pivoted, they couldn't withstand the failure patterns that ultimately caused their demise.

Shifting to a new business model later in a venture's life—when the original plan isn't working as expected—can have advantages. First, a team that's been in business for a while should have a good grasp of customers' unmet needs. Essentially, by running the venture for months or years, they've completed a thorough round of customer discovery research, so they should be less vulnerable to false starts and false positives as they consider new solutions. Second, such a startup typically has ample resources that its leaders can draw upon to execute a pivot, including experienced engineers and marketers, as well as capital. By contrast, founders implementing an early pivot are often still busy assembling resources as they also search for the right business model.

A late pivot does have two potential drawbacks, however. First, once a venture has been more fully developed, it takes more energy to shift direction. Management must coordinate the efforts of many more employees and explain the changes to existing suppliers and customers. The latter, in particular, may be confused and alienated by the shift. Pivoting at this juncture is akin to trying to turn a big cargo ship around—you need to travel miles to change its course.

Fab.com ran into this problem when Jason Goldberg pivoted away from Fab's early focus on drop-shipped flash sales in order to offer a broader selection of goods held in in-house inventory. The pivot made sense strategically: The following year, Fab's rival Wayfair successfully completed an IPO by leveraging a similar model. However, the pivot took months for Fab to complete: Engineers had to redesign its website, operations personnel had to develop processes for packing and shipping orders, merchandising teams had to negotiate terms with existing and new suppliers, and so forth. The pivot might have worked if Goldberg had simultaneously slowed the company's growth, giving his team more time to refine merchandise selection and marketing programs. Instead, he tried to sustain Fab's high growth rate during and after the pivot by spending heavily on customer acquisition. As a consequence, the venture suffered an LTV/CAC squeeze and burned through its capital.

The second drawback is that a startup may not have enough runway left to complete the pivot successfully. Recall Eric Ries's definition of "runway": the number of pivots that a startup can complete before cash balances are exhausted. That number may be zero if the startup has just enough cash to commence a pivot but—absent an infusion of fresh capital—cannot survive long enough to see whether the pivot is working.

That's essentially what happened to Quincy Apparel: co-founder

Nelson, after assuming the CEO role, trimmed the range of sizes that Quincy offered to reduce operational complexity and inventory requirements. This was probably a smart move, but we cannot know for sure, since the pivot came too late. Similarly, as Triangulate was running low on cash, Nagaraj pivoted away from Wings to DateBuzz. Again, the pivot made sense: Revealing profile photos only after users voted on other "bite-sized" profile elements redistributed daters' attention and satisfied an unmet customer need. But Triangulate lacked the capital to build awareness of this innovation, and Nagaraj wasn't able to raise more.

In summary, late pivots take longer to execute. And with a bigger team, the venture is consuming capital at a higher rate. As a result, the startup may need a cash infusion before it's clear whether the pivot is working as expected. In response, investors—especially new ones—may say "Let's wait and see" before committing more capital.

Seeking New Investors. Every failed startup profiled in this book tried unsuccessfully to raise money from new investors: Jibo, Quincy, Triangulate, Baroo, Fab, Dot & Bo, and Better Place were all at an inflection point—just a few months away from exhausting the proceeds from their most recent funding round—when they courted new investors. Their founders could point to some achievements, but they couldn't yet make a convincing case that they had a clear path to long-term profitability. An optimistic new investor might have seen a glass half full. But skeptics and glass-half-empty pessimists prevailed.

It's not unusual for entrepreneurs to seek a new investor to lead their next funding round, rather than inviting existing investors to do so. A new investor will bring additional expertise and contacts. Also, when bidding against other VCs, a new investor must offer a high enough share price to win the right to lead the round. A high share price means less dilution for existing shareholders, including the founders. And, since each new round tends to be substantially larger than the last one, existing investors might not be able to provide all of the capital required, even if they were inclined to do so.

When a startup's performance has fallen short of expectations and its team is debating corrective measures, existing investors may have other reasons to encourage the startup's CEO to try to raise capital from new investors. The startup's prospects are shrouded with uncertainty, so existing investors may be second-guessing their decision to back the venture. Or, these existing investors, having put their professional reputation on the line, might have their judgment about the startup's prospects clouded by ego-defensive biases ("Of course the venture isn't off the rails. I only invest in winners."). In either scenario, if the CEO can persuade a new, impartial investor that the startup's prospects are positive, existing investors will welcome the validation.

On the other hand, this gambit can backfire. As prospective new investors complete due diligence, they want to know: Will existing investors take their *pro rata* allocation in the new round? The terms of an earlier round often grant that round's investors the right (but not the obligation) to contribute enough capital in subsequent rounds to maintain the same percentage ownership stake that they held when they made their original investment. If a startup is doing well, this right can be very valuable, so VCs usually take their pro rata allocation—assuming they have enough capital left in their current fund to do so. Hence, it's disconcerting for prospective new investors if existing investors hedge ("We're still sorting that out") when asked if they'll "take pro rata." Lindsay Hyde had an even worse experience with her disgruntled angel investor, who scared off prospective new backers by criticizing Baroo's leadership during due diligence talks.

Selling the Company. After failing to raise capital from new investors, the next step is often an effort to sell the startup. Investors on the board of directors, knowing that the alternative to selling the company would require them to invest more capital themselves, may wish to explore merger and acquisition (M&A) options.

Typically, it's not difficult for an entrepreneur who puts his venture up for sale to find an audience. Logical candidates will be rivals or big companies operating in the same space. And even if they aren't serious about buying the startup, these players may express interest as a means of learning more about the venture's strategy, financial performance, intellectual property, employee compensation, and so forth.

Most of the startups profiled in this book went through this dance. For example, Anthony Soohoo at Dot & Bo engaged an investment banking firm to manage the sale process but concluded that the bankers fell short of Soohoo's goals for industry introductions. He was also acutely aware that potential acquirers, having learned through their due diligence about Dot & Bo's shrinking cash balance, could use that knowledge to gain negotiating leverage. He said, "They dragged us along to wear us down." Dot & Bo eventually received a few bids, including one for $50 million—which would have been a good outcome, since only $19.5 million had been invested in the startup up to that point. Unfortunately, after rival One Kings Lane was sold for a disappointing price, Dot & Bo's acquisition offers evaporated.

Lindsay Hyde likewise initiated discussions to sell Baroo. She received two offers. Her board accepted one of them, but after completing the agreed-upon thirty-day due diligence period, the suitor walked away for undisclosed reasons. When Hyde then circled back to the company that had made the other offer, its CEO replied simply, "No, thanks. I went out on a limb with my board to get approval for our original bid; I'm not doing that again." Next, a third company offered $1 million for Baroo—again, contingent on a thirty-day due diligence period. If completed, this deal would yield a loss for investors, who'd committed $4.5 million to Baroo. They would, at least, get some money back—but this offer, too, eventually disappeared.

Hyde's experience points to one of the challenges with using an acquisition as an escape path for struggling startups: It takes time to shop the venture, complete due diligence, and then consummate a merger. Hyde estimated that the third suitor might have required another ninety days beyond the initial thirty days of pre-purchase due diligence to finalize legal work and close the deal.

Another potential challenge is the founder's ambivalence about life after a merger. Selling the company might return capital to investors and provide a landing pad for employees. However, an acquisition typically will be contingent on some members of the senior management team committing to continued employment—often for an eighteen- to twenty-four-month "lockup" period. If the merger yields little or no personal financial upside for the founder—as would have been the case for Hyde—the prospect of becoming someone else's employee, instead of pursuing a new venture, is even less appealing. This is especially true for the type of person who opted to start her own business in the first place rather than work for someone else.

Another problem: There simply may not be any buyers. Avni Patel Thompson, founder of Poppy, the on-demand childcare service mentioned in Chapter 2, had this experience. She recalled that after shopping Poppy to rivals, "It turned out everyone else was struggling with margins, too. No one had buckets of cash to spend on acquisitions. Even the companies who were interested would not be able to move quickly enough to get a deal done in under six months, during which time we would be under immense pressure to not let the core business falter."

Moreover, as VC Fred Destin notes, if the acquisition process is unsuccessful, the startup becomes "damaged goods." He describes the scenario: "M&A goes so-so. Maybe the offers are low, maybe a suitor takes you all the way to the altar and drops you. You hear a lot of 'this is a bit early to sell, you should fix X and Y' (which you knew already). Your 'asset' is now burnt in the market and it will be a year or two before you can re-spin your story. You remember that advice about 'good businesses get bought, not sold' and it makes more sense now."

Bridge Financing. If a CEO fails to raise more capital from new investors and cannot consummate a merger, the next step is to seek bridge financing from existing investors. Sometimes, these investors can't or won't commit more money. For example, when Quincy's founders proposed a bridge loan, their investors deflected the request and instead offered introductions to angels who might be interested—discussions that went nowhere.

Negotiations over a bridge round can get nasty because they may require a "cram down" that significantly dilutes the equity stake of any existing investors who don't participate. Terms vary, but basically, those who step up to provide more capital to a troubled venture will often only do so at a very low stock price. When that's true, a huge number of new shares will be issued in the bridge round; afterward, investors whose preferred shares were acquired in earlier rounds will own a much smaller percentage of the company. The same is true for founders and employees who hold common shares. To keep managers motivated after their equity stake is diluted, a restructuring plan may also include provisions to issue them new stock or options. It takes a board vote to approve any new financing round, so board members can end up at an impasse if some investors refuse to commit more capital but won't accept the cram down.

This happened to Hyde after she asked her board to consider a $500,000 bridge loan to help Baroo operate until the $1 million acquisition offer mentioned above could be completed. The request triggered heated discussions among the investors. One board member agreed to fund the bridge loan, provided that he—and any other investors willing to join him—received 100 percent of exit proceeds until they had earned back six times the value of their new infusion of capital. In practical terms, this meant that the acquisition proceeds of $1 million would be distributed entirely to the bridge investors—a nice return on their $500,000 new investment. The other shareholders were prepared neither to bear this risk nor to approve this deal.

Head Count Reduction. If their startup's performance has been disappointing, many entrepreneurs conclude that they must cut head count to slow their cash burn rate so as to buy more time for further fundraising and M&A efforts, or for a pivot to play out. In doing so, they confront four decisions about a reduction in their workforce.

First, how transparent should we be with employees about the company's situation? This decision logically precedes the others below. In his book *Lost and Founder,* Rand Fishkin, founder of Moz, a startup that provides search engine optimization software, expressed regrets about not being more transparent with his staff before a big layoff. The company had invested heavily over several years in broadening its product line to encompass a full suite of tools for digital marketing (e.g., social media tracking, monitoring blog content). To stem the cash outflow after these new products stalled, Moz laid off 59 of its 210 employees. Fishkin recounts the aftermath:

> There were tears and anger, nasty writeups about the company on blogs, review sites, and social media, lost friendships, lost trust, and lost reputation. Worst of all was that this news came as a complete surprise to most of our team. Of all the missteps and poor decisions, the one I regret most is the lack of transparency our leadership team, myself among them, showed in the months leading up to that event. . . . If we'd really intended to invest in these multiple products knowing that we might need to lay off a substantial portion of the team, we should have said so upfront. . . . When trust is lost like that, it's incredibly hard to win back.

Second, how deeply should we cut? Conventional wisdom says that a CEO should cut deeply enough to avoid the need for a second round of layoffs. A second round could shatter morale and spur the departure of talented employees the company would like to retain because they no longer trust management or have confidence that the venture will survive. However, making mass reductions in one fell swoop has its drawbacks, too. In his postmortem analysis of Fab's failure, Jason Goldberg regretted imposing massive layoffs in Europe and rapidly reducing Fab's U.S. team from four hundred to eighty-five. He recalled:

> Truth be told, it became a death spiral. The only thing we became good at was reducing the burn rate, but the business it-

self was floundering and losing value. I slammed on the brakes of a speeding rocket ship and that's incredibly hard to do, and I failed miserably at it. I was too quick to focus on slashing costs and narrowing scope vs. taking a step back and devising a plan with our board to preserve value for our shareholders. Everyone always says: "Cut fast and cut deep." I now disagree. It should rather be: "Cut smart, cut with a plan, and cut with help."

Third, who should we cut? Senior managers may be appealing targets because their compensation is high. But letting go of senior people tends to draw unwanted attention to the fact that the company is in trouble. For example, Goldberg's decision to fire a number of his direct reports led to some blowback in the business press. He recalled:

> The press made a big deal out of senior managers leaving. The implication was they left in frustration with my management style. But the press got only one side of the story, because at the time I had resolved to not blame anyone for Fab's problems but myself. I've never regretted those departures: we had too many high salaried people and many of them were not performing well. In most cases, I fired them and let their #2 reports run things. That was a very concerted decision, made with board support. Their #2s had been doing the actual work and they were capable of doing a better job.

Instead of dismissing senior managers, some CEOs ask them to take a pay cut, which can help the startup avoid deeper cuts in frontline ranks. Hyde did this, and her management team at Baroo was willing to defer their salaries. However, Hyde's lawyer subsequently informed her that in Massachusetts, a CEO is personally liable for nonpayment of deferred salaries, often with mandatory triple damages—and Directors & Officers insurance held by most firms does not cover this type of liability. So, the company immediately paid out the $250,000 worth of deferred salaries due—except for Hyde's—which nearly emptied Baroo's bank account and triggered its shutdown.

Finally, how much severance should we pay to laid-off employees? When Moz was planning for its big layoff, Fishkin battled with his fellow board members over how much severance to pay. He argued that the loyalty and morale of remaining employees would be bolstered if Moz paid at least six weeks of severance to laid-off colleagues with more than four years' tenure. A VC board member countered that many tech companies offered just two weeks of severance, and six was the most he'd ever seen. Did the company really want to spend 20 percent of its remaining cash on severance? Fishkin prevailed but said that in the process he "burned bridges—relationships with board members that I'd spent years building."

Pulling the Plug

If none of the strategies described above have panned out, an entrepreneur will face a stark choice: Is it time to throw in the towel? My conversations with entrepreneurs and investors unearthed several reasons why so many founders are inclined to keep running on empty—past the point where the odds of a turnaround have become vanishingly small.

In early-stage settings, a founder has sole discretion over whether to keep going or shut down his startup because that's the only time he still controls a majority share of votes on the startup's board of directors—if a board exists at all. Of course, even if the founder/CEO controls a majority of board votes, he still has an obligation to keep his board fully informed of the company's situation and to seek its advice on how to proceed. In late-stage ventures, however, when outside directors outnumber management on the board, shutting down becomes a decision for the entire board.

As they decide whether their startup has enough potential to warrant more effort, founders will want to take enough time to work through the array of rescue options listed in the prior section:

pivots, courting new investors, etc. Failed founder Andrew Lee commented on this impulse: "I found some striking parallels between end-of-life startup decisions and end-of-life medical decisions. . . . As in medicine, we can make decisions to 'prolong' the life of a startup."

Beyond this impulse to exhaust rescue options, there are several other reasons why entrepreneurs may be inclined to delay a shutdown, despite the dwindling odds of their venture's success. They include the following:

• Typically, **failure is a slow-motion affair:** Growth sputters, then prospective investors hedge with "We need more time to think this over." The ambiguity of such statements allows founders to hold on to a glimmer of (usually false) hope, but it is difficult to determine whether the situation is in fact hopeless.

• **Surviving on life support is often feasible,** especially for early-stage startups. To conserve cash, a small team can terminate its office lease and set up shop in the founder's apartment. Loyal employees who have committed to the vision from the very start may be willing to take pay cuts "until we raise the next round."

• Founders are constantly told that great entrepreneurs are gritty. This creates **a mindset that a quitter cannot be a great entrepreneur.** So, to preserve his self-image, a founder will be disposed to soldier on. Founders are also told that persistence pays; they revel in stories of eleventh-hour rescues. And, having invested so much effort and emotion in the venture, they tend to see what they want to see.

This way of thinking was evident in a series of heart-wrenching posts by Mike Gozzo, who titled his then-anonymous blog "My Startup Has 30 Days to Live." Chronicling the dying days of the startup he founded, Gozzo admits, "I did see the metrics. I reported my concerns to the 'board' (whatever this looks like in a seed-stage startup) and to our investors. However, when I look back on these reports, I see that I was so used to crafting a positive, hopeful story that I continued to do so when I really should have been honest with myself. I was always one deal away from hitting the targets I missed last month. Trying so desperately to stay on track that I forgot that the rails were leading me to a cliff."

• **Many founders lack a sounding board;** they face this existential crisis—in Gozzo's words—"utterly alone." Entrepreneurs must project unwavering confidence to keep their startups afloat. When team members, partners, or customers ask how things are going, founders invariably accentuate the positive, knowing that a balanced and more honest appraisal might trigger team defections and accelerate their startup's demise. In particular, while attempting to raise more capital, founders may withhold bad news from those best equipped to provide counsel: current investors. Consequently, few individuals are sufficiently informed to give the founder good advice about whether, and when, to pull the plug.

While the impulse to hide the company's troubles can be difficult to overcome, founders who do reach out for help typically find that it is readily forthcoming. Andrew Lee, Esper's founder, wrote, "Everyone (not just investors) is willing to help. Although I felt embarrassed and guilty, once I reached out, I realized how common my situation was and how empathetic others were. I wish I had reached out sooner."

• Even if they have come to grips with the reality, **founders may feel a moral obligation to persevere** on behalf of employees who depend upon the firm for their livelihood, customers who rely upon its products, and investors who were inspired by the founder's vision. As Steve Carpenter, founder of the failed "fin tech" startup Cake Financial, told my students, "Once you take other people's money, you can't quit."

Echoing that theme, Gozzo said, "What tore me apart in the middle of the night was the responsibility I felt toward people who had shared in my vision and took part in clarifying it and building it with me. What would failure mean for them? Would their careers really recover from the sacrifices they made chasing this dream? Would failure of a business sever friendships and relationships the way the reading of a will can tear a family apart?"

Gozzo was later heartened by his team's reaction when he told them their venture was in trouble: "I called a meeting and gave everyone a long, hard look at our financials. I was the only one with the quiver of sadness in my voice. My team stepped up, re-affirmed their alignment with our shared vision and made a ton of sacrifices to ensure we could continue executing it. This passion is what being elite is all about."

When visiting my MBA class on entrepreneurial failure, startup coach Jerry Colonna cautioned that, while loyalty to one's team is admirable, sticking with a venture *strictly* out of a sense of obligation to others "creates a risk of toxicity. Leaders have power, and there's a danger they'll use it badly when they resent others or loathe themselves."

• **A founder's ego takes a big hit** when his venture fails, and this pain is compounded if failure is stigmatized in the circles he runs in. If failure seems likely, the founder must decide whether to confront this ego blow now or push it off as far as possible into the future. The pain that entrepreneurs feel when they know their startups are failing is palpable.

As Gozzo put it: "I've often heard that in our final moments, our life starts to flash before our eyes. Over the last 24 days I feel like I've experienced a lifetime of trials, failures, successes and emotions as I came to terms with the fate of my startup. The past month has been a torrent of emotions, a series of lows, each lower than the last as I retreated into a shell, neglected my health and came to terms with our only chance at a strategic acquihire [i.e., an *acqui*rer that only wants to *hire* the venture's team] ending with a shitty Skype chat where we were told we just weren't good enough to work with the successful Silicon Valley startup in our space."

But despite all the factors that encourage an early-stage founder to delay a shutdown, there are also countervailing forces at work. In particular, investors may push for an early shutdown if they've concluded that a turnaround is unlikely. They'd rather dissolve the venture before it has consumed all of its capital, so they can get some of their money back. Also, investors who serve on the startup's board will view that time commitment as having a high opportunity cost. Since early-stage startup boards typically meet at least ten times per year and require lots of additional time outside of regularly scheduled meetings, VCs face a practical constraint in terms of the number of board seats they can hold. If a spot on their "dance card" is filled by a venture with dubious prospects, that decreases their overall odds of reaping a unicorn-size reward.

Seasoned entrepreneurs who've shut down a venture have good advice for first-time founders wrestling with this decision. They suggest 1) specifying milestones that must be met, and setting deadlines for meeting them; 2) asking trusted advisers—who know you, your venture, and what it takes for an entrepreneur to succeed—whether it makes sense to persist; and 3) asking yourself regularly whether the following are true:

- **Are you out of moves?** Specifically, have you exhausted the options listed at the beginning of this chapter—pivoting, raising capital from new investors, M&A, etc.? This question was what ultimately led Gozzo to pull the plug on his venture: "It wasn't a failed pivot. It wasn't a fight. It wasn't a sudden change in life situation. It wasn't bad advice that was blindly followed. In fact, it's really hard to pin down what it was that made me recognize the prognosis and end the self-delusion. *I knew the moment that I was out of moves.* I realized that even if I had a longer runway, and some awesome bridge loan was on the table, I could not accept it with a clear conscience."

- **Are you miserable?** Do you hate your job, your co-founder, your team, your investors? How you are treating your family? And has this been true for weeks on end? As Jasper Diamond Nathaniel, co-founder of the failed sports nutrition startup Revere, recounts the period leading up to his pulling the plug: "I was *so fucking* exhausted, physically, mentally and emotionally. I'd barely been sleeping. My mood had been completely unstable—I was living and dying with every investor meeting, every uptick and downturn in sales. I was neglecting friends and family, and my relationship was failing.

And I was lonely. Feeling the need to keep a strong front, I had walled myself off, hiding my inner turmoil from my employees and investors, and avoiding talking about it with people outside of the business who I was sure just couldn't understand. I'd been telling myself that this was all normal, this was part of the entrepreneurial journey, but suddenly it all caught up to me. I tried to dig deep and find something to help me keep fighting, but I came up empty—any passion once there had now been sapped."

• **Do you still believe in the vision that motivated you in the first place?** With Baroo's cash running out, Lindsay Hyde was preparing to pitch another VC firm for funding when she was informed that an elderly diabetic cat had died in the care of a Baroo employee— Baroo's first such fatality. As a result, she walked into the VC meeting feeling distraught. Even though a veterinarian later determined that Baroo's employee had not been at fault, the incident shattered Hyde's confidence and the pitch bombed. The investor later told her, "I know you and I believe in you. But I didn't believe that *you* believed your own story." She reflected, "In that moment, I suppose that I really didn't believe we could succeed. Once an entrepreneur has lost energy—that little bit of crazy that allows you to say, 'Just wait: It'll be amazing in 24 months'—you are done."

• **Is the window for a "graceful" shutdown closing?** By *graceful,* I mean a shutdown in which you honor your commitments to customers; you pay in full all outstanding vendor bills; you not only pay employees their compensation, you also offer some severance; and your investors receive at least some of their money back. While a failure may tarnish a founder's reputation—at least to some extent—a graceful shutdown will lessen that. There's a trade-off, however: Running the venture beyond the point where a graceful shutdown is possible gives a founder more time to search for additional funding or a merger partner.

To calculate exactly when this window might close, a founder must have a clear grasp of the venture's commitments and its cash burn rate. Wallace had this date in mind when she proposed a shutdown to Quincy's board, and her co-founder Nelson ultimately timed the shutdown so that the venture offered employees a small severance payment, reimbursed all of its creditors, and returned a small percentage of investors' capital. Hyde, by contrast, missed the window to meet all of Baroo's financial obligations. While it paid its employees in full, Baroo ended up not being able to repay about $100,000 to vendors.

Once they've made the decision to pull the plug and they've communicated that decision to their team, many founders experience a form of catharsis—a great release of emotional pressure. Hyde said, "It was a relief to end the turmoil over the bridge loan. I had a moment of great clarity, because at that point, I legitimately felt that we had run down every path we could for our investors. We had poured our heart and soul into trying to get their money back."

Having decided that his venture cannot survive as an independent entity, a founder has more choices to make. Among them: Should he simply quit and let someone else wind down the company? And: Should the team pursue an "acquihire" by a company that wants to hire the venture's team but not continue running it as a going concern?

Quitting or Stepping Down. On rare occasion, a founder/CEO in effect tosses the car keys on the table and announces to his board or co-founders that he's leaving the startup: "I'm done driving. You can finish." The impulse is understandable, given the pressure a founder has been under and the fact that the endgame promises more of the same—with no prospect of equity upside. Or, a founder might elect to step down from the CEO position—but continue working full-time in another role—if some of the factors listed above have weakened his resolve to continue as CEO.

There are two good reasons for not quitting. First, seeing the venture through to the bitter end can be a learning experience for a founder. Second, no founder wants to get the reputation as the kind of captain who would abandon a sinking ship. Venture capitalist Aileen Lee told me about a founder who simply walked away from his struggling venture, asserting that there just wasn't enough personal financial upside to justify spending several months winding things down. The board and investors were furious: The founder had convinced them to invest in his vision only to walk away, leaving the investors to clean up the mess. They all agreed to never work with the founder again.

Acquihires. An acquihire is a common exit path for failing startups with venture capital backing. The upside of an acquihire is that investors typically earn a modest positive return on their investment, and some of the venture's employees get a job. On the other hand, founders may have to cope with the kind of behavior Gozzo experienced in his acquihire negotiations: "We're being courted by men who've seemingly forgotten the struggle and are intent on toying with their prey. Both those that have approached us and those who we've approached have acted similarly, circling our bleeding body in the water, perhaps to sadistically toy with us. Though likely, they're waiting until the lights go out before looting."

An acquihire constitutes a "make vs. buy" decision for the acquiring company, as relates to engineering and entrepreneurial talent. And, by the way, the acquirer isn't interested in taking everyone: They'll conduct interviews to figure out who'll make the cut. They're essentially asking, how does the cost of purchasing an intact team that has shown it can build something and work together compare to the cost of hiring and training a similarly competent team from scratch? This calculation means that acquihires are rarely completed at a big multiple of the total capital raised by a venture. That would make buying talent too expensive, compared to hiring and building a team the old-fashioned way.

Due to liquidation preferences negotiated by VCs, investors receive all of the exit proceeds from an acquihire until they've earned back their original capital contribution. Given the modest purchase proceeds, once the preferred shareholders (i.e., the VCs) have received their share, there may not be much, if anything, left to distribute to the common shareholders—that is, the founders and any employees who hold stock or options.

The fact that founders and team members will earn little or no equity payoff can cause some complications, since the acquirer will make its purchase contingent on the retention of key team members. The easiest solution for the acquirer is to offer those team members side deals, for example, a signing bonus or stock in the acquiring company that vests over time. From the acquirer's perspective, side deals are attractive—as long as they don't significantly increase the total cost of the acquisition. Of course, the startup's investors will look askance at any side deals made at their expense. It can be challenging for a founder to thread this needle, simultaneously keeping his team intact, keeping the deal on the rails, and satisfying his board of directors—which must approve the acquisition.

A founder who's emotionally connected to his company and to his colleagues may feel distress at seeing the team he's built being grilled in a cold-blooded diligence process and then ultimately dismembered and dispersed: "We'll keep these two, but not that loser." As a result, Andrew Lee advises founders to ask their teams what they really want before acquisition talks commence. He recalls that the acquihire process "split our team apart for interviews—or what felt like interrogations—and took us on an emotional roller coaster of uncertainty that quickly left a sour taste in our mouths."

Winding Down

You've reached the end of the road and found no white knights with last-minute funding or acquisition offers. So, how do you wind down your venture responsibly?

Advisers. The first step, if you haven't already taken it, is to find a lawyer and an accountant who can guide you through the shutdown process. These advisers should have experience with the complexities of legal and tax obligations and prudent shutdown management practices—for example, who gets paid first if liquidation proceeds fall short of amounts due; how to use escrow accounts to hold funds in reserve, pending final settlements; and how to terminate employees so they can claim unemployment benefits. Advisers can also help you complete the government paperwork required to shut down a company—for example, canceling state licenses and obtaining a certificate of dissolution.

The law firm you've been working with up to this point—on incorporation, employment and supplier contracts, regulatory issues, patent filings, and so forth—may or may not have someone on staff who's experienced with shutdowns. If they don't, they should be able to steer you to a specialist. This lawyer is likely to charge a mostly flat fee, up front. Pay it promptly: Your attorney will be justifiably concerned about reimbursement, and you don't want him bailing out midstream. If you can't afford to retain a lawyer, you can find good advice online at sites like NOLO.com and Rocket Lawyer.

Approach. The next step is to decide, with your advisers' assistance, which of three basic approaches you'll follow for liquidating assets and paying creditors. Before you commence the process, you'll need to inventory all of the assets you can sell and all of the claims for payment you must deal with. Also, you or your advisers should review contracts associated with the claims, to see if any of them grant the claimant the right to be paid first when you liquidate assets.

Regardless of which approach you use, the order in which you pay various claimants will be governed to a large extent by state laws and regulations. In most jurisdictions, you must 1) pay all taxes that are due, 2) pay employee wages and benefits, and 3) refund any customer deposits before you settle any secured claims, such as a bank loan that is secured by your receivables or inventory. If you cannot repay the loan, the bank will collect the receivables and sell the inventory—and keep all of the proceeds until the loan is repaid. It's very important to understand whether any of your assets serve as collateral for secured claims. If you sell them without the claimant's permission, you'll be in legal jeopardy.

Unsecured claims are next in line, and you may have some discretion over which of them to repay, depending on which shutdown approach you employ. If there's any cash left after all the claims are dealt with, you'll make a distribution to preferred shareholders. Last in line: common shareholders like you, the founder.

Here are the three basic approaches for managing the shutdown of a startup:

• **Bankruptcy.** With a bankruptcy filing, all claims on the venture are wiped out. A trustee appointed by the bankruptcy court liquidates assets and resolves claims. This reduces the founder's workload, compared to a do-it-yourself, out-of-court workout (described below). However, bankruptcy has disadvantages. It's a public process; it can take a long time to complete; and liquidation tends to yield less value than other processes—especially after the trustee takes a commission on asset sales. And finally, the founder forfeits discretion over which unsecured claims are repaid.

• **Assignment for the Benefit of Creditors (ABC).** With an ABC process, the startup grants a third party the legal right to liquidate assets and resolve claims, in exchange for a fee. An ABC process has several advantages. First, it's less time-consuming for the founder than an out-of-court workout. Second, an ABC process is usually completed more quickly than a bankruptcy. Third, since most ABC firms have industry-specific expertise with liquidating assets and negotiating claims, they may recover more value than would be recouped via a bankruptcy court or workout. Finally, sophisticated buyers of expensive assets will typically prefer to work with either an ABC firm or a bankruptcy court—and not an individual self-managing an asset sale. The buyers want to avoid legal complications that will ensue if the assets they acquire are secured by another claim; ABC firms and bankruptcy courts take care to ensure that assets aren't encumbered in this way.

However, the ABC process has downsides as well. For one, ABC firms prefer to work with larger startups because they generate bigger fees. And second, their priorities may not align with those of the founder or shareholders. For example, Dot & Bo paid a $250,000 fee to an ABC firm retained by the bank whose loan to Dot & Bo was secured by a large portion of the startup's assets. Anthony Soohoo was disappointed with the results. He said, "The firm running the ABC process didn't care much about what happened after they recovered enough to pay back the bank loan. They weren't focused on paying back vendors everything they were owed, or on returning some capital to shareholders."

• **Workout.** A do-it-yourself, out-of-court workout is often the preferred approach for smaller startups because it allows them to avoid the fees and commissions associated with the other two approaches. With a workout, the founder personally manages asset sales and negotiates settlements with creditors that release the startup from further liability. The process can be time-consuming but gives the founder more leeway to specify which creditors get repaid and how much. According to NOLO, an online repository of legal resources, creditors know they'll have a hard time collecting once you are out of business, so they will often agree to settle a claim if you can offer them between 30 percent and 70 percent of what they are owed. In advance of these negotiations, it's important to notify unsecured creditors (via certified letter) that you are shutting down and are requesting claims during a time window that conforms to state requirements. Claims submitted by notified parties beyond this time frame are not valid; however, parties who are not notified can submit late claims. After reaching a settlement with a creditor, you should be sure to obtain a signed release from future claims.

Communications. Having decided to shut down, a founder must determine how to share the news with stakeholders. He'll contact creditors through one of the processes described above. Other important stakeholders include customers, investors who aren't board members, and employees.

When dealing with customers, it's wise to collect receivables before notifying them that a shutdown is pending; otherwise, it may prove difficult to collect payment. Customers will want to know exactly when service will end. For a truly graceful shutdown, a startup will smooth the customers' transition to a new service provider. In the case of Baroo, Hyde arranged for Rover, an online rival, to onboard both Baroo's walkers and its customers, who were offered a $40 credit to get started on Rover.

Some entrepreneurs are better than others at keeping investors who aren't board members informed. Updates tend to become less frequent as a startup begins to struggle—after all, it's never fun to deliver bad news—so its shutdown may come as a surprise to some investors. Those who've invested in many other startups will see the failure as part of the "circle of life" and most won't be bitter. However, they deserve a full accounting of what happened and a thank-you for their support.

When informing employees that a shutdown is coming, a founder should address several points. First, how much severance (if any) will they receive? Second, how do they file for unemployment? Third, do they have the option to continue medical benefits, for example, through a self-funded COBRA program? Fourth, the founder should assure employees that he will take steps to help them find new jobs—for example, serving as a reference and calling other companies to inform them that talented candidates will be on the market. Finally, the founder and his top managers should tell employees how much they appreciate their service, that the employees bear no responsibility for the firm's failure, and that everyone should be proud of the work they did together.

This chapter traces the logistical challenges on the path toward a shutdown. But a founder will face emotional tests over the course of the journey, too. During the first phase—the prelude to the fall—his emotions will swing wildly as he tries to save the venture. His hopes will rise and fall as pivots get off to a good start and then falter, as investors proffer term sheets and then withdraw them, and as merger partners send conflicting signals.

During the middle phase, he'll wrestle—perhaps alone—with the existential question: Is it time to pull the plug? This question will stir a mix of strong emotions: guilt at having let down his team and investors, anger with white knights who promised salvation and then rode off, self-doubt about whether he was fit to lead in the first place, and sorrow at the prospect that his "change-the-world" dream is failing.

The endgame starts with emotional catharsis: finally sharing the news that it's all over. Then, for a few weeks, the founder will probably be too busy winding down the business to ruminate. But after that flurry of activity, once his team is gone, negotiations with creditors are complete, and dissolution paperwork is filed, he'll have plenty of time to mourn, try to figure out what happened and what he might have done differently, and start thinking about what he'll do next. Strategies for how to cope with this final phase are explored in the next chapter.

CHAPTER 11

Bouncing Back

Christina Wallace felt devastated after she was forced out of Quincy during its dying days. She spent three weeks alone in her apartment, ordering in meals from Seamless and watching all seven seasons of *The West Wing*. Wallace dreaded explaining to her friends what was happening at Quincy, because, despite not being on speaking terms with her best friend and co-founder Alexandra Nelson, she felt a strong sense of duty to the startup they had built. Wallace avoided "How's it going?" conversations with acquaintances in the tightly knit New York City startup community. If word spread about Quincy's problems, it would be more difficult for Nelson to pull a rabbit out of the hat and find more funding. So, Wallace emerged from her apartment only once while Quincy was in its death throes. She attended a holiday charity ball where she spoke to no one but posted some selfies on Instagram to make it look like everything was normal.

Wallace resolved to shake off her funk out of sheer necessity, to deal with a looming personal financial crisis. She'd invested all of her savings in Quincy and had accrued considerable credit card debt just for living expenses; now, her student loans were due. She didn't qualify for unemployment benefits; she had no significant other to lean on; and her family didn't have money to lend her. She had to find a job, and fast. After Quincy failed, over a thirty-day period, she had coffee with seventy friends and professional contacts. She asked each of them, "What do you think I'm good at?" From these conversations, Wallace concluded that she excelled at storytelling and selling an organization's mission, and that she rose to the challenge of creating something from nothing. This pointed her toward her next job: opening a New York City expansion campus for the Startup Institute, which offered immersive training for career switchers.

The path that Wallace followed was an accelerated version of a three-phase journey that awaits most founders as they try to bounce back from their venture's failure. The first phase is **recovery** from the emotional battering that the shutdown inflicts. The founder must cope with the grief, depression, anger, and guilt that can accompany any major personal setback—often, as with Wallace, while confronting the stark reality of having no income or personal savings. During the second phase, **reflection,** the founder ideally moves beyond blaming the failure on others or on uncontrollable external events. Through introspection, she gains a deeper understanding of what went wrong, what role she played in her venture's demise, and what she might have done differently. In the process, she also gains new insights about her motivations and her strengths and weaknesses as an entrepreneur, manager, and leader. In the final phase, **reentry,** the founder leverages these insights to decide whether to pursue another startup or choose a different career track.

This chapter will examine these three phases and offer advice for entrepreneurs on how to heal, learn, and ultimately rebound from a startup's failure.

Recovery

A startup's failure can severely derail an entrepreneur in three ways. First, her personal finances may be in disarray. Many, like Wallace, invest all of their savings in their venture. Some max out credit cards to keep it running. To stretch their firm's runway, most pay themselves little or, like Lindsay Hyde at Baroo, defer their own salary.

Second, the entrepreneur's personal relationships may be in a shambles because she neglected friends, family, and her significant other while working eighty-hour weeks for months on end. "Sorry about that, but I need your emotional support now" may not immediately find a sympathetic ear. Fearing that rejection, and embarrassed about what happened, the founder may avoid trying to reboot or repair relationships. Self-isolation—especially initially—is a common response.

As Josh Carter, founder of the now-defunct developer services company BrightWork, described this painful period, "The thoughts of what we could have done better drown out the faint voices of the morning news. . . . I sit at home trying to find a path back from this deep sense of failure that has been eating away at me like a virus. The feeling is paralyzing as I stare blankly at my screen and continue to seek some sense of purpose. I have failed those that rely on me and I have to find a way to put on a good face for my family and friends. Today, it's nearly impossible."

Finally, the failure of her venture can inflict deep emotional distress on a founder as she wrestles with a toxic brew of guilt, shame, regret, and disappointment. Unfortunately, guilt and shame paired with the instinct to hide or withdraw can be a dangerous combination. If the entrepreneur is socially isolated, these emotions take center stage and can launch her into a vicious downward spiral. "My first instinct was to apologize—to [my co-founder] Marcin, to my team, to my investors, to the loyal community we'd built," recalls Nikki Durkin, who shut down her startup, 99dresses, in 2014. "I felt shame, guilt, embarrassment—like a shepherd who'd led her sheep off a cliff when it was my responsibility to keep them safe. I logically knew that I shouldn't feel these things, but emotions aren't always logical. In fact, I didn't really know *what* I should be feeling. I'd been working on this company ever since I finished high school, so 99dresses was all I'd ever known. It was a huge part of my identity—I was 'that 99dresses girl.' Who was I without this startup? I had no idea."

Elisabeth Kübler-Ross's "Five Stages of Grief" provides a useful framework for understanding the emotions a founder might feel during this period—and how they evolve over time. Kübler-Ross famously observed that individuals coping with a life-altering loss often cycle through five responses—although the sequence may vary, and some responses may not surface at all.

- *Denial:* In this initial state of shock, a typical response is "This can't be happening." For example, Anthony Soohoo's initial reaction to Dot & Bo's shutdown was: "It just didn't seem real."
- *Anger:* In this stage, the sentiment is "This isn't fair!" and the question is "Who's to blame?" Entrepreneurs may rant about co-founders who dropped the ball, investors who pushed too hard for growth, or partners who failed to deliver on promises. Therapists advise grieving patients to express such anger fully, because it's a natural response that helps rebind them to reality; founders may benefit from this technique as well.
- *Bargaining:* To cope with feelings of helplessness and vulnerability, people in this stage aim to regain control by constructing a narrative that explains their loss. Accordingly, the founder will ruminate over "What ifs?"—"What if we'd pivoted earlier? What if we'd slowed our growth? What if we'd never entered the European market?"
- *Depression:* At some point, a grieving individual may be overwhelmed by feelings of hopelessness and emptiness and may not wish to be around others. At this stage, with a diminished sense of self-worth, a founder may be thinking, "What's the point of launching another venture? I clearly don't have what it takes to win."
- *Acceptance:* This is the goal for the end of the recovery phase: a founder who's at peace with what happened and feels, "I'm going to be okay."

The recovery phase tends to be gradual; time *does* heal, but sometimes quite slowly. Therapists encourage grieving patients to acknowledge their pain—keeping a journal can help—and to expect erratic progress as they work through their loss, with some backsliding. Establishing a daily routine can help restore a sense of control.

Likewise, physical fitness can be therapeutic. Anthony Soohoo, for example, spent the first two weeks after Dot & Bo's demise at a friend's house, doing little more than meditating and exercising. And, of course, talking through her feelings can help a founder move forward. A psychologist can play this role—though a failed founder may no longer have healthcare coverage and may not be able to afford professional counseling.

Revisiting old hobbies or activities—and finding new ones—can provide a welcome distraction from unproductive rumination and help the founder rebuild self-confidence. And taking some first steps on the professional front—starting a job search, taking on a consulting project, or jotting down early thoughts about a new venture—can provide motivation and hope. Notre Dame professor Dean Shepherd, who has studied the psychology of failed entrepreneurs, observes that alternating between distractions of this nature and ruminating on the recent failure can be restorative.

This is borne out by the experience of Avni Patel Thompson, founder of the failed high-touch childcare service Poppy: "Talking about Poppy's failure with other founders and with my husband helped immensely," she recalls. "In some ways it felt like I had disappeared. But looking back, a lot happened. My family moved to Vancouver, I took the summer to learn how to code full-time, and I spent a lot of time talking to parents—dozens of them. I was still captivated by challenges with household operations and the 'invisible workload' which falls disproportionately on the shoulders of women. The entrepreneurial flicker was starting to come back."

Wise advice from Adi Hillel, founder of the failed startup Hubitus, a virtual hub and online framework for freelancers, sums up these steps: "Fighting it won't help. Let go. Allow yourself to fail without judging. Do nothing. Go to the cinema, you probably haven't seen a decent movie in six months. Meet some friends. Answer 'I don't know' when you're asked about your plans for the future. . . . Be gentle with yourself. Remember that everything is temporary, and that you are temporarily depressed. Very often, our negative predisposition towards our negative feelings is the thing that holds us back, not the feelings themselves. Take the time to process your loss. Accept it. And know that you're about to get strong again."

Reflection

After cycling through the strong emotions triggered by loss, a founder will be ready to move to the next phase of her post-failure journey: reflecting on what happened and learning from her start-up's demise. Absorbing lessons from the failure of one's startup is not easy for two reasons. First, when things go wrong, our ego-defensive wiring often leads us to blame others, or external circumstances, rather than our own shortcomings. Second, grief can impair learning, and the strong emotions experienced by a failed founder can pose such an obstacle.

For these reasons, some skip the reflection phase altogether, or learn precious little from it. These founders tend to cluster around one of the two ends of a "Who's to blame?" continuum. At one end, a founder concludes that she made a series of big mistakes that doomed her startup because she is hopelessly inept—that she was, and in the future forever will be, truly unfit to lead a startup. For someone who's feeling dejected and despondent after a shutdown, this interpretation is a natural extension of the sense of diminished self-worth that often accompanies feeling depressed.

At the other end of the spectrum are founders—especially the narcissistic ones—who are convinced that they made all the right moves: an interpretation that's sure to salve a wounded ego. In this view, the venture failed either due to the irresponsible or malevolent actions of others—actions that the entrepreneur believes she could not have foreseen or forestalled—or due to misfortunes beyond her control, say, a sudden change in regulation or a capital market meltdown that shut off the funding spigot for healthy startups.

Now, some entrepreneurs really are ill-suited to lead a startup and should find another line of work. And, as we've seen, startup failure is sometimes due solely to misfortune rather than either an entrepreneur's errors or a mix of misfortune and mistakes. So, some founders legitimately belong at the ends of the "Who's to blame?" continuum. But too many others place themselves at these extremes on the basis of a flawed self-analysis. When this happens, both they and society lose out. When individuals who might actually be competent or even talented entrepreneurs walk off the playing field because they're convinced they lack the "right stuff," the world will never get to see the ventures they might have built. And when their cocksure counterparts at the other end of the continuum get back on the horse and risk repeating the same mistakes that threw them out of the saddle on their previous ride, they, along with a new set of teammates and investors, are likely to land with another thud.

How to avoid these extremes and absorb the right lessons from a venture's demise? First, you should allow the passage of time to work its healing powers. With some distance from the shutdown, its emotional sting will diminish, making it easier to see what went wrong, what mistakes you made, and what you might have done differently. Second, you should write up your postmortem analysis; this can help you make sense of what happened, as writing compels you to present an argument, exposing any gaps or logical inconsistencies. Finally, you should test your conclusions with people who know you and the story of your failed venture well, asking, "Do these lessons ring true?"

All of the founders whose failed ventures were profiled in previous chapters went through a process like this—and all of them learned a lot from it. Of course, the conclusions from such in-depth self-reflection will vary markedly from founder to founder. But Jason Goldberg's postmortem analysis of his role in Fab's failure offers useful guidance to failed founders. As he wrote in a blog post:

Every founder should go through a soul-searching exercise after failure. They should ask themselves a series of questions along the lines of:

- Was failure avoidable? Could I/should we have done more or something different to create or preserve value? (You'll be asking yourself this for years, replaying the events over and over again in your head and in conversations with others.)

- Is a startup really for me?
- If I had to do it all over again, would I?
- What did I learn from the experience?
- What did the experience teach me about what I'm personally good at and where I need to improve?
- Would people follow me into battle again? Should they?
- Would people invest in me again? Should they?

Much like Christina Wallace, who asked seventy friends and professional contacts "What am I good at?" Goldberg also shared his resulting self-assessment with "co-founders, board members, team members, my executive coach, investors, my husband—to make sure I wasn't missing anything. [I learned that I] was well-suited to be a startup founding CEO, but that in order to avoid future failure, I would need to either commit to learning how to scale operations more professionally and/or empower others to do it for me."

Goldberg—who ultimately bounced back and went on to co-found Moxie, a platform that connects consumers with fitness and yoga instructors—offers the following advice for failed founders on the rebound: "Home in on something that you are really, really, good at, and get back to basics doing that. Prove to yourself and to others that you still have mad skills that can have a positive impact, whether inside of an established company, at another startup, writing a book, teaching, volunteering, and so on. Just find one thing after your failure that reminds you that you are still very good at something valuable."

Reentry

After this period of reflection, an entrepreneur will be better equipped to confront the question "What next?" A surprisingly large percentage of failed founders get back on that horse after the demise of their ventures. When I examined the career paths of a random sample of fifty entrepreneurs who shut down their venture capital–backed startups in 2015, I found that 52 percent of serial entrepreneurs (those who had founded at least one other startup prior to the one that failed in 2015) went on to launch yet another venture, and 48 percent of first-time entrepreneurs launched another venture within five years of their 2015 failure.

For those who want to try their hand at another new venture but are afraid their failure will carry an indelible stigma, there's some good news: For most founders—especially those who preserved relationships with team members and investors by engineering a graceful shutdown—the problem doesn't appear to be as acute as many of them feared. Founders interviewed by the late Jason Cope of Lancaster University all found attractive opportunities after their venture failed and didn't experience meaningful stigmatization or rejection, as some had expected. The same is also true for the entrepreneurs profiled in this book (see the sidebar "What They Did Next").

The best way to avoid being stigmatized is to take responsibility for the failure of your venture and explain clearly what you've learned and how those lessons will influence the way you'll manage and lead in the future. Lindsay Hyde believes it was important to acknowledge that Baroo was a failure, rather than trying to spin the outcome: "Because we ultimately sold our assets, we could have claimed that we exited and called that a victory. Many founders of failed startups do that. But I wanted to publicly take responsibility and own the narrative."

When pitching their reentry plans, founders will get a better reception if they can say how their failure shaped those plans. For example, Rand Fishkin at Moz (the marketing software startup whose failed product line expansion nearly tanked the venture and caused a large layoff) expressed his discomfort with the way that VCs push entrepreneurs to "swing for the fences." As a result, he insists that when he launches another startup, "I won't pursue venture capital. For me, it's too restrictive. Venture capital forces a binary outcome—either succeed spectacularly (a true rarity) or collapse (far more common). It's absolutely the right call for those seeking to go truly big, but I want the freedom to choose a path of slow, profitable growth, perhaps never selling at all and simply building a business that yields profits for employees and a reliable, high-quality product for customers."

Lindsay Hyde took the opposite viewpoint. Reflecting on Baroo's failure, she said she was "100 percent ready" to be a founder again in the future: "What I have learned about myself is that I like to grow things fast. I like the challenge of building something with scale." Hyde recognized that given these goals, raising venture capital would be necessary to "pour gas on the fire."

If, after a period of introspection, you've addressed the questions Jason Goldberg posed in the "Reflection" section above, you should have a good sense of whether launching another startup is the right next move. You now have a more complete view of the skills and attitudes that are required for entrepreneurial success—and whether you have them. Based on your experience with your last venture, you've amassed countless tactical dos and don'ts—like whether to seek VC funding. Finally, you've closely examined your motivations. In particular, how much risk are you willing to bear? How important is independence—being your own boss? Accumulating personal wealth? The challenge of leading a great team? Making the world a better place?

Armed with new insights on what it takes to succeed as an entrepreneur as well as deeper self-knowledge and self-awareness, you'll be ready to decide whether to take another ride on the startup roller coaster.

What They Did Next

The entrepreneurs profiled in this book all landed on their feet after their ventures failed.

- After Jibo's shutdown, **Steve Chambers** served as chief marketing officer of Sense Labs, a green tech startup, earned master's degrees in applied psychology from the University of Southern California and in educational technology from Harvard's Graduate School of Education (GSE), and is currently a doctoral student at GSE.
- After Quincy Apparel's failure, **Christina Wallace** launched the New York City campus of the Startup Institute. She then founded BridgeUp, an ed-tech startup affiliated with the American Museum of Natural History that inspires young women and minorities to pursue STEM college degrees and careers. Next, Wallace was VP-Growth for Bionic, a consulting firm that helps Fortune 100 corporations launch entrepreneurial ventures. In 2020, she joined the faculty of Harvard Business School, where she teaches entrepreneurship.
- After Quincy failed, co-founder **Alexandra Nelson** joined Google as a product manager. Two years later, she moved to Anheuser-Busch InBev, where she leads new venture efforts.
- After shutting down Triangulate, **Sunil Nagaraj** spent six years as a VC at Bessemer Venture Partners, then launched his own seed stage fund, Ubiquity Ventures.
- After Baroo's failure, **Lindsay Hyde** spent two years as a venture partner at Moderne Ventures, then joined the Wildflower Foundation, where she leads efforts to create a network of entrepreneur-run, community-connected Montessori "micro schools."
- After Fab and Hem were sold, **Jason Goldberg** co-founded four Berlin-based startups, most recently Moxie, a platform that connects consumers seeking online fitness and yoga classes with instructors.

• After Dot & Bo shut down, **Anthony Soohoo** joined Walmart as executive vice president of its Home Division—a business with billions of dollars in revenue.

• **Shai Agassi** founded another clean tech startup after Better Place failed: Newrgy, which remains in stealth mode but is speculated to focus on public transportation solutions.

Letter to a First-Time Founder

Dear Founder:

Congratulations for taking the plunge—for committing to work full-time on that startup concept you've been pursuing. You asked me to share some advice based on the work I've done on entrepreneurial failure. I hope that all you've read in the preceding chapters has been helpful. Here, I want to leave you with a few more words about the challenges you'll face when running an early-stage venture. Believe me, leading a late-stage startup brings an entirely new set of thorny problems. But before you can tackle them, you've got to run the early-stage gauntlet. If you make it through that, I'll write you a follow-up letter!

As a first-time founder, you've probably heard all of the conventional wisdom about what makes a great entrepreneur. But while this advice is mostly sound, following it *blindly* might actually boost your odds of failing. If you read books and blogs that offer encouragement to first-time founders like you, you'll see six points emphasized repeatedly:

1. **Just Do It!** Great entrepreneurs have a bias for action; they make things happen and they move fast to capture opportunity. They trust their instincts and don't overanalyze a situation. All of

this makes sense. Lacking the resources of big corporations pursuing the same opportunities, being decisive and nimble is one of the few advantages that an entrepreneur has—and it's a big one.

And yet, a bias for action may tempt you to truncate exploration (searching for a compelling solution to a pressing problem) and move too soon toward expansion (building and selling a product). As we've seen, the exploration phase is critical: That's when you do the research needed to identify unmet customer needs and consider alternative solutions to satisfy them. If you are champing at the bit to build and sell and you decide to skip this research, you may find yourself locked prematurely into a flawed solution—and a **false start.**

2. **Be Persistent!** Entrepreneurs encounter setbacks over and over again. Products have glitches or are delayed. Rivals and regulators spring unwanted surprises. Prospective customers, investors, and employees repeatedly say "No, thanks!" A true entrepreneur dusts herself off and goes back at it; she must be persistent and resilient.

However, if persistence turns into stubbornness, you may have difficulty recognizing a *false start* for what it is. Also, you may be reluctant to pivot when it should be clear that your solution isn't working well. Delaying a pivot eats up scarce capital, reducing your venture's runway.

3. **Bring Passion!** Like persistence, passion—a burning desire to have a world-changing impact—can power an entrepreneur through the most daunting challenges. And passion can motivate employees, investors, and partners to help make your dream a reality.

But in the extreme, passion can translate into overconfidence: the conviction that you've already divined the right solution to a crucial problem, so there's no need for up-front research. This increases your risk of a *false start*. Likewise, passion can blind you to the fact that your product isn't meeting customer needs, thereby delaying a necessary pivot. Finally, early adopters may identify with and share your ardent desire to find a solution to their problems. This can lead to a **false positive** failure if you craft a solution that appeals to these loyal, supportive early adopters but not to mainstream customers.

4. **Grow!** Y Combinator's Paul Graham says, "A startup is a company designed to grow fast . . . if you get growth, everything else tends to fall into place. Which means you can use growth like a compass to make almost every decision you face"—for example, how much to spend on marketing and which employees to hire. Rapid growth is a magnet for investors and talent, and gives a team a great morale boost, too.

On the other hand, the constant pressure to grow may tempt you to curtail customer discovery research and prematurely launch your product, making a *false start*. And remember that rapid growth puts heavy demands on team members and partners. If you have **bad bedfellows,** growth may exacerbate quality problems and depress profit margins.

5. **Focus!** Resources are limited in an early-stage startup, and as an entrepreneur you can only do so much. So, you should focus on what's most important. Find your target customers and create a product that dazzles them. Anything that distracts from that priority is a problem! Scuttle your side projects. Skip the conference speaking engagement.

But excessive focus comes with risks. If you concentrate all of your efforts on a single customer segment, your logical target will be early adopters. But focusing only on them and ignoring the needs of mainstream customers can yield a *false positive*. Likewise, if you haven't tried to sell your product to any other customers segments, or you have only employed a single marketing method, you may have trouble identifying options when it comes time to pivot.

6. **Be Scrappy!** Because resources are limited, entrepreneurs must conserve them by being frugal and figuring out clever ways to make do with less.

True enough, but if your startup cannot consistently deliver on its value proposition because your team lacks crucial skills, you'll face the decision of whether to hire new employees with those skills. If those candidates demand high compensation, a scrappy, frugal founder might say, "We'll just have to do without them"—and risk being stuck with *bad bedfellows*.

So, you should follow the conventional advice—most of the time. You should be scrappy, passionate, and persistent—most of the time. You should move decisively and put a laser-like focus on your top priorities, including growth—most of the time.

In other words, you should view these principles less as gospel and more as a tool for making decisions when the stakes are low, or on those rare occasions when you must make a split-second, high-stakes decision and you just don't have enough time to assess the trade-offs thoroughly.

Complex decisions that can, if bungled, boost your odds of failure—for example, shifting from exploring to expanding; balancing the needs of early adopters and mainstream customers; pivoting; or hiring experts—should *not* be made according to simple rules. Rather, you should weigh your options and trade-offs deliberately. In particular, be careful with the widely held presumption that entrepreneurs should trust and follow their gut instincts. Under the pressure of bet-the-company decisions, your gut will be wracked by strong emotions—and that can obscure the right move. Sleep on these decisions—maybe for two nights. Then, write up your analysis of options and trade-offs, and share it with team members and investors. I truly believe that with crucial choices, what Nobel Prize–winning economist Daniel Kahneman calls "slow thinking" will boost your odds of survival.

The fact that you've already committed to an entrepreneurial path, knowing full well that your odds of failure are high, suggests to me that you've come to terms with that possibility. You're likely aware that while failure may be painful, the entrepreneurial path is, for many people, an irresistible draw—a career calling. You may well be one of them.

Several years ago, when startup valuations were booming, I worried that my current students—who were in middle school when the late 1990s Internet bubble burst—were launching startups without appreciating the implications of another industry bust. I feared they were running headfirst, like a herd, toward a bruising outcome. So, I wrote to a number of my former students who'd launched ventures during 1999 and 2000—almost all of which failed when nuclear winter set in. I asked them: Do you regret founding your startup?

To my surprise, all but one alumni founder insisted they had no regrets whatsoever. Instead, they spoke about their pride in building a product, a team, and a business. They pointed to everything they had learned, and to the incredible experience they got from being a general manager, in charge of every aspect of their venture—with a level of responsibility that paled in comparison to what they would have had as an employee. And a couple of them added, "I'm glad that I won't have to tell my grandchildren that when the Internet took off, I watched from the sidelines, working at an investment bank."

So, founder, I hope that after reading this book, you're ready to get off the sidelines. It will be an amazing ride, creating something out of nothing. To do that, think fast *and* think slow. And don't lose sight of why you got behind the wheel in the first place. The world needs entrepreneurs like you to create jobs and produce the kind of innovation we need to solve society's problems. Go build something great!

Best wishes,
Tom Eisenmann

Acknowledgments

Launching a new venture takes a team; so does writing a book. A terrific team contributed to *Why Startups Fail*. I'm enormously grateful to the hundreds of people who shared insights and helped with my research.

I first want to acknowledge an intellectual debt to the many practitioners whose trailblazing ideas about startup management shaped my thinking in profound ways. Foremost among them are Steve Blank, Paul Graham, Reid Hoffman, Ben Horowitz, Geoffrey Moore, Eric Ries, Peter Thiel, and Fred Wilson.

I'm likewise beholden to the founders who shared the stories that this book is built around: Steve Chambers, Jason Goldberg, Lindsay Hyde, Sunil Nagaraj, Alexandra Nelson, Anthony Soohoo, and Christina Wallace. These founders also generously and candidly recounted their experiences to my MBA students, as did Katia Beauchamp, Steve Carpenter, Jerry Colonna, Rand Fishkin, Mike Gozzo, Justin Joffe, Chet Kanojia, Avni Patel Thompson, and Ted Wiley. It's easy to visit a classroom to trumpet one's success; it takes more courage to talk openly and thoughtfully about setbacks. By doing so, these founders have given a great gift to the next generation of entrepreneurs. For that, for the trust they showed in me, and for the insights I've gained from them, I'm deeply appreciative.

I interviewed many other entrepreneurs and investors when researching this book, and in particular I wish to thank James Currier, Abby Falik, Adam Kanner, Samir Kaul, Aileen Lee, Mike Maples, and Dipish Rai for their thoughts about startup failure. I'm also obliged to Paul Baier, Ellen Chisa, and Cathy Han for their valuable feedback on a draft of the book. I'm grateful to the hundreds of founders who completed my survey on drivers of early-stage startup performance, along with the four entrepreneurs who helped me debug the survey questionnaire: Cathy Han, Lindsay Hyde, Michael Schrader, and Avni Patel Thompson.

Harvard Business School (HBS) has been my professional home for the past twenty-seven years, and I owe a tremendous debt of gratitude to many members of its community for their ideas and encouragement—and to the HBS Division of Research for the generous financial support provided for this multiyear project.

Foremost, it's been exciting and rewarding to teach several thousand dazzling students at HBS, and to stay in touch with them after they graduate. I'm constantly learning from my current students and from alumni. In particular, I wish to thank the students who took a chance and signed up for version 1.0 of my MBA elective "Entrepreneurial Failure." Our discussions battle-tested and greatly improved the concepts that found expression in *Why Startups Fail*.

Many past and present faculty colleagues have been my collaborators in building courses and writing cases about startups; they've taught me a lot and I've had great fun working with them. These colleagues were also partners in developing and refining the conceptual frameworks used in this book, including the diamond-and-square model, the Six S's of scaling, and the RAWI test. For their rich insights and invaluable feedback, I wish to thank Julia Austin, Joe Fuller, Shikhar Ghosh, Felda Hardymon, Scott Kominers, Josh Krieger, Joe Lassiter, Stig Leschly, Alan MacCormack, Jim Matheson, Ramana Nanda, Jeffrey Rayport, Mark Roberge, Toby Stuart, Noam Wasserman, and Russ Wilcox. Special thanks to Jeff Bussgang, Frank Cespedes, and Mitch Weiss not only for the opportunity to collaborate over the years but also for providing comments on a draft of *Why Startups Fail* and for guidance on the publishing process.

I'm immensely grateful to two senior colleagues who, as mentors, have had a huge influence on my research and teaching: Bill Sahlman and Howard Stevenson, who together built the HBS Entrepreneurial Management Unit. Bill taught the MBA elective "Entrepreneurial Finance" for over thirty years and also launched "The Entrepreneurial Manager," HBS's required first-year MBA course on entrepreneurship. I'm greatly honored to hold the chaired professorship named for Howard, who proffered the definition of entrepreneurship that we've used at HBS for decades: the pursuit of opportunity beyond resources controlled. Bill and Howard have inspired countless students to launch new ventures, and they've recruited and trained dozens of entrepreneurship scholars and educators.

Over the past several years, I've enjoyed the support of many terrific HBS researchers who've helped collect and analyze data on failed startups and co-authored the teaching cases that I draw upon in this book and use in my MBA courses. They include Halah AlQahtani, Sarah Dillard, Alex Godden, Olivia Graham, David Kiron, Ann Leamon, Susie Ma, Lisa Mazzanti, Chris Payton, Jasper Rollmann, Stephan Rollmann, Jacey Taft, and Michael Zarian. Past and present colleagues at the HBS California Research Center have likewise assisted with case writing and by arranging interviews for this book; they include Lauren Barley, Allison Ciechanover, George Gonzalez, Jeff Huizinga, Nicole Keller, Liz Kind, and Alison Wagonfeld. Miltos Stefanidis deserves special thanks for managing the survey of early-stage startups that informs this book, and for helping me analyze the survey data.

I wish to thank my literary agent, Rafe Sagalyn, for his early and infectious enthusiasm for my book proposal, and for his wise counsel at every step along the way.

An author is lucky to have one great editor. I had three! Special thanks to my extraordinary editorial adviser, Phyllis Strong, who brought insight, incisive questions, and a flair for storytelling to the project. I'm likewise deeply grateful to my editor at Crown, Talia Krohn, for her thoughtful and thorough guidance. Talia has a discerning eye; she is a master at streamlining and restructuring a manuscript, and at flagging flaws in logic and gaps in evidence. She manages to make a book better while bolstering a writer's confidence and being fun and easy to work with. Finally, I wish to thank Roger Scholl, my editor at Crown prior to his retirement, for his confidence in my initial vision and his early stewardship of the project. Roger suggested the book's title, encouraged me to undertake a founder survey, brainstormed chapter topics, and helped me select case studies.

As I write this, I haven't yet met the team at Crown that will help with the book's marketing and publicity. Talia says that they are amazing, and I can't wait to work with them.

Saving the best for last: Thanks to my family! My son, Jack, a software engineer at a late-stage startup, helped me debug the book's cases, rubber ducking them while we walked our dog, Stan. My daughter, Caroline, was my secret weapon: She's a literary agent, and with that hat on, she provided keen guidance on key decisions throughout the publishing process. Finally, I'm deeply grateful to my wife, Jill, for her patience and for encouraging me to finally finish this project. I began outlining the book in 2014; for a long time its working title was *False Start*. Jill pointed out the irony of repeatedly starting and stopping work on a book with that title. In 2018, she said, "Enough: Make it happen!" That push, and sheltering in place for six months without distractions, were what it took to finish. Jack, Caroline, and Jill: With all my love, I dedicate this book to you.

Appendix

Early-Stage Startup Survey

To explore factors that contribute to startup failure and success, I conducted a survey of early-stage founder/CEOs in the spring of 2020. Based on PitchBook data, the survey targeted all U.S-based startups founded in 2013 or later that raised a first major funding round of $500,000 to $3 million between January 1, 2015, and April 30, 2018 (and no more than $250,000 prior to this first major round). This time frame allowed the ventures to develop their businesses for at least two years after their first funding round, yielding a spread in performance outcomes. The sample excluded biotech, energy, and material science–based startups, due to their distinctive performance drivers. These criteria yielded 3,263 candidates. For 2,822 of them, PitchBook had current contact information for the individual who was CEO when the startup raised its first major round. I reached out to all of them, and 470 founder/CEOs completed the survey: a solid 17 percent response rate.

Of the 470 who responded, 89 percent led startups that were still *operating and independent* when they completed the survey, 8 percent had *sold* their ventures, and 3 percent had *shut down*. This compares to 8 percent sold and 7 percent shut down among the 2,822 startups invited to participate. Consequently, shutdowns are somewhat underrepresented in the sample—but there are enough of them to draw statistically valid inferences about differences between less and more successful ventures.

Measuring Performance

My measure of performance was the change in the value of equity raised in a startup's first major funding round: Did the value of this equity increase, stay roughly the same, or decrease—at the extreme, going to zero? Specifically, the founder/CEOs of startups still operating were asked, *"As of December 31, 2019, before news of the coronavirus pandemic became widespread, how much would someone have paid for your startup's first round equity/convertible notes?"* The multiple-choice options were 1) >150 percent of the amount originally invested; 2) 50 percent to 150 percent; or 3) <50 percent. Respondents were also told, *"We know that first round equity and convertible notes cannot normally be sold—but imagine that they could. How much might an experienced, well-diversified investor have paid your largest first round investor to take over their position on December 31, 2019? Assume that equity or notes would be transferred with terms intact (e.g., liquidation preferences, discounts, caps)."*

Respondents whose startups were sold or shut down were asked the same question about the value (if any) of proceeds distributed to early investors. Specifically: Compared to the amount these investors originally invested, were any proceeds they received worth >150 percent; 50 percent to 150 percent; or <50 percent?

In my analysis below, the >150 percent outcome is labeled "High Valuation," while the <50 percent outcome is designated "Low Valuation." Of those surveyed, 63 percent reported a high valuation. Low valuations accounted for 10 percent of overall responses, consisting of 64 percent of the startups that had shut down, but only 7 percent of the ventures still operating.

To explore factors that contribute to startup failure, I decided to compare low and high valuation outcomes, rather than surveying startups that had actually shut down and then comparing them to successful going concerns. I did this for two reasons. First, to obtain a sufficient number of shutdowns for statistical analysis, I would have had to sample startups further into the past. That expanded time frame would have posed problems with the reliability of respondents' recollections.

Second, and more important, recall this book's definition of failure: *A venture has failed if its early investors did not—or never will—get back more money than they put in.* By that definition, failure seems like a distinct possibility for a startup that, while still operating today, has a current equity valuation that's less than one-half of the original value of the seed capital it raised. Some of these low valuation ventures might be turned around and ultimately succeed. And, many of the high valuation ventures will ultimately fail. However, since those outcomes can't be reliably predicted, the goal here is to compare groups of early-stage startups that, based on the book's definition, are *trending toward failure* with those *trending toward success.*

Since valuation outcomes were self-reported, it's possible some respondents inflated their performance to massage their egos, even though I had promised I would not divulge their identities when presenting survey results. Nevertheless, even if such inflation happened, I believe that the findings below would still hold. To explain: If some respondents exaggerated their performance, then the high valuation responses I observed would be a blend of data from startups that truly do have a high valuation and those that inflated their valuation. If a factor genuinely has a strong, positive impact on a startup's valuation, this kind of blending would reduce the reported impact of that factor. Consequently, if the survey shows that a factor has a strong impact, we can presume that its impact would be even stronger if any inflated valuations could be corrected.

Analyzing the Survey Data

Below, I explore relationships between valuation outcomes and various factors using both *bivariate* and *multivariate analysis.*

- *Bivariate analysis* asks whether there is a statistically significant relationship between two variables—say, A and B—ignoring the possible influence of other variables.
- However, if one or more *other* variables are correlated with *both* A and B, then we need to exercise caution before using A to predict outcomes for B.

• For example, the bivariate analysis below shows that *founders' age* and *founders' years of prior work experience in their startup's industry* each have a positive, statistically significant relationship with valuation outcomes: Older and more experienced founders are more likely to lead high valuation startups. However, age and experience are also positively correlated with each other: Individuals with more years of experience tend to be older. Consequently, we can't reliably predict the impact of age or experience on valuation outcomes using bivariate analysis alone. We need to look at their *joint* impact, using *multivariate analysis*.

• Multivariate analysis asks which, if any, "independent" variables reliably predict a "dependent" (i.e., outcome) variable. By examining the collective influence of multiple independent variables (also called "predictors"), multivariate analyses can show the extent to which the relationship between a given predictor and the outcome is unique—that is, independent of the influence of other predictors.

In the section that follows, I'll first examine how startup age, location, and industry sector are related to valuation outcomes. Next, for factors related to the various elements of the diamond-and-square framework presented in Chapter 2 (e.g., customer value proposition, marketing, founders, investors, etc.), I'll report 1) the results of bivariate analysis, then 2) results for any statistically significant predictors based on multivariate analysis, and finally 3) founders' relevant responses to the survey question, "If you could wind back the clock, what's the single most important thing you'd do differently in managing and leading your startup?"

In the tables below presenting the results of bivariate analysis, I'll show the percentage of founder/CEOs leading low valuation startups who selected one of the multiple-choice options for a given survey question, and then I'll compare that to the response from founder/CEOs of high valuation startups. For ease of interpretation, I'll omit the middling (50 percent to 150 percent) valuation results. Valuation outcomes and most of the factors are *categorical variables,* that is, their values fall into distinct categories (e.g., low, middling, and high in the case of valuation). Accordingly, I use a *chi square test of independence* to measure the strength of the relationship between a given factor and valuation outcomes. In the tables below, bolded figures are statistically significant with at least 95 percent confidence.

My multivariate analysis employs *multinomial logistic regression*. For a categorical dependent variable, multinomial regression separately estimates for each outcome category the collective influence of a set of independent variables on the probability of observing that outcome. In the text below, for variables in my regression model that are statistically significant predictors of low valuation with at least 90 percent confidence, I'll show—bolded—the predicted probability of observing a low valuation outcome as the focal variable is ranged from its lowest possible survey response to the highest possible response, while holding the level of all other independent variables constant at their respective sample means. When gauging the impact of these variables, note that the baseline predicted probability of a low valuation (with *all* variables at their sample mean) is 10 percent.

When interpreting results, remember that **correlation does not always imply causation.** If a certain factor—say, a strong company culture—is more often associated with high valuation startups than low valuation counterparts, it might be true that a strong culture leads to strong performance. Or, the reverse might be true. The statistical techniques I use here cannot determine causation.

Age, Location, and Industry Sector

Startups in the sample with low and high valuation were founded, on average, 5.1 and 4.9 years ago, respectively. This difference isn't statistically significant. Compared to counterparts headquartered elsewhere, startups located in California, accounting for 32 percent of the sample, were somewhat more likely to have both low valuations (13 percent for California vs. 9 percent elsewhere) and high valuations (65 percent vs. 62 percent). While these differences aren't large or statistically significant, the pattern suggests that entrepreneurs in California—perhaps in the sway of Silicon Valley's cultural norms—might be more inclined to "swing for the fences," managing in ways that boost both failure and success odds.

Based on multivariate analysis, the predicted probability of low valuation for startups offering information technology (accounting for 53 percent of the sample) was **8 percent,** compared to **12 percent** for startups in other sectors—a modest but statistically significant difference.

Customer Value Proposition

Founder/CEOs leading low valuation startups conducted significantly less customer research before launching their products than did their high valuation counterparts. They also were less likely to complete rigorous MVP tests and less likely to have a very deep understanding of customer needs and competitors. In contrast to their high valuation counterparts, more founder/CEOs of low valuation startups admitted that they had completed too few or too many pivots. In multivariate analysis, pivoting too often had a big impact, increasing the predicted probability of a low valuation to **19 percent** (vs. **6 percent** for an optimal level of pivoting). Likewise, not pivoting often enough increased the probability of a low valuation to **22 percent.**

These themes were echoed in founders' responses to the survey question, "What's the single most important thing you'd do differently?" Fourteen percent of all respondents cited a need to gain deeper understanding of customer needs and to validate demand for their solution by conducting more up-front research and MVP tests. Many of these respondents also said they'd aim for more focus in their product feature set, product line breadth, and range of customer segments served. For several founders, "do-over" priorities included launching faster to get early customer feedback and pivoting more rapidly.

These survey results are consistent with the False Start pattern described in Chapter 4: Founders who skip up-front research are more likely to need to pivot away from an initially flawed solution. Furthermore, a false start consumes capital, reducing the number of pivots that the startup can ultimately complete.

In addition, founder/CEOs of low valuation startups reported greater differences between the needs of early adopters and mainstream customers than their high valuation counterparts. This divide would increase their exposure to the False Positive failure pattern described in Chapter 5.

In terms of other performance drivers related to a venture's customer value proposition, high valuation startups were more likely to pursue new product categories and faced fewer direct rivals; and their founder/ CEOs were more likely to say that their products had a big edge over those of their most important rivals, in terms of unique features and performance benefits. However, the impact of these factors was neither strong nor statistically significant in bivariate analysis. This suggests that it takes more than just a great product to build a great company.

Customer Value Proposition Factors

Factors	Criteria	Low Valuation	High Valuation
Customer research before product launch	Six or more person months completed	38%	53%
Use of MVPs	One or more rigorous MVPs completed	29%	47%
Pivots	Did too few/too many	40%/13%	15%/4%
Early adopter vs. mainstream customer needs	Needs were different/ nearly identical	33%/2%	25%/16%
Understanding of customer needs before product launch	Very deep	15%	29%
Product category maturity	Category existed for less than two years	44%	53%
Number of direct competitors	Ten or more	35%	25%

Factors	Criteria	Low Valuation	High Valuation
Understanding of competition at product launch	Very deep	21%	32%
Product had unique features and superior performance	We/rivals had a big edge	31%/23%	38%/9%

Technology and Operations

Factors related to technology and operations did not have a statistically significant impact on valuation outcomes. Likewise, they were mentioned by only 3 percent of survey respondents as "the most important thing they'd do differently." Low valuation startups were somewhat less likely to follow a highly structured approach to managing the engineering function; were less reliant on proprietary intellectual property; and, consistent with the Bad Bedfellows failure pattern described in Chapter 3, were more likely to report that they relied too much or too little on third-party providers for technology and operational capability.

Technology and Operations Factors

Factors	Criteria	Low Valuation	High Valuation
Engineering management	Followed highly structured approach	17%	21%
Proprietary intellectual property	Was extremely important	8%	28%
Reliance on 3rd-party technology and operations providers	Too little/too much	23%/25%	20%/16%

Marketing

Founder/CEOs of low valuation startups were much more likely to say they spent too much money on generating demand. Based on multivariate analysis, startups that overspent significantly on demand generation had a **26 percent** predicted probability of low valuation, compared to only **6 percent** for those that spent at optimal levels.

There were no material differences between low and high valuation startups in terms of their reliance on channel partners to acquire customers. And, when they did rely on channel partners, low and high valuation startups were equally likely to report dissatisfaction with their partners' performance.

Only 4 percent of survey respondents mentioned factors related to marketing as their top "do-over" priority. Most of these founders led high valuation startups and said that they should have spent more—and spent earlier—on marketing.

Marketing Factors

Factors	Criteria	Low Valuation	High Valuation
Spending to generate demand	Overspent modestly or significantly	47%	21%
Relied upon channel partners to acquire customers	Not at all	61%	65%
Satisfaction with channel partners (if the startup used them)	Low or very low	41%	41%

Profit Formula

With respect to their startup's profit formula, founder/CEOs of low and high valuation ventures were equally likely to report a high level of confidence in their estimate of their startup's total addressable market (TAM). Confidence in this estimate matters: In our multivariate regression model, moving from low to high confidence in TAM estimates reduced the predicted probability of low valuation from **15 percent** to **10 percent**.

By contrast, founder/CEOs leading low valuation startups were much less confident than their high valuation counterparts in their estimates of unit economics, LTV/CAC ratios, and six-month cash flow projections. Confidence in LTV/CAC estimates was a particularly strong predictor of valuation performance. In multivariate analysis, moving from low to high confidence regarding estimates of LTV/CAC ratios reduced the predicted probability of low valuation from **18 percent** to just **2 percent**.

Not surprisingly, founder/CEOs leading low valuation startups also were more likely to report an excessive cash burn rate and were less confident that their ventures had a clear path to long-term profitability. In multivariate analysis, startups that reported a burn rate that was "much too high" had a **32 percent** predicted probability of low valuation. Those that had a very low level of confidence in their path to profitability had a **36 percent** predicted probability of low valuation, compared to just **2 percent** for startups that reported a very high level of confidence.

Interestingly, low valuation startups that are still operating were significantly more likely than their high valuation counterparts to report that they currently have positive operating cash flow. We might surmise that some of these low valuation startups are what some VCs call "zombies": They can generate enough cash to survive but are unlikely ever to yield a positive return to investors.

Ten percent of survey respondents cited better financial management as their top "do-over" priority; their comments focused mostly on burn rates. Founders who said they wished they'd reduced their early burn rate (or, equivalently, wished they'd focused more on earning early revenue) outnumbered those who said they should have spent more aggressively by a seven-to-one margin.

Profit Formula Factors

Factors	Criteria	Low Valuation	High Valuation
Confidence in total addressable market estimate	High	48%	50%
Confidence in unit economics estimates	High	21%	40%
Confidence in LTV/ CAC estimates	High	2%	23%
Confidence in six-month cash flow projections	High	21%	39%
Confidence in having clear path to long-term profitability	High or very high	13%	53%
Burn rate	Much too high	23%	4%
Operating cash flow (for startups still operating and independent)	Is now positive	35%	20%

Founders

Compared to high valuation startups, low valuation startups were somewhat less likely to be led by a sole founder and more likely to have a CEO who was young and/or had, prior to founding, less than two years of full-time work experience.

Consistent with the Bad Bedfellows failure pattern, founder/CEOs of low valuation startups had significantly less prior work experience in the industry in which their startup operates. They were also much more likely to report a lack of clarity between co-founders over roles, along with frequent conflict between co-founders and with other senior team members.

Compared to counterparts leading high valuation startups, founders leading low valuation startups were also somewhat less likely to be serial founders; equally likely to have a PhD; more likely to have an MBA; and more likely have a degree from one of the world's top fifty universities (as ranked by *US News & World Report*). However, relationships between these factors and valuation performance were not statistically significant.

Due to bias in survey response rates, I do not analyze the relationship between gender and valuation outcomes. Within the full set of 2,822 startups invited to participate in the survey, female founder/CEOs led 12 percent of all ventures that had shut down. By comparison, within my sample of 470 survey respondents, female founder/CEOs led 29 percent of all startups that had shut down. Put another way, failed female founders were much more willing to accept my invitation to complete the survey than their failed male counterparts. Since failed female founders are overrepresented in my sample, inferences about any relationship between gender and valuation performance would not be valid.

Founder Factors

Factors	Criteria	Low Valuation	High Valuation
Number of founders	One	15%	21%
Serial founder	Founded a venture before this one	48%	52%
Has degree from one of world's top fifty universities	Top fifty based on *US News & World Report* rankings	54%	37%
Has MBA or similar management-focused master's degree		44%	33%
Has PhD		8%	8%
CEO age	<30 years old	21%	16%

Factors	Criteria	Low Valuation	High Valuation
CEO full-time work experience before founding	Less than two years	13%	4%
CEO experience in the startup's industry	Four or more years	52%	63%
Role clarity among senior team members	Not very or not at all clear	17%	6%
Frequency of conflict between senior team members	Frequent or almost daily	33%	18%

Compared to their counterparts leading high valuation startups, founder/CEOs of low valuation ventures were less likely to co-found with former co-workers and more likely to do so with former classmates, family members, and—as with Quincy Apparel—friends. However, these results weren't statistically significant.

CEO's Relationship with Co-Founders Before Founding

	Low Valuation	High Valuation
Co-workers	27%	43%
Classmates	17%	12%
Family	10%	7%
Friends	46%	38%

Founder/CEOs that lead low valuation startups reported similar motivations for pursuing an entrepreneurial career as their high valuation counterparts, but for each motivation, founder/CEOs of low valuation startups were somewhat less likely to report that this was "a crucial concern."

CEO's Motivations to Be an Entrepreneur:
"A Crucial Concern"

	Low Valuation	High Valuation
Independence/be own boss	33%	40%
Build something new, enduring, important	81%	90%
Accumulate wealth	17%	27%

Low and high valuation founder/CEOs for the most part reported similar self-assessed personality traits. Both groups cited "resilient," "visionary," and "charismatic" as the top three attributes that others would say "describes me well" or "describes me very well." A few interesting—but not statistically significant—differences emerged. Compared to their high valuation counterparts, low valuation founders were somewhat more likely to assess themselves as *charismatic* and *overconfident*. These are personality traits of the monomaniacal founders who often contribute to the Cascading Miracles failure pattern described in Chapter 9.

CEO's Self-Assessed Personality Traits:
"Describes Me Well/Very Well"

	Low Valuation	High Valuation
Charismatic	73%	68%
Consensus Builder	44%	52%
Control Freak	19%	18%
Headstrong	46%	48%
Introverted	17%	16%
Judgmental	25%	22%
Methodical	33%	51%

	Low Valuation	High Valuation
Overconfident	31%	21%
Perfectionist	25%	37%
Resilient	88%	96%
Risk Averse	15%	9%
Visionary	73%	81%

While some of the attributes of founders listed above had a statistically significant relationship with valuation outcomes in bivariate analysis, none of them were statistically significant predictors in multivariate regression. Put another way, it seems that a wide range of different founder types can succeed. And while choosing a talented "jockey" may be important for venture success, it isn't easy to pick the right leader based only on readily observable characteristics like age or personality type.

Founder issues were cited by 20 percent of respondents as their top "do-over" priority—second only to team issues. About half of these comments related to co-founder conflict. Poor co-founder fit—with respect to both skills and attitude—was frequently mentioned; it often resulted in a messy "divorce." Many other founders said they wished they'd done a better job understanding their co-founders' capabilities, motivations, and leadership style before agreeing to work together. Lack of clarity of roles and lack of agreement over goals were recurrent problems.

Other comments were self-directed, with founders sharing ideas for improving their own leadership style. On this front, recommendations were diverse and only a handful were mentioned more than once. Some examples include 1) show more confidence, 2) do a better job of prioritizing, 3) delegate more, 4) trust my instincts more and be less reliant on investors' guidance or team consensus, 5) focus more on strategy, 6) focus less on strategy and more on execution, 7) learn from other founders' experiences, 8) learn more about technology, 9) learn more about finance, 10) learn how to manage the personal stress that comes with founder life, 11) be less timid about spending, 12) go faster, 13) go slower—there's no rush, 14) be realistic about how long it will take to build a business, and 15) know when to throw in the towel.

The list above includes some contradictory recommendations. This says something, I suppose, not only about "mentor whiplash," but also about the vexing challenges that founders confront. With those challenges in mind, one comment captured much wisdom:

> Enjoy the ride and celebrate milestones more! Being an entrepreneur means subjecting yourself to one of the most insane roller coaster rides you could possibly imagine. You will encounter massive highs and brutal lows. Each challenge in the moment might seem insurmountable. Each win might seem like you have struck gold. I'll never forget when we secured our first $25,000 line of credit from a regional bank and thought our business problems were solved! But the goalpost marking "Success Here!" always seems to be just beyond your reach. Cherish memories that are earned and never waste a single bite of life!

Team

With respect to team factors, founder/CEOs of low valuation startups were more likely to report that their company lacked formal structure for managing human resources (e.g., recruitment, training, promotions, etc.). Not surprisingly, they were also significantly less likely to say their startup had a strong company culture. In multivariate analysis, moving from "much weaker" to "much stronger" when assessing the strength of one's company culture relative to that of peer startups reduced the probability of low valuation sharply, from **23 percent** to **6 percent**. As noted above, however, this correlation does not necessarily imply causation. A weak culture might be a consequence of the startup's problems, rather than the cause of its struggles.

In recruiting, low valuation startups were somewhat more likely to put too much emphasis on both skill and attitude. In multivariate analysis, the penchant to overemphasize skills had a small but statistically significant impact. Moving from "about optimal" to "too much" emphasis on skill increased the predicted probability of low valuation from **9 percent** to **14 percent**.

Team Factors

Factors	Criteria	Low Valuation	High Valuation
Human resources management	Had almost no HR structure	35%	16%
Company culture	Stronger than peer startups	42%	64%
Balance in hiring for skill vs. attitude	Too much or way too much emphasis on skill/attitude	31%/23%	21%/21%

When asked about the *performance* of their startup's heads of various functions, relative to the founder/CEO's *expectations,* the founder/CEOs of low and high valuation startups reported similar rates of dissatisfaction. On average, about one-quarter of the function heads were disappointments. A smaller percentage of those disappointing function heads were actually fired or demoted. Notably, in each function, dismissal rates were lower for low valuation startups; the difference was especially stark for the head of sales. In multivariate analysis, startups that never dismissed a sales head had a **13 percent** predicted probability of low valuation, compared to only **5 percent** for those that did.

Performance of Function Heads: "Below Expectations/Fired or Demoted"

Function	Low Valuation	High Valuation
Engineering	19%/17%	17%/21%

Function	Low Valuation	High Valuation
Product management	29%/13%	21%/19%
Operations	19%/13%	17%/16%
Marketing	35%/19%	33%/22%
Sales	29%/15%	33%/31%
Finance	25%/6%	12%/8%

Issues with building and managing a team comprised 28 percent of responses to the question, "If you could wind back the clock, what's the single most important thing you'd do differently?" No other topic received more comments. "Hire slow and fire fast" was mentioned by a full 5 percent of founders. A similar fraction recommended hiring A-quality rather than B-quality employees and advised more care and effort in recruiting—for example, by checking references carefully, insisting on a "tryout" before committing to a full-time position, and not hiring founders' friends.

Interestingly, only a handful of founders cited a need for more employees with relevant industry expertise; instead, 7 percent of respondents cited talent gaps in specific functions, including, in roughly equal numbers, sales, marketing, product management, engineering, and finance. Recruiting a stronger senior management team earlier was mentioned by another 4 percent of founders.

Many other team-related priorities were each mentioned by one or just a few founders, including 1) focusing more effort on company culture; 2) hiring an HR head earlier; 3) having a founder initially perform a function—especially sales—to better understand recruiting requirements; 4) introducing Objectives and Key Results (OKRs) or other goal-setting processes earlier to boost employee accountability; 5) better balancing the rate of hiring across different areas, for example, engineering versus business functions, or marketing versus sales; and 6) putting more emphasis on hiring for diversity.

Investors

Compared to high valuation counterparts, low valuation startups were somewhat more likely to have their first major investment round led by angels rather than by venture capital firms. Likewise, their first round was slightly less likely to include a "top 100" investor (as ranked by investors' number of first round investments among the 2,822 startups invited to participate in the survey). However, these relationships between investor type and valuation performance were not statistically significant.

Consistent with the Bad Bedfellows failure pattern, low valuation startups were more likely than their high valuation counterparts to have raised less capital than they'd targeted in their first round of fundraising. In multivariate analysis, raising less than 75 percent of a startup's initial funding goal resulted in an **18 percent** predicted probability of low valuation, compared to **7 percent** for startups that raised more than 125 percent of their initial goal. However, this is another variable for which correlation may not imply causation. Some startups may fail to meet their fundraising goals because it's evident to investors that they've enlisted a weak team or targeted a bad idea—or both. These startups may ultimately be shut down due to a lack of capital, but the root cause of their failure was a "jockey and/or horse" problem.

Founder/CEOs of low valuation startups were more likely to have been disappointed with the quality of advice they received from their investors, and more likely to report frequent, serious, and divisive conflict with investors over strategic priorities.

Investor Factors

Factors	Criteria	Low Valuation	High Valuation
First round investor type	Angel-led	19%	12%
Top 100 investor in first round		25%	29%

Factors	Criteria	Low Valuation	High Valuation
1st round amount of capital raised vs. goal	<75% of goal	25%	11%
Quality of advice from investors	Much less than expected	35%	22%
Amount of conflict with investors over priorities	Was frequent, serious, and divisive	10%	4%

Seventeen percent of founders' "do-over" comments concerned fundraising. More than half of those comments focused on the amount of capital raised in startups' seed round, with founders saying they should have raised more capital outnumbering those wishing they'd raised less by a five-to-one margin. Several founders also said they should have continued bootstrapping and avoided raising venture capital altogether. Five percent expressed dissatisfaction with their investors, frequently citing bad advice or conflict over strategic priorities.

To sum up, the survey results offer strong support for the early-stage failure patterns presented in Part I of this book. They also strongly show that entrepreneurial failure is due to a diverse set of factors rather than a single cause.

Notes

Introduction

3 **And, since more than two-thirds:** My startup failure rate estimate is based on multiple sources that present different mortality rates. Robert Hall and Susan Woodward, "The Burden of the Non-Diversifiable Risk of Entrepreneurship," *American Economic Review* 100, no. 3 (2010): 1163–1194, finds that three-quarters of venture capital–backed companies never return any equity proceeds to their entrepreneurs. Deborah Gage, "The Venture Capital Secret: 3 Out of 4 Startups Fail," *Wall Street Journal,* Sept. 20, 2012, summarizes unpublished research by Shikhar Ghosh that is consistent with Hall and Woodward's finding. Ghosh examined investments in over two thousand startups that received at least $1 million in venture capital funding from 2004 through 2010. He determined that 75 percent did not return investors' capital. Using a methodology similar to Ghosh's and analyzing returns for all startups that received a first round of venture capital financing between 1985 and 2009, a 55 percent failure rate is reported in William Kerr, Ramana Nanda, and Matthew Rhodes-Kropf, "Entrepreneurship as Experimentation," *Journal of Economic Perspectives* 28, no. 3 (2014): 25–48. This estimate is lower than Ghosh's due in part to the fact that Kerr et al. assume that all acquired startups that did not announce the value of their exit proceeds—the preponderance of acquisitions—were sold at a profit, for 1.5x the total capital they'd raised. In fact, many acquisitions yield a loss for investors. Most other estimates of startup failure rates fall between 50 percent and 90 percent. Differences in startup failure rate estimates depend largely on researchers' definitions of "startup" and "failure." Reported rates tend to be *lower* when failure is defined as an outright shutdown due to financial distress. However, this definition excludes "living dead" startups that survive but will never earn a positive return for investors, and also excludes acquisitions with proceeds less than total capital raised. Mortality rates tend to be *higher* if startups are defined as any entity that aims to pursue an entrepreneurial opportunity rather than just those that have raised a threshold amount of external funding. See Grace Walsh and James Cunningham, "Business Failure and Entrepreneurship: Emergence, Evolution and Future Research," *Foundations and Trends in Entrepreneurship* 12, no. 3 (2016): 163–285, for a summary of failure rate esti-

mates from various academic studies. Definitions of "startup" and "failure" are discussed in Ch. 1 of this book.

4 **Our alumni have founded:** PitchBook Data, Inc., "PitchBook Universities: 2019," PitchBook website. PitchBook is also the source for the list of HBS "unicorns" later in the paragraph.

5 **To get started:** There's a vast literature exploring failure in domains beyond entrepreneurship. Overviews include Megan McArdle, *The Up Side of Down: Why Failing Well Is the Key to Success* (New York: Viking, 2014); and Sarah Lewis, *The Rise: Creativity, the Gift of Failure, and the Search for Mastery* (New York: Simon & Schuster, 2014). Scott Sandage, *Born Losers: A History of Failure in America* (Cambridge, MA: Harvard University Press, 2005), provides a historical perspective on societal attitudes toward failure. Charles Perrow, *Normal Accidents: Living with High-Risk Technologies* (New York: Basic Books, 1984), analyzes the failure of complex systems such as nuclear power plants. Eliot Cohen and John Gooch, *Military Misfortunes: The Anatomy of Failure in War* (New York: Free Press, 1990, examines failure in battle. Richard Neustadt and Ernest May, *Thinking in Time: The Uses of History for Decision Makers* (New York: Free Press, 1989), contrasts foreign and domestic policy successes and failures. Atul Gawande, *The Checklist Manifesto: How to Get Things Right* (New York: Metropolitan Books, 2009), explores medical failures and how to avoid them.

5 **"If you cannot fail":** Eric Ries, *The Lean Startup: How Today's Entrepreneurs Use Radical Innovation to Create Successful Businesses* (New York: Currency, 2011), p. 56. The role of falsifiability in theory development and testing is discussed in Karl Popper, *The Logic of Scientific Discovery* (London: Hutchison, 1959). Sim Sitkin, "Learning through Failure: The Strategy of Small Losses," *Research in Organizational Behavior* 14 (1992): 231–266, similarly argues that "failure is an essential prerequisite for learning" because it stimulates experimentation. Sitkin explores factors that promote learning in organizational settings.

5 **By studying failure:** A. Bandura, *Social Learning Theory* (Englewood Cliffs, NJ: Prentice Hall, 1977), describes the process of vicarious learning and contrasts it to learning from direct experience. Jerker Denrell, "Vicarious Learning, Undersampling of Failure, and the Myths of Management," *Organization Science* 14, no. 3 (2003): 227–243, argues that when individuals in organizations learn vicariously, they are too likely to focus on successful rather than failed initiatives. According to Denrell, if risky strategies are more likely to result in both more successes *and* more failures, compared to safer strategies, then undersampling failures may lead to an inference that risky strategies are more attractive than they really are.

6 **Humans are wired:** Hans Hansen, "Fallacies," *The Stanford Encyclopedia of Philosophy* (online; Summer 2020 ed.), discusses John Stuart Mill's analysis of the single cause fallacy, which Mill categorizes as a fallacy of generalization of the type *post hoc ergo propter hoc.*

6 **Furthermore, we're prone:** Lee Ross, "The Intuitive Psychologist and His Shortcomings: Distortions in the Attribution Process," *Advances in Experimental Social Psychology* 10 (1977): 173–220, coins the term "fundamental attribution error." The BMW example is from Patrick Enright, "Road Rage Can Churn the Calmest of Hearts," NBCNews.com, May 15, 2007.

7 **However, that meant:** Dean Shepherd and Randall Tobias, eds., *Entrepreneurial Failure* (Northampton, MA: Edward Elgar, 2013), is a compilation of thirty-six academic articles on the causes and consequences of entrepreneurial failure.

8 **These patterns run counter:** Paul Gompers, Will Gornall, Steven Kaplan, and Ilya Strebulaev, "How Do Venture Capital Investors Make Decisions?" *Journal of*

Financial Economics 135, no. 1 (2020): 169–190, surveys 885 venture capital professionals about factors that drove their investment decisions. The most important factor was the quality of the management team, ranked number one by 47 percent of respondents; in total, 37 percent ranked one of four "horse" factors (business model, product, market, or industry) as most important. A typical investor view is expressed by Roger Ehrenberg, a venture capital partner at IA Ventures, in an October 26, 2010, response to a Quora question, "Why do so many startups fail?" He replies, "THE WRONG PEOPLE, hands down. All other problems are derivative." Likewise, in "Is It the Jockey or the Horse?" on the Seraf website, Christopher Mirabile, Seraf founder/CEO, briefly interviews nine prominent angel investors. Six say the jockey is more important; three say both jockey and horse are important.

9 **When the information service CB Insights:** CB Insights, "The Top 20 Reasons Startups Fail," Research Briefs, CB Insights website, Nov. 6, 2019.

9 **After all, Lean Startup methods:** Ries, *The Lean Startup,* builds upon Steve Blank, *Four Steps to the Epiphany: Successful Strategies for Products That Win* (Louisville, KY: Cafepress, 2005), which introduces the crucial concept of customer discovery. See also Steve Blank, "Why the Lean Start-Up Changes Everything," *Harvard Business Review,* May 2013.

11 **To my surprise:** Hans Swildens and Eric Yee, "The Venture Capital Risk and Return Matrix," Industry Ventures blog, Feb. 7, 2017, presents analysis of PitchBook data for all VC investments in late-stage ventures from 2006 through 2016, showing that 29 percent of investments return 0x to 1x and 28 percent earn 1x to 2x. Since this book defines failure as not earning a return *greater* than 1x, some portion of the 28 percent earning 1x to 2x are assumed to be failures.

13 **To win such a gamble:** Alan Patricof, "VC: Too Many Entrepreneurs' Business Models Rely on a 'Cascade of Miracles,' " Business Insider website, Mar. 10, 2015. Patricof explains the concept of "cascading miracles" and attributes the phrase to the late Monty Shapiro, the former CEO of cable set-top box manufacturer General Instruments. I first heard about cascading miracles from Liberty Media CEO John Malone, who once worked for Shapiro.

13 **In the early 1970s:** Roger Frock, *Changing How the World Does Business: FedEx's Incredible Journey to Success—The Inside Story* (San Francisco: Berrett-Koehler, 2006).

Chapter 1: What Is Failure?

17 **"The servers out there":** Jeffrey Van Camp, "My Jibo Is Dying and It's Breaking My Heart," *Wired,* Mar. 8, 2019.

17 **Jibo was a social robot:** Background in the next several paragraphs on the robot and the startup's history through February 2015 is drawn from Jeffrey Bussgang and Christine Snively, "Jibo: A Social Robot for the Home," HBS case 816003, Dec. 2015 (May 2016 rev.).

18 **The team was also close:** Author's interview with former Jibo CEO Steve Chambers, July 11, 2019.

18 **Because Breazeal's research:** Author's interview with Chambers is the source for details and his quotes on the next few pages about Jibo's fundraising, product development, early marketplace reception, and ultimate shutdown.

19 **An Indiegogo campaign:** Campaign results are reported in Bussgang and Snively, "Jibo: A Social Robot."

20 **In the meantime:** Chris Welch, "Amazon Just Surprised Everyone with a Crazy Speaker That Talks to You," The Verge website, Nov. 6, 2014.

21 **One camp maintained:** Total capital raised is from Crunchbase.

22 **Who Is an Entrepreneur?:** This section is adapted from Thomas Eisenmann, "Entrepreneurship: A Working Definition," Harvard Business Review blog, Jan. 10, 2013.

22 **For the past thirty years:** HBS professor Howard Stevenson first defined entrepreneurship as "the pursuit of opportunity beyond the resources you currently control" in "A Perspective on Entrepreneurship," HBS working paper 384–131, 1983.

24 **A standard definition of failure:** See Walsh and Cunningham, "Business Failure and Entrepreneurship" for a discussion of different ways to define entrepreneurial failure.

24 **Two hundred years ago:** Tom Nicholas, *VC: An American History* (Cambridge, MA: Harvard University Press, 2019), Ch. 1.

26 **As a matter of fact:** Noam Wasserman, *The Founder's Dilemmas: Anticipating and Avoiding the Pitfalls That Can Sink a Startup* (Princeton, NJ: Princeton University Press, 2012), p. 299.

26 *Wired* **reporter Jeffrey Van Camp:** Jeffrey Van Camp, "Review: Jibo, Social Robot," *Wired,* Nov. 7, 2017; the quote that follows is from Van Camp, "My Jibo Is Dying."

27 **For example, failed ventures:** Barry Sardis, "How Can Social Robots Benefit Seniors Aging in Place?" TechForAging website, Dec. 1, 2019, describes several social robots designed for elder care.

27 **For example, team members:** Jerry Kaplan, *Startup: A Silicon Valley Adventure* (Boston: Houghton Mifflin, 1994), recounts GO Corp's history; Kaplan was the startup's CEO.

29 **"The company was dependent":** Author's email correspondence with Jeff Bussgang, July 2019.

29 **"Amazon just surprised everyone":** Welch, "Amazon Just Surprised."

30 **Chambers and his team:** Author's interview with Chambers is the source for details about product design decisions in this paragraph and CTO hiring decisions in the next one.

31 **For example, in a survey:** J. P. Eggers and Lin Song, "Dealing with Failure: Serial Entrepreneurs and the Cost of Changing Industries Between Ventures," *Academy of Management Journal* 58, no. 6 (2015): 1785–1803.

31 **"all failed companies":** Peter Thiel, *Zero to One: Notes on Startups, or How to Build the Future* (New York: Currency, 2014), p. 34. For academic research supporting the "blame the horse" viewpoint, see Steven Kaplan, Berk Sensoy, and Per Stromberg, "Should Investors Bet on the Jockey or the Horse? Evidence from the Evolution of Firms from Early Business Plans to Public Companies," *Journal of Finance* 64, no. 1 (2009): 75–115.

31 **"There's just one mistake":** Paul Graham, "The 18 Mistakes That Kill Startups," Paul Graham blog, Oct. 2016.

32 **In a survey of venture capital:** Michael Gorman and William Sahlman, "What Do Venture Capitalists Do?" *Journal of Business Venturing* 4, no. 4 (1989): 231–248.

32 **In another survey:** Ian Macmillan, Lauriann Zemann, and P. N. Subbanarasimha, "Criteria Distinguishing Successful from Unsuccessful Ventures in the Venture Screening Process," *Journal of Business Venturing* 2, no. 2 (1987): 123–137.

32 **Research by my HBS colleagues:** Paul Gompers, Anna Kovner, Josh Lerner, and David Scharfstein, "Performance Persistence in Entrepreneurship," *Journal of Financial Economics* 96, no. 1 (2010): 18–32.

33 **Unfortunately, researchers aren't much in agreement:** Robert Baron and Gideon

Markman, "Beyond Social Capital: The Role of Entrepreneurs' Social Competence in Their Financial Success," *Journal of Business Venturing* 18 (2003): 41–60 shows that higher scores on measures of social competence (e.g., adaptability, persuasiveness) predict higher income for entrepreneurs. Sabrina Artinger and Thomas Powell, "Entrepreneurial Failure: Statistical and Psychological Explanations," *Strategic Management Journal* 37, no. 6 (2016): 1047–1064, shows that overconfident entrepreneurs are more prone to enter overcrowded markets in lab experiments. Hao Zhao, Scott Seibert, and G. T. Lumpkin, "The Relationship of Personality to Entrepreneurial Intentions and Performance: A Meta-Analytical Review," *Journal of Management* 36, no. 2 (2010): 381–404, shows that four of the "Big Five" stable personality attributes—conscientiousness, openness to experience, extraversion, and emotional stability—were positively correlated with entrepreneurial firm performance. By contrast, M. Ciavarella, A. Bucholtz, C. Riordan, R. Gatewood, and G. Stokes, "The Big Five and Venture Survival," *Journal of Business Venturing* 19 (2004): 465–483, finds that the only statistically significant Big Five predictor of venture survival is a positive relationship with conscientiousness.

33 **Unsurprisingly, research shows:** For academic research on the performance consequences of entrepreneurs' industry experience, see Rajshree Agarwal, Raj Echambadi, April Franco, and M. B. Sarkar, "Knowledge Transfer through Inheritance: Spin-out Generation, Development, and Survival," *Academy of Management Journal* 47, no. 4 (2004): 501–522; Aaron Chatterji, "Spawned with a Silver Spoon? Entrepreneurial Performance and Innovation in the Medical Device Industry," *Strategic Management Journal* 30, no. 2 (2009): 185–206; and Charles Eesley and Edward Roberts, "Are You Experienced or Are You Talented? When Does Innate Talent Versus Experience Explain Entrepreneurial Performance?" *Strategic Entrepreneurship Journal* 6 (2012): 207–219. Eggers and Song, "Dealing with Failure," shows that serial founders whose previous venture failed are more inclined to blame the external environment than their own ability, and thus are more likely to change industries when pursuing a new venture, compared to counterparts whose previous venture was successful. Furthermore, Eggers and Song show that changing industries hurts the performance of a serial entrepreneur's subsequent venture—regardless of the entrepreneur's success or failure with their previous venture. This lends strong support to the notion that industry experience drives success odds.

Chapter 2: Catch-22

39 **To break through this impasse:** Eisenmann, "Entrepreneurship: A Working Definition," presents the four tactics to break the Catch-22.

42 **The Diamond-and-Square Framework:** Richard Hamermesh and Thomas Eisenmann, "The Entrepreneurial Manager, Course Overview: 2013 Winter Term," HBS course note 813155, Jan. 2013, summarizes the framework, which I developed in 2013 for HBS's required MBA course on entrepreneurship and refined with assistance from my teaching group colleagues. The diamond elements are analyzed in greater detail in Thomas Eisenmann, "Business Model Analysis for Entrepreneurs," HBS course note 812096, Dec. 2011 (rev. Oct. 2014).

44 **Finally, *sustaining* this differentiation:** Thiel, *Zero to One*, emphasizes the importance of proprietary competitive advantage and discusses ways to achieve it.

44 **Examples include trusted brand names:** Fiona Southey, "Rouqette 'Significantly Increases' Pea Protein Supply Deal with Beyond Meat," Food Navigator website, Jan. 16, 2020.

44 **With network effects:** For perspective on how network effects influence customer perceptions of a product's value, see Thomas Eisenmann, Geoffrey Parker, and Marshall Van Alstyne, "Strategies for Two-Sided Markets," *Harvard Business Review,* Oct. 2006; Thomas Eisenmann, "Platform-Mediated Networks: Definitions and Core Concepts," HBS course note 807049, Sept. 2006 (Oct. 2007 rev.); Geoffrey Parker, Marshall Van Alstyne, and Sangeet Choudary, *Platform Revolution: How Networked Markets Are Transforming the Economy and How to Make Them Work for You* (New York: W. W. Norton, 2017); James Currier, "The Network Effects Manual: 13 Different Network Effects (and Counting)," NfX blog; and Anu Hariharan, "All about Network Effects," Andreessen Horowitz blog, Mar. 7, 2016.

48 **Poppy, a failed startup:** Thomas Eisenmann and Jeff Huizinga, "Poppy: A Modern Village for Childcare," HBS case 820715, Nov. 2017; and Thomas Eisenmann, Scott Kominers, Jeff Huizinga, and Allison Ciechanover, "Poppy (B)," HBS case 820715, Mar. 2020.

51 **"The number one reason":** Blake Masters, "Peter Thiel's CS183: Startup—Class 10 Notes Essay," Blake Masters blog, May 8, 2012.

51 **For example, the video:** Thomas Eisenmann, Michael Pao, and Lauren Barley, "Dropbox: It Just Works," HBS case 811065, Jan. 2011 (Oct. 2014 rev.).

52 **Consistent with this risk, the Startup Genome:** Startup Genome Project, "A Deep Dive into the Anatomy of Premature Scaling," Startup Genome website, Sept. 2, 2011.

53 **LTV/CAC Ratio:** For more guidance on calculating LTV and CAC, see Tom Eisenmann, "Business Model Analysis, Part 6: LTV and CAC," Platforms & Networks blog, July 27, 2011; David Skok, "What's Your TRUE Customer Lifetime Value (LTV)—DCF Provides the Answer," for Entrepreneurs blog, Feb. 23, 2016; and Eric Jorgenson, "The Simple Math Behind Every Profitable Business— Customer Lifetime Value," *Medium,* Mar. 16, 2015.

55 **As I explained:** See Wasserman, *Founder's Dilemmas,* for in-depth analysis of founders and the choices they make.

56 **Industry Experience:** See references in Ch. 1 to academic research on the link between performance and entrepreneurs' industry experience.

56 **It's well documented:** See in particular Arnold Cooper, Carolyn Woo, and William Dunkelberg, "Entrepreneurs' Perceived Chances for Success," *Journal of Business Venturing* 3, no. 2 (1988): 97–108; L. W. Busenitz and Jay Barney, "Differences between Entrepreneurs and Managers in Large Organizations: Biases and Heuristics in Strategic Decision-Making," *Journal of Business Venturing* 12, no. 1 (1997): 9–30; and Antonio Bernardo and Ivo Welch, "On the Evolution of Overconfidence and Entrepreneurs," *Journal of Economics & Management Strategy* 10, no. 3 (2001): 301–330. Colin Camerer and Dan Lovallo, "Overconfidence and Excess Entry: An Experimental Approach," *American Economic Review* 89, no. 1 (1999): 306–318, presents experimental results showing that overconfident individuals are, in a simulation, more likely to launch ventures in a market with uncertain prospects, resulting in excess entry and financial losses. Mathew Hayward, Dean Shepherd, and Dale Griffin, "A Hubris Theory of Entrepreneurship," *Management Science* 52, no. 2 (2006): 160–172, analyzes attributes of ventures that are likely to increase founder overconfidence and posits reasons why overconfident founders are more likely to fail.

57 **So, a founder's level of confidence:** This section is based in part on Tom Eisenmann, "Head Games: Ego and Entrepreneurial Failure," O'Reilly Radar website, July 9, 2013. For academic research on the performance consequences of entrepreneurs' overconfidence, see Artinger and Powell, "Entrepreneurial Failure";

and Robin Hogarth and Natalia Karelaia, "Entrepreneurial Success and Failure: Confidence and Fallible Judgment," *Organization Science* 23, no. 6 (2012): 1733–1747.

58 **One decision about team composition:** For a VC viewpoint supporting hiring for attitude, see Mark Suster, "Whom Should You Hire at a Startup (Attitude over Aptitude)?" *TechCrunch,* Mar. 17, 2011. Wasserman, *Founder's Dilemmas,* Ch. 8, also addresses hiring choices.

59 **In early-stage startups:** For analysis of early-stage funding decisions, see Brad Feld and Jason Mendelson, *Venture Deals: Be Smarter Than Your Lawyer and Venture Capitalist* (Hoboken, NJ: Wiley, 2011); Jeffrey Bussgang, *Mastering the VC Game: A Venture Capital Insider Reveals How to Get from Start-up to IPO on YOUR Terms* (New York: Portfolio, 2011); Jason Calacanis, *Angel: How to Invest in Technology Startups* (New York: Harper Business, 2017); and Scott Kupor, *Secrets of Sand Hill Road: Venture Capital and How to Get It* (New York: Portfolio, 2019).

61 **As my HBS colleague Bill Sahlman:** Wasserman, *Founder's Dilemmas,* p. 291.

61 **Marc Andreessen suggests:** Marc Andreessen, "Part 6: How Much Funding Is Too Little? Too Much?" The Pmarca Guide to Startups website, July 3, 2007.

64 **Sticking with the maritime metaphor:** Marc Andreessen, "Part 5: The Moby Dick Theory of Big Companies," The Pmarca Guide to Startups website, June 27, 2007. Dharmesh Shah, "Advice for Partnering with the Big and Powerful: Don't," OnStartups blog, Oct. 7, 2008, discusses the same issue.

64 **Along these lines, Dropbox:** Eisenmann et al., "Dropbox: It Just Works."

Chapter 3: Good Idea, Bad Bedfellows

67 **Alexandra Nelson and Christina Wallace:** The sources for all facts about Quincy Apparel and quotes from the founders in this chapter are Thomas Eisenmann and Lisa Mazzanti, "Quincy Apparel (A)," HBS case 815067, Feb. 2015 (Apr. 2016 rev.); and Eisenmann and Mazzanti, "Quincy Apparel (B)," HBS case 815095, Feb. 2015 (Apr. 2016 rev.).

73 **So, what can founders:** For additional guidance on recruiting employees for early-stage startups, see Julia Austin, "Hard to Do, and Easy to Screw Up: A Primer on Hiring for Startups," Being FA and Other Ponderings blog, Oct. 25, 2015; Dan Portillo, "Debugging Recruiting," Greylock Partners website, May 23, 2016; David Skok, "Recruiting—the 3rd Crucial Startup Skill," for Entrepreneurs blog; Sam Altman, "How to Hire," Sam Altman blog, Sept. 23, 2013; and Fred Wilson, "MBA Mondays: Best Hiring Practices," AVC blog, June 11, 2012.

74 **According to analysis by Noam Wasserman:** Wasserman, *Founder's Dilemmas,* Ch. 4.

76 **Wasserman's research shows:** Wasserman, *Founder's Dilemmas,* p. 131.

76 **In this situation:** For additional guidance on how to choose a co-founder and how to manage co-founder conflict, see Naval Ravikant, "How to Pick a Co-Founder," Venture Hacks blog, Nov. 12, 2009; Simeon Simeonov, "When to Fire Your Co-Founders," Venture Hacks blog, Jan. 28, 2010; Jessica Alter, "Three Biggest Mistakes When Choosing a Cofounder," OnStartups website, Apr. 18, 2013; and this interview of Steve Blank: "Looking for Love in All the Wrong Places—How to Find a Co-Founder," First Round Review website.

81 **So, how do founders find:** In addition to the references cited for the previous chapter's discussion of funding challenges, for guidance on choosing early-stage investors, see Geoff Ralston, "A Guide to Seed Fundraising," Y Combinator blog, Jan. 7, 2016; Chris Dixon, "What's the Right Amount of Seed Money to Raise?"

cdixon blog, Jan. 28, 2009; Rob Go, "How a Seed VC Makes Investment Decisions," NextView blog, Apr. 8, 2015; Mark Suster, "How to Develop Your Fundraising Strategy," Both Sides blog, Jan. 17, 2012; and Roger Ehrenberg, "Thoughts on Taking VC Money," informationarbitrage blog, Dec. 5, 2009.

84 **Unfortunately, there's not much:** For discussion of strategies for negotiating with a more powerful partner, see Peter Johnston, *Negotiating with Giants: Get What You Want Against the Odds* (Cambridge, MA: Negotiation Press, 2012).

Chapter 4: False Starts

89 **Sunil Nagaraj founded Triangulate:** The sources for all facts about Triangulate and quotes from Nagaraj are Thomas Eisenmann and Lauren Barley, "Triangulate," HBS case 811055, Jan. 2011; Eisenmann and Barley, "Triangulate (B): Post Mortem," HBS case 819080, Nov. 2018; and Eisenmann, Shikhar Ghosh, and Christopher Payton, "Triangulate: Stay, Pivot or Exit?" HBS case 817059, Oct. 2016.

92 **In his book *The Lean Startup*:** Ries, *The Lean Startup,* p. 160.

100 **Nagaraj reflected:** For additional analysis of challenges confronting online dating startups, see Andrew Chen, "Why Investors Don't Fund Dating," @andrewchen blog.

104 **The full process can be depicted:** Design Council, "What Is the Framework for Innovation? Design Council's Evolved Double Diamond," Design Council website.

104 **In the pages that follow, I lay out:** My mapping of tasks to the Double Diamond stages is drawn from an unpublished course note, Tom Eisenmann, "Design Workshop," Nov. 2018. In addition to the references listed below for specific research techniques, see also Bella Martin and Bruce Hanington, *Universal Methods of Design: 100 Ways to Research Complex Problems, Develop Innovative Ideas, and Design Effective Solutions* (Beverley, MA: Rockport, 2012); Jeanne Liedtka and Tim Ogilvie, *Designing for Growth: A Design Thinking Toolkit for Managers* (New York: Columbia Business School Publishing, 2011); Tom Kelley, *The Art of Innovation: Lessons in Creativity from IDEO, America's Leading Design Firm* (New York: Currency, 2001); Jake Knapp, *Sprint: How to Solve Big Problems and Test New Ideas in Just Five Days* (New York: Simon & Schuster, 2016); and Laura Klein, *UX for Lean Startups: Faster, Smarter User Experience Research and Design* (Beverley, MA: O'Reilly, 2013).

105 **Iteration should stop only:** The positioning statement is adapted from a version in Geoffrey Moore, *Crossing the Chasm: Marketing and Selling Disruptive Products to Mainstream Customers* (New York: Harper, 1991; 3rd ed. 2014), p. 186.

106 **Customer Interviews:** Best practices for customer interviewing are presented in Frank Cespedes, "Customer Visits for Entrepreneurs," HBS course note 812098, Nov. 2011 (Aug. 2012 rev.); Elizabeth Goodman, Mike Kuniavsky, and Andrea Moed, *Observing the User Experience: A Practitioner's Guide to User Research* (Waltham, MA: Morgan Kaufmann, 2012), Ch. 6; Rob Fitzpatrick, *The Mom Test: How to Talk to Customers* (Scotts Valley, CA: CreateSpace, 2013); and Cindy Alvarez, *Lean Product Development: Building Products Your Customers Will Buy* (Boston: O'Reilly, 2014).

106 **Lean Startup guru Steve Blank:** Blank, *Four Steps,* Ch. 3.

107 **But early adopters:** See Moore, *Crossing the Chasm,* Ch. 2, for analysis of the differences between early adopters and mainstream customers.

109 **User Testing of Existing Solutions:** For user testing best practices, see Goodman et al., *Observing the User Experience,* Ch. 11; and Steve Krug, *Rocket Surgery*

Made Easy: The Do-It-Yourself Guide to Finding and Fixing Usability Problems (Berkeley, CA: New Riders, 2010).

109 **Focus Groups and Ethnography:** For best practices, see Goodman et al., *Observing the User Experience,* Ch. 7 for focus groups and Ch. 9 for ethnography. See also Ellen Isaacs, "The Power of Observation: How Companies Can Have More 'Aha' Moments," GigaOm website, Sept. 15, 2012.

109 **Journey Mapping:** For how and why to use journey maps, see Sarah Gibbons, "Journey Mapping 101," Nielsen Norman Group website, Dec. 9, 2018.

110 **Competitor Analysis:** For best practices with competitor analysis, see Goodman et al., *Observing the User Experience,* Ch. 5.

111 **Customer Surveys:** For best practices when conducting customer surveys, see Goodman et al., *Observing the User Experience,* Ch. 12; and SurveyMonkey, "Surveys 101," SurveyMonkey website.

112 **The best way to synthesize:** For best practices when developing personas, see Goodman et al., *Observing the User Experience,* Ch. 17; and Alan Cooper, *The Inmates Are Running the Asylum: Why High-Tech Products Drive Us Crazy and How to Restore the Sanity* (Carmel, IN: Sams-Pearson Education, 2004).

112 **Also known as structured ideation:** For best practices when brainstorming, see Scott Berkun, "How to Run a Brainstorming Session," Scott Berkun blog; and Tina Seelig, "Brainstorming—Why It Doesn't (Always) Work," *Medium,* Jan. 8, 2017.

113 **Jeff Hawkins, inventor:** Alberto Savoia, "The Palm Pilot Story," *Medium,* Mar. 2, 2019.

113 **Early in the solution development process:** The distinction between "works like" vs. "looks like" prototypes is a widely accepted principle in design. For a good explanation of the distinction—and why designers should use both types—see Ben Einstein, "The Illustrated Guide to Product Development (Part 2: Design)," Bolt website, Oct. 20, 2015.

113 **When creating "looks like" prototypes:** For further discussion of trade-offs when selecting the level of fidelity for a prototype, see John Willshire, "Want to Improve Your Design Process? Question Your Fidelity," Mind the Product website, Mar. 17, 2015; and Lyndon Cerejo, "Design Better and Faster with Rapid Prototyping," Smashing Magazine website, June 16, 2010.

114 **To explore perceptions of value:** The questions that follow were adapted from a January 2017 "MBA Startup Bootcamp" class presentation by Keith Hopper, founder/CEO of Danger Point Labs.

115 **MVP Testing:** In addition to Ries, *The Lean Startup,* for further discussion of MVP testing logic and best practices, see Thomas Eisenmann, Eric Ries, and Sarah Dillard, "Hypothesis-Driven Entrepreneurship: The Lean Startup," HBS course note 812095, Dec. 2011 (July 2013 rev.); and Steve Blank, "An MVP Is Not a Cheaper Product; It's about Smart Learning," Steve Blank blog, July 22, 2013.

115 **The goal is to quickly:** Ries, *The Lean Startup,* p. 8.

115 **MVPs come in four basic types:** Eisenmann et al., "Hypothesis-Driven Entrepreneurship," pp. 7–8. See also Tristan Kromer, "Concierge versus Wizard of Oz Prototyping," Kromatic website.

Chapter 5: False Positives

118 **Lindsay Hyde founded Baroo:** The sources for all facts about Baroo and quotes from Hyde in this chapter are Thomas Eisenmann and Susie Ma, "Baroo: Pet Concierge," HBS case 820011, Aug. 2019; and Eisenmann and Ma, "Baroo (B)," HBS case 820026, Aug. 2019.

131 **If the root cause of false positives:** Moore, *Crossing the Chasm,* provides a detailed account of how and why managers in technology companies may fail to perceive differences between early adopters and mainstream customers, and strategies they should employ once they understand those differences.

132 **Consider the approach:** Lit Motors' approach to validating demand is described in Thomas Eisenmann and Alex Godden, "Lit Motors," HBS case 813079, Dec. 2012 (Nov. 2014 rev.).

133 **There are various options:** Moore, *Crossing the Chasm,* assumes that mainstream customers are more likely than early adopters to require a "whole product solution"—that is, one that minimizes the need for customer self-service and provides easy access to any complements required to use the product. The chasm framework also assumes that mainstream customers will not find references from early adopters credible because the two groups have such different requirements. Accordingly, Moore recommends a "D-Day invasion" when entering the mainstream market: a reengineered whole-product solution, delivered with allies who can provide any necessary complements, and marketed with intensity to compensate for a lack of credible reference customers.

133 **Dropbox took the last approach:** Eisenmann et al., "Dropbox: It Just Works."

Chapter 6: Out of the Frying Pan

137 **Surprisingly, about one-third of them:** Swildens and Yee, "The Venture Capital Risk and Return Matrix."

138 **Others innovate by exploiting:** Magdelena Petrova, "This Green Cement Company Says Its Product Can Cut Carbon Dioxide Emissions by Up to 70%," CNBC website, Sept. 28, 2019.

139 **To assess the likelihood:** I developed the "Six S" framework with Jeffrey Rayport in 2017 for the HBS MBA elective course "Scaling Technology Ventures." The framework adapts elements of McKinsey's "7-S" framework, described in Tom Peters and Robert Waterman, *In Search of Excellence: Lessons from America's Best-Run Companies* (New York: Harper & Row, 1982).

141 **Growth can be self-reinforcing:** In addition to the references cited for Ch. 2's discussion of network effects, for analysis of factors that encourage startups to accelerate customer acquisition, see Reid Hoffman and Chris Yeh, *Blitzscaling: The Lightning-Fast Path to Building Massively Valuable Companies* (New York: Currency, 2018); Albert Wenger, "Hard Choices: Growth vs. Profitability," Continuations blog, Oct. 12, 2015; Michael Skok, "Scaling Your Startup: The Deliberator's Dozen," LinkedIn blog, July 16, 2013; Thomas Eisenmann, "Scaling a Startup: Pacing Issues," HBS course note 812099, Nov. 2011 (Nov. 2014 rev.); and Eisenmann, "Internet Companies' Growth Strategies: Determinants of Investment Intensity and Long-Term Performance," *Strategic Management Journal* 27, no. 12 (2006): 1183–1204.

142 **Facebook is an example:** John Gramlich, "10 Facts About Americans and Facebook," Pew Research Center website, May 16, 2019.

144 **Geographic Reach:** For further analysis of how and why startups expand geographically, see John O'Farrell, "Building the Global Startup," Andreessen Horowitz blog, June 17, 2011—the first of a five-part series; and Steve Carpenter, "A Startup's Guide to International Expansion," *TechCrunch,* Dec. 23, 2015.

144 **Uber, for example, launched:** Olivia Solon, "How Uber Conquers a City in Seven Steps," The Guardian website, Apr. 12, 2017.

145 **The leading online marketplace:** Thomas Eisenmann, Allison Ciechanover, and Jeff Huizinga, "thredUP: Think Secondhand First," HBS case 817083, Dec. 2016;

thredUP's strategy for European entry was described by co-founder/CEO James Reinhart during an HBS class visit in February 2017.

145 **If entrepreneurs don't grasp:** J. Stewart Black and Tanya Spyridakis, "EuroDisneyland," Thunderbird case TB0195, June 15, 1999.

146 **Entrepreneurs in late-stage startups:** The arc of product evolution is discussed in Steve Sinofsky, "Everyone Starts with Simplicity; No-One Ends There (and That's Okay)," Learning by Shipping blog, May 13, 2014.

148 **For mature corporations, management scholars:** For analysis of financial returns to corporations making acquisitions, see Jay Barney, "Returns to Bidding Firms in Mergers and Acquisitions: Reconsidering the Relatedness Hypothesis," *Strategic Management Journal* 9, no. S1 (1988): 71–78; and Sara Moeller, Frederik Schlingemann, and Rene Stulz, "Wealth Destruction on a Massive Scale? A Study of Acquiring-Firm Returns in the Recent Merger Wave," *Journal of Finance* 60, no. 2 (2005): 757–782.

150 **This phenomenon is known:** For a description of the winner's curse, see Richard Thaler, *The Winner's Curse: Paradoxes and Anomalies of Economic Life* (Princeton, NJ: Princeton University Press, 1994), Ch. 5.

151 **VC Fred Wilson has estimated:** Fred Wilson, "Why Early Stage Venture Investments Fail," Union Square Ventures blog, Nov. 30, 2007.

151 **As Fred Wilson advises:** Fred Wilson, "The Finance to Value Framework," AVC blog, May 20, 2018.

152 **Funding Risk:** For a discussion of financing risk and its impact on entrepreneurial innovation, see Ramana Nanda and Matthew Rhodes-Kropf, "Investment Cycles and Startup Innovation," *Journal of Financial Economics* 110 (2013): 403–418; and Nanda and Rhodes-Kropf, "Financing Risk and Innovation," *Management Science* 63, no. 4 (2017): 901–918.

152 **CEO Succession:** Wasserman, *Founder's Dilemmas,* Ch. 10, describes the incidence, antecedents, and consequences of startup CEO succession. See also Steve Blank, "I've Seen the Promised Land. And I Might Not Get There with You," Steve Blank blog, Jan. 21, 2010.

152 **Board Priorities:** For further discussion of governance issues confronting startup boards, see Brad Feld and Mahendra Ramsinghani, *Startup Boards: Getting the Most Out of Your Board of Directors* (Hoboken, NJ: Wiley, 2013); Matt Blumberg, *Startup CEO: A Field Guide to Scaling Up Your Business* (Hoboken, NJ: Wiley, 2013), Part 4; a series of AVC blog posts by Fred Wilson in March and April 2012; a series of VCAdventure blog posts by Seth Levine, titled "Designing the Ideal Board Meeting," Oct. and Nov. 2018; and Jeff Bussgang, "Board Meetings vs. Bored Meetings," *Business Insider,* Apr. 5, 2011.

153 **The first three S's pertain:** Portions of the sections on Staff and Structure that follow are adapted from Thomas Eisenmann and Alison Wagonfeld, "Scaling a Startup: People and Organizational Issues," HBS course note 812100, Jan. 2012 (Feb. 2012 rev.). Other perspectives on human capital management challenges in scaling startups are available in Ben Horowitz, *The Hard Thing about Hard Things* (New York: HarperCollins, 2014); Hoffman and Yeh, *Blitzscaling,* Part IV; Blumberg, *Startup CEO,* Part 2; Sam Altman, "Later Stage Advice for Startups," Y Combinator blog, July 6, 2016; Brian Halligan, "Scale-Up Leadership Lessons I've Learned over 9 Years as HubSpot's CEO," *Medium,* Jan. 10, 2016; Mark Suster, "This Is How Companies 'Level Up' after Raising Money," Both Sides blog, Apr. 10, 2014; and Wasserman, *Founder's Dilemmas,* Chs. 8 and 10, which address hiring challenges and CEO succession, respectively.

153 **"Managing at scale":** Horowitz, *The Hard Thing,* p. 193.

154 **VC Fred Wilson estimates:** Fred Wilson, "MBA Mondays: Turning Your Team," AVC blog, Aug. 12, 2013.

155 **Some founder/CEOs:** Steve Blank, "The Peter Pan Syndrome: The Startup to Company Transition," Steve Blank blog, Sept. 20, 2010. The phrase was first applied to grown men who behave in a childlike manner by Dan Kiley, *The Peter Pan Syndrome: Men Who Have Never Grown Up* (New York: Dodd, Mead, 1983).

155 **Venture capitalist John Hamm:** John Hamm, "Why Entrepreneurs Don't Scale," *Harvard Business Review,* Dec. 2002.

155 **According to research by Yeshiva:** Wasserman, *Founder's Dilemmas,* p. 299.

157 **"Technical founders often think":** Eisenmann and Wagonfeld, "Scaling a Startup: People and Organizational Issues."

157 **Adding *product managers:*** For an overview of the product manager role, see Jeffrey Bussgang, Thomas Eisenmann, and Rob Go, "The Product Manager," HBS course note 812105, Dec. 2011 (Jan. 2015 rev.).

157 **Adding the position of *chief operating officer:*** For a contrary view, see Mark Suster, "Why Your Startup Doesn't Need a COO," Both Sides blog, Sept. 13, 2013.

158 **Adding Management Systems:** For research on patterns of system adoption by startups, see Anthony Davila, George Foster, and Ning Ja, "Building Sustainable High-Growth Startup Companies: Management Systems as an Accelerator," *California Management Review,* Spring 2010. The OKR (objectives and key results) system for performance management, used in many tech companies, is described in John Doerr, *Measure What Matters: How Google, Bono, and the Gates Foundation Rock the World with OKRs* (New York: Portfolio, 2018); and First Round Review, "AltSchool's CEO Rebuilt Google's Performance Management System to Work for Startups—Here It Is," First Round Review website, which interviews Max Ventilla, who discusses adapting OKRs to startups.

158 **Venture capitalist Ben Horowitz defines:** Ben Horowitz, *What You Do Is Who You Are: How to Create Your Business Culture* (New York: HarperCollins, 2019). For additional perspectives on managing a scaling startup's culture, see Horowitz, *The Hard Thing;* Blumberg, *Startup CEO,* Ch. 9; Hoffman and Yeh, *Blitzscaling,* Part IV; Dharmesh Shah, "Does HubSpot Walk the Talk on Its Culture Code?" OnStartups blog, Apr. 11, 2013; Kristi Riordan, "You Hire for Culture, but Have You Established What Your Culture Is?" *Medium,* May 30, 2016; and Steve Blank, "The Elves Leave Middle Earth—Sodas Are No Longer Free," Steve Blank blog, Dec. 21, 2009.

159 **"Some companies' cultures":** Adapted from Jerry Colonna, *Reboot: Leadership and the Art of Growing Up* (New York: Harper Business, 2019), p. 185.

159 **First, "old guard versus new guard":** For additional perspective, see Rands, "The Old Guard," *Medium,* Jan. 27, 2016.

160 **Dropbox offers a good example:** Justin Randolph, Peter Levine, and James Lattin, "Dropbox," Stanford Graduate School of Business case E471, Apr. 20, 2013 (May 15, 2015, rev.).

164 **Samir Kaul and his partners:** Author interview with Samir Kaul, July 19, 2019.

165 **Lit Motors:** Eisenmann and Godden, "Lit Motors."

165 **E Ink, whose primary business:** William Sahlman and Matthew Lieb, "E Ink: Financing Growth," HBS case 800252, Dec. 1999.

Chapter 7: Speed Trap

167 **The first, a venture:** Ben Popper, "Demolition Man: Why Does Fab's CEO Keep Building Companies That Suddenly Implode?" The Verge website, Nov. 26, 2013.

167 **His second, a service:** Adam Penenberg, "Fab.com: Ready, Set, Reset!" *Fast Company,* May 16, 2012, is the source for facts in this chapter's first four paragraphs, unless otherwise noted.

168 **Customers found great appeal:** Allison Shontell, "The Tech Titanic: How Red-Hot Startup Fab Raised $330 Million and Then Went Bust," Business Insider website, Feb. 6, 2015.

168 **To prepare for further expansion:** 2012 funding total is from Crunchbase.

168 **That year, the venture sold:** Total 2012 sales are from Penenberg, "Ready, Set, Reset!" Total 2011 sales are from Jason Goldberg, "On the Rebound from Epic Failure," Hackernoon blog, June 20, 2016.

168 **However, Fab's business model:** The $90 million loss is cited in Erin Griffith, "Fab's Eyes Are Bigger Than Its Wallet. That's Nothing $100 Million Can't Fix," *Pando Daily,* Apr. 30, 2013.

168 **Because to supercharge:** Marketing spending is from Erin Griffith, "The Samwer Brothers May Have the Last Laugh on Fab after All," *Pando Daily,* Nov. 26, 2013.

168 **"By the summer of 2012":** Author's interview with Jason Goldberg, July 3, 2019.

169 **Compounding the cash drain:** Facts in this paragraph are from Griffith, "Samwer Brothers."

169 **"had cloned us":** Author's interview with Goldberg.

169 **To jump-start its move:** Shontell, "Tech Titanic," is the source for facts in this paragraph, except otherwise noted.

169 **By August:** Sarah Perez, "Fab: Europe Will Be 20% of Fab's 2012 Revenue," *TechCrunch,* Aug. 7, 2012.

170 **In April 2013, Goldberg:** Alex Konrad, "Fab Pivots Away from Flash Sales; Sets Sights on Amazon and IKEA," Forbes website, Apr. 30, 2013.

170 **"a good way to draw people":** Author's interview with Goldberg.

170 **By that point:** Konrad, "Fab Pivots." Eleven thousand products is from Zachary Crockett, "Sh*t, I'm F*cked: Jason Goldberg, Founder of Fab," The Hustle website, Oct. 17, 2017.

171 **"It was capital intensive":** Author's interview with Goldberg.

171 **"We started to lose":** Crockett, "Sh*t, I'm F*cked."

171 **With the pivot in place:** This paragraph and the next are drawn from Goldberg, "On the Rebound."

171 **Fab's cash burn rate peaked:** Ingrid Lunden, "Fab Was Burning through $14 Million/Month before Its Layoffs and Pivot," *TechCrunch,* Oct. 20, 2014.

171 **Fab laid off 80 percent:** Goldberg, "On the Rebound."

172 **In October 2014:** Crockett, "Sh*t, I'm F*cked."

172 **Hem was subsequently sold:** Ingrid Lunden, "Hem.com Is on the Block; Swiss Furniture Maker Vitra Likely Buyer," *TechCrunch,* Dec. 30, 2015.

174 **"I allowed silos":** Shontell, "Tech Titanic."

174 **Uber, for example:** Kate Taylor and Benjamin Goggin, "49 of the Biggest Scandals in Uber's History," Business Insider website, May 10, 2019.

174 **Zenefits, a licensed health insurance broker:** Claire Suddath and Eric Newcomer, "Zenefits Was the Perfect Startup. Then It Self-Disrupted," *Bloomberg Businessweek,* May 9, 2016.

175 **It helps to have a radar detector:** The origins of the RAWI test are shrouded in mystery, but I believe my HBS colleague Shikhar Ghosh should be credited with the invention, with some assistance from me, Felda Hardymon, Toby Stuart, and other members of our teaching group for the required HBS MBA course on entrepreneurship.

176 **A startup is *ready* to scale:** Marc Andreessen coined the term "product-market fit" in "Part 4: The Only Thing That Matters," The Pmarca Guide to Startups

blog, June 25, 2007. See also Andrew Chen, "When Has a Consumer Startup Hit Product-Market Fit?" @andrewchen blog; Sean Ellis, "Using Product/Market Fit to Drive Sustainable Growth," *Medium: Growth Hackers,* Apr. 5, 2019; and Brian Balfour, "The Neverending Road to Product-Market Fit," Brian Balfour blog, Dec. 11, 2013.

176 **Long-term profitability:** See citations for LTV/CAC calculations in Ch. 2.

176 **Businesses with high fixed expenses:** The target 3.0 ratio is referenced in, among many other sources, Jared Sleeper, "Why Early-Stage Startups Should Wait to Calculate LTV: CAC, and How They Should Use It When They Do," for Entrepreneurs blog.

177 **For this reason:** For further discussion of cohort analysis, see David Skok, "SaaS Metrics 2.0—A Guide to Measuring and Improving What Matters," for Entrepreneurs blog; Nico Wittenborn, "Cohort Analysis: A (Practical) Q&A," The Angel VC blog, Mar. 14, 2014; and Sean Ellis and Morgan Brown, *Hacking Growth: How Today's Fastest-Growing Companies Drive Breakthrough Success* (New York: Currency, 2017), Ch. 7.

178 **The following table:** The cohort and CAC tables in this section are adapted from supplemental materials that accompany Mark Roberge and Thomas Eisenmann, "eSig: Growth Analysis," HBS case 817009, Aug. 2019 (Nov. 2019 rev.).

179 **My HBS colleague Mark Roberge:** Mark Roberge, *The Science of Scaling,* forthcoming ebook.

180 **Conducting cohort analysis:** Jeff Bussgang, "Your LTV Math Is Wrong," *Seeing Both Sides,* Oct. 24, 2015, discusses entrepreneurs' penchant to inflate LTV projections and mistakes they frequently make when calculating LTV.

181 **VC Jeff Bussgang likens this:** Jeff Bussgang, "Why Metrics Get Worse with Scale," *HuffPost,* Feb. 12, 2015.

181 **"We spent $200 million":** Shontell, "Tech Titanic."

182 **"Our original sin":** Author's interview with Goldberg, which is also the source for the quote in the next paragraph.

183 **According to press accounts:** Shontell, "Tech Titanic."

184 **While Fab had some issues:** Shontell, "Tech Titanic."

184 **As Reid Hoffman says:** Hoffman and Yeh, *Blitzscaling,* pp. 217–218.

185 **"A startup is a company":** Paul Graham, "Startup = Growth," Paul Graham blog, Sept. 2012.

188 **Network Effects:** For references regarding network effects, see citations in Ch. 2.

190 **Fortunately, it's possible:** For further guidance on conducting conjoint analysis, see Elie Ofek and Olivier Toubia, "Conjoint Analysis: A Do-It-Yourself Guide," HBS course note 515024, Aug. 2014.

192 **LTV calculations:** For more guidance on how and why to calculate viral coefficients, see Adam Nash, "User Acquisition: Viral Factor Basics," Psychohistory blog, Apr. 4, 2012.

193 **Switching Costs:** Portions of this section on switching costs and the next section on scale economies are adapted from Thomas Eisenmann, "Note on Racing to Acquire Customers," HBS course note 803103, Jan. 2003 (Sept. 2007 rev.).

199 **Is de-escalation:** The discussion of de-escalation and when it might work that follows is adapted from Eisenmann, "Note on Racing."

Chapter 8: Help Wanted

202 **Dot & Bo was founded:** Unless otherwise noted, all facts about Dot & Bo and quotes from Anthony Soohoo and his Dot & Bo colleagues in this chapter are from Thomas Eisenmann, Allison Ciechanover, and George Gonzalez, "Anthony

Soohoo at Dot & Bo: Bringing Storytelling to Furniture E-Commerce," HBS case 820036, Sept. 2019 (Dec. 2019 rev.); and Eisenmann, Ciechanover, and Gonzalez, "Anthony Soohoo: Retrospection on Dot & Bo," HBS case 820037, Sept. 2019 (Dec. 2019 rev.).

206 **Meanwhile, the news broke:** Jason DelRay, "One Kings Lane Sold for Less Than $30 Million after Being Valued at $900 Million," *Vox recode,* Aug. 23, 2016.

207 **Venture capital is prone:** For analysis of the causes and consequences of VC boom-bust cycles, see Paul Gompers and Josh Lerner, *The Money of Invention: How Venture Capital Creates New Wealth* (Boston: Harvard Business School Press, 2001), Ch. 6; Gompers and Lerner, *The Venture Capital Cycle* (Cambridge, MA: MIT Press, 2004); Paul Gompers, Anna Kovner, Josh Lerner, and David Scharfstein, "Venture Capital Investment Cycles: The Impact of Public Markets," *Journal of Financial Economics* 87 (2008): 1–23; and Nicholas, *VC: An American History,* Ch. 8.

209 **Entrepreneurs leading later-stage startups:** For additional perspective on how to manage through boom-bust valuation cycles, see Eisenmann, "Note on Racing." For a summary of research on the relationship between capital market overvaluation and product market overinvestment, see Thomas Eisenmann, "Valuation Bubbles and Broadband Deployment," Ch. 4 in Robert Austin and Stephen Bradley (eds.), *The Broadband Explosion: Leading Thinkers on the Promise of a Truly Interactive World* (Boston: Harvard Business School Press, 2005).

212 **Echoing these points:** See two posts by Ben Horowitz: "Old People," Andreessen Horowitz blog, December 5, 2012, and "Why Is It Hard to Bring Big Company Execs into Little Companies?" Business Insider website, Apr. 22, 2010.

213 **"struggled, since its inception":** Rand Fishkin, *Lost and Founder: A Painfully Honest Field Guide to the Startup World* (New York: Portfolio, 2018), Ch. 5.

213 **So, how to proceed?:** See references cited in Ch. 6 for recruiting best practices.

214 **"Startups can get by":** Thomas Eisenmann and Halah AlQahtani, "Flatiron School," HBS case 817114, Jan. 2017.

215 **In contrast to early-stage startups:** This paragraph and the next one are adapted from Eisenmann and Wagonfeld, "Scaling a Startup: People and Organizational Issues."

Chapter 9: Moonshots and Miracles

217 **"We wanted flying cars":** Daniel Weisfield, "Peter Thiel at Yale: We Wanted Flying Cars, Instead We Got 140 Characters," Yale School of Management website, Apr. 27, 2013.

217 **He founded the startup Better Place:** Unless otherwise noted, facts in the first three paragraphs of this chapter are from Max Chafkin, "A Broken Place: The Spectacular Failure of the Startup That Was Going to Change the World," *Fast Company,* May 2014.

217 **Agassi joined SAP's executive board:** Roles at SAP are from Elie Ofek and Alison Wagonfeld, "Speeding Ahead to a Better Place," HBS case 512056, Jan. 2012 (Mar. 2012 rev.).

217 **"This is a better job":** Brian Blum and Shlomo Ben-Hur, "Better Place: An Entrepreneur's Drive Goes Off Track," IMD case 940, Oct. 2018.

218 **With help from Peres:** Tax rates are from Brian Blum, *Totaled: The Billion-Dollar Crash of the Startup That Took on Big Auto, Big Oil and the World* (Sherman Oaks, CA: Blue Pepper, 2017), p. 27.

218 **Next, Agassi turned to fundraising:** Better Place's fundraising details in this chapter are from PitchBook.

218 **Siblings and former SAP colleagues:** Team member backgrounds are from Blum and Ben-Hur, "Better Place: An Entrepreneur's Drive."

218 **Agassi selected his native Israel:** Launch market criteria in this paragraph and the projected costs and capacity of charge spots and exchange stations in the next two paragraphs are from Ofek and Wagonfeld, "Speeding Ahead."

219 **70 percent of family sedans:** Blum, *Totaled*, p. 225.

219 **He and his team eventually:** Chris Nuttal, "Better Place's $200M Round to Expand Electric Car Networks," *Financial Times*, Nov. 22, 2011.

219 **So, Better Place commissioned market research:** Ofek and Wagonfeld, "Speeding Ahead."

220 **Although Agassi had promised:** Vehicle and subscription pricing are respectively from p. 200 and p. 205 of Blum, *Totaled*.

220 **Better Place would pay:** Cost of the vehicle and battery are respectively from p. 201 and p. 190 of Blum, *Totaled*; 2008 projection for battery cost is from Ofek and Wagonfeld, "Speeding Ahead."

220 **In addition to vehicle:** Ofek and Wagonfeld, "Speeding Ahead" cites a $600 cost for electricity to drive twelve thousand miles and "a few hundred dollars" per customer annually for maintenance. To this, I've added $70 for depreciation of charge spots and exchange stations, assuming, based on figures cited in "Speeding Ahead," specifically 1) a cost of $250 per charge spot and $400,000 per exchange station, and 2) two charge spots per customer and two thousand customers per exchange station. I assumed a ten-year depreciation life for both charge spots and exchange stations.

221 **Better Place's corporate headquarters:** Blum, *Totaled*, p. 86, lists offices and project locations.

221 **Creating the vehicle's software:** OSCAR is described in Blum, *Totaled*, p. 64 and p. 135.

221 **According to tech journalist Brian Blum:** The $60 million cost estimate is from Blum, *Totaled*, p. 67.

221 **he'd become something:** *Time* magazine list is mentioned in Blum and Ben-Hur, "Better Place: An Entrepreneur's Drive." TED Talk was on April 19, 2009.

222 **"The confidence he has":** Chafkin, "Broken Place."

222 **"I've never seen someone":** Vauhini Vara, "Software Executive Shifts Gears to Electric Cars," *Wall Street Journal*, Oct. 29, 2007.

222 **"the born salesman's ability":** Clive Thompson, "Batteries Not Included," *New York Times Magazine*, Apr. 16, 2009.

222 **For example, in a 2008 meeting:** The GM meeting is described in Chafkin, "Broken Place"; and Ch. 6 of Blum, *Totaled*.

222 **Meanwhile, Better Place's relationship:** Relations with Renault-Nissan's new electric vehicle manager and the "smart screw" debate in the next paragraph are described in Ch. 10 of Blum, *Totaled*, and fast charging trade-offs are referenced on p. 61.

223 **The Leaf was launched:** Peter Valdes-Dapena, "The Nissan Leaf Will Cost $25,000," CNN Money website, Mar. 30, 2010.

223 **Charge spots would ultimately cost:** Blum, *Totaled*, p. 219, cites an estimated Better Place charge spot cost, including installation, of $2,000 to $3,000 and average installation costs for U.S. charge spots of $1,350.

223 **General Electric started selling:** Leslie Guevarra, "GE and Lowe's Partner to Power EV Charging at Home," GreenBiz website, July 19, 2011.

223 **Similarly, the twenty-one exchange stations:** A cost per station in excess of $2 million is cited in Chafkin, "Broken Place."

223 **A consultant hired early:** Blum, *Totaled*, pp. 62–63.

224 **At a June 2010 meeting:** Blum, *Totaled,* pp. 172–174.

224 **He berated employees:** Blum, *Totaled,* pp. 158–159.

224 **Meanwhile, Renault-Nissan was late:** Blum, *Totaled,* p. 193, cites delays in delivering the Fluence.

224 **According to Blum:** Blum, *Totaled,* pp. 186–188, discusses digging restrictions.

224 **Also, while existing gas stations:** Blum, *Totaled,* p. 181, discusses gas station regulation.

224 **And, Renault's distributor in Israel:** Blum, *Totaled,* pp. 202–204.

224 **However, the goal had been:** Blum, *Totaled,* p. 195.

225 **When Better Place finally began:** Chafkin, "Broken Place," cites a $500,000 daily burn rate.

225 **Moreover, leasing companies:** Blum, *Totaled,* p. 226, discusses the usage tax and p. 228 cites residual value concerns.

225 **According to Blum:** Blum, *Totaled,* pp. 210–212; "Friends are either true or not friends" is cited on p. 232.

226 **Normally a CFO:** Blum, *Totaled,* pp. 192–194.

226 **In late August:** Failed fundraising and Agassi's departure are described in Chafkin, "Broken Place," which is also the source for "fewer than 1,500 cars." Efforts by Agassi's successors as CEO are described in Blum, *Totaled,* Ch. 19.

228 **Contrary to the predictions:** Blum, *Totaled,* p. 258, cites data on usage by Better Place customers.

228 **Tesla opened a battery exchange station:** Kristen Korosec, "Telsa's Battery Swap Program Is Pretty Much Dead," Fortune website, June 10, 2015.

231 **"escalation of commitment":** Barry Staw, "The Escalation of Commitment to a Course of Action," *Academy of Management Review* 6, no. 4 (1981): 577–587. A propensity to "double down," increasing one's commitment in the wake of a bad outcome, is also consistent with the core tenet of prospect theory: that individuals tend to be risk averse in the domain of gains (i.e., when they've experienced good outcomes and have a lot to lose if a bet goes badly) and risk seeking in the domain of losses, as shown in Daniel Kahneman and Amos Tversky, "Prospect Theory: An Analysis of Decision under Risk," *Econometrica* 47, no. 2 (1979): 263–292. Likewise, escalation of commitment is broadly consistent with a threat-rigidity response: a tendency by individuals or organizations, when under duress, to revert to a familiar strategy rather than search for a new one, as described in Barry Staw, Lance Sandelands, and Jane Dutton, "Threat-Rigidity Effects in Organizational Behavior: A Multilevel Analysis," *Administrative Science Quarterly* 26, no. 4 (1981): 501–524.

235 **Iridium is another example:** Details in this paragraph are from John Bloom, *Eccentric Orbits: How a Single Man Saved the World's Largest Satellite Constellation from Fiery Destruction* (New York: Atlantic Monthly Press, 2016); market research projections are described on p. 196 and the $6.4 billion investment is cited on p. 209.

235 **"If I had asked people":** Patrick Vlaskovits, "Henry Ford, Innovation, and That 'Faster Horse' Quote," Harvard Business Review blog, Aug. 29, 2011.

236 **Dean Kamen, the inventor:** Details in this paragraph are from Steve Kemper, *Code Name Ginger: The Story Behind Segway and Dean Kamen's Quest to Invent a New World* (Boston: Harvard Business School Press, 2003). ADL projections are cited on p. 63; the initial consumer rider test is described on p. 227.

236 **the company sold just thirty thousand:** Jordan Golson, "Well, That Didn't Work: The Segway Is a Technological Marvel. Too Bad It Doesn't Make Any Sense," *Wired,* Jan. 16, 2015.

236 **After selling Segways:** Johnny Diaz, "Segway to End Production of Its Original Personal Transporter," *New York Times,* June 24, 2020.

236 **So did GO Corp:** Details in this paragraph and the next on GO Corp's product development decision are from Josh Lerner, Thomas Kosnik, Tarek Abuzayyad, and Paul Yang, "GO Corp," HBS case 297021, Sept. 2016 (Apr. 2017 rev.). Facts in the next paragraph about GO Corp's failure are from Jerry Kaplan, *Startup: A Silicon Valley Adventure* (New York: Penguin, 1994), Ch. 13.

237 **Iridium's satellite phones:** Bloom, *Eccentric Orbits,* p. 180.

238 **To illustrate the last point:** Frederick Brooks, *The Mythical Man Month: Essays on Software Engineering* (Boston: Addison-Wesley, 1975).

239 **"There comes a time":** Kemper, *Code Name Ginger,* p. 36.

239 **Iridium, too, launched:** Bloom, *Eccentric Orbits,* p. 182.

240 **"We're here to put a dent":** The provenance of this quote attributed to Jobs is disputed, according to Quora responses to the question: Where and when did Steve Jobs say, "We're here to put a dent etc."? One response speculates that the quote was written for the movie *Pirates of Silicon Valley;* another cites Jobs's 1985 *Playboy* interview; still others note multiple references to "dent in the universe" in Walter Isaacson's biography, *Steve Jobs* (New York: Simon & Schuster, 2011).

240 **"do to the car":** The car/mainframe quote is from Kemper, *Code Name Ginger,* p. 93; the fastest-growing company assertion is from p. 50; "entertaining and irresistible" is from p. 49.

241 **"Narcissistic Leaders: The Incredible Pros":** Michael Maccoby, "Narcissistic Leaders: The Incredible Pros, the Inevitable Cons," *Harvard Business Review,* Jan. 2001.

241 **While startups of all types:** Chad Navis and O. Ozbek, "The Right People in the Wrong Places: The Paradox of Entrepreneurial Entry and Successful Opportunity Realization," *Academy of Management Review* 41, no. 1 (2016): 109–129, argues that overconfident and narcissistic individuals are more likely to be drawn to bold, novel opportunities because they will overestimate success odds (due to overconfidence) and will crave the attention that comes with doing something big and new (due to narcissism). Navis and Ozbek also argue that overconfidence and narcissism inhibit learning in ways that reduce success odds with novel ventures.

243 **Elizabeth Holmes is an example:** John Carreyrou, *Bad Blood: Secrets and Lies in a Silicon Valley Startup* (New York: Knopf, 2018), p. 43.

244 **To confront this problem:** Blumberg, *Startup CEO,* Ch. 37. For additional guidance on best practices for managing a board, see the references for the section "Board Priorities" in Ch. 6.

245 **Federal Express did:** Frock, *Changing How the World Does Business.*

Chapter 10: Running on Empty

249 **"Failure is not the worst thing":** Andrew Lee, "Startup Mortality: What End-of-Life Care Teaches Us about Startup Failure," *Medium: Startup Grind,* Nov. 28, 2017.

251 **As noted previously:** In addition to Wasserman, *Founder's Dilemmas,* Ch. 10, Michael Ewens and Matt Marx, "Founder Replacement and Startup Performance," *Review of Financial Studies* 31, no. 4 (2018): 1532–1565, presents data on the incidence of founder/CEO replacement in struggling startups and shows that performance tends to improve after the founder/CEO of a struggling startup is replaced.

251 **For example, PayPal began:** Eric Jackson, *The PayPal Wars: Battles with eBay, the Media, the Mafia, and the Rest of Planet Earth* (Los Angeles: World Ahead, 2004).

251 **Likewise, YouTube started:** Jason Koebler, "Ten Years Ago Today, YouTube Launched as a Dating Website," Vice website, Apr. 23, 2015.

252 **The second drawback:** Wilson, "Why Early Stage Venture Investments Fail," notes that of eleven portfolio companies on which he earned more than 5x his investment, seven had pivoted successfully, but only one of five failures in his portfolio had done so. Wilson attributes this to "the large unsustainable burn rates they had built up."

254 **Will existing investors take:** For additional perspective, see Fred Wilson, "The Pro Rata Participation Right," AVC blog, Mar. 4, 2014; and Mark Suster, "What All Entrepreneurs Need to Know about Prorata Rights," Both Sides blog, Oct. 12, 2014.

254 **Selling the Company:** For additional perspective on selling a startup, see Chris Dixon, "Notes on the Acquisition Process," cdixon blog, Sept. 10, 2012; Ben Horowitz, "Should You Sell Your Company?" Andreessen Horowitz blog, Jan. 19, 2011; Chris Sheehan, "Corporate Development 101: What Every Startup Should Know," OnStartups blog, Apr. 2, 2014; John O'Farrell, "Knowing Where the Exits Are," Andreessen Horowitz blog, May 30, 2012; and James Altucher, "The 9 Most Important Things to Remember If You Want to Sell Your Company," TechCrunch website, June 13, 2011.

255 **"They dragged us along":** Eisenmann, Ciechanover, and Gonzalez, "Anthony Soohoo: Retrospection."

255 **"No thanks":** Lindsay Hyde class visit, HBS MBA "Entrepreneurial Failure" course, Feb. 2019.

255 **Another potential challenge:** Guidance for founders who sell their startup to a big company is provided in Scott Weiss, "The 'I-Just-Got-Bought-by-a-Big-Company' Survival Guide," Andreessen Horowitz blog, Feb. 2, 2013.

256 **"It turned out everyone else":** Eisenmann et al., "Poppy (B)."

256 **"M&A goes so-so":** Fred Destin, "How to Get Really Screwed by Your Board and Investors in a Scaled Startup," *Medium,* Sept. 30, 2016.

256 **Bridge Financing:** For additional perspective on bridge financing, see Fred Wilson, "Financing Options: Bridge Loans," AVC blog, Aug. 15, 2011; and Jason Lemkin, "How Bridge Rounds Work in Venture Capital: Messy, Full of Drama, and Not Without High Risk," SaaStr blog, June 20, 2019.

257 **Head Count Reduction:** For additional perspective on managing head count reductions, see Erick Schonfeld, "Email from Jason Calacanis: How to Handle Layoffs," TechCrunch website, Oct. 22, 2008; and Fred Wilson, "MBA Mondays: How to Ask an Employee to Leave the Company," AVC blog, July 2, 2012.

258 **"There were tears and anger":** Fishkin, *Lost and Founder,* Ch. 17.

258 **"Truth be told":** Goldberg, "On the Rebound."

259 **"The press made a big deal":** Author's interview with Goldberg.

260 **"burned bridges":** Fishkin, *Lost and Founder,* Ch. 17.

261 **"I found some striking parallels":** Lee, "Startup Mortality."

261 **Beyond this impulse:** Dawn DeTienne, Dean Shepherd, and Julio De Castro, "The Fallacy of 'Only the Strong Survive': The Effects of Extrinsic Motivation on the Persistence Decisions for Under-Performing Firms," *Journal of Business Venturing* 23 (2008): 528–546, presents a theoretical model for why entrepreneurs may persist with a struggling venture, and tests the model through conjoint analysis. One factor positively associated with persistence that isn't on my list is the entrepreneur's past record of venture success. According to DeTienne et al., pre-

viously successful entrepreneurs are more apt to persist because they assume they have a winning formula.

261 **"I did see the metrics"**: Mike Gozzo, My Startup Has 30 Days to Live blog, *Tumblr,* 2013.

262 **"utterly alone"**: Gozzo, 30 Days.

262 **"Everyone (not just investors)"**: Lee, "Startup Mortality."

262 **"Once you take"**: Steve Carpenter, class visit to HBS MBA course "Entrepreneurial Failure," Feb. 2019.

262 **"What tore me apart"**: Gozzo, 30 Days.

263 **"creates a risk of toxicity"**: Jerry Colonna, class visit to HBS MBA course "Entrepreneurial Failure," Mar. 2019.

263 **"I've often heard"**: Gozzo, 30 Days.

264 **"It wasn't a failed pivot"**: Gozzo, 30 Days.

264 **"I was so *fucking* exhausted"**: Jasper Diamond Nathaniel, "When Your Startup Fails," Medium: Noteworthy blog, Apr. 15, 2019.

265 **"I know you and I believe"**: Eisenmann and Ma, "Baroo (B)."

265 **Wallace had this date**: Shutdown specifics for Quincy are based on the author's personal experience as an investor.

266 **While it paid its employees**: Eisenmann and Ma, "Baroo (B)."

266 **"It was a relief"**: Eisenmann and Ma, "Baroo (B)."

266 **Venture capitalist Aileen Lee**: Author's interview with Aileen Lee, July 9, 2019.

267 **An acquihire is a common exit**: For additional perspective on acquihires, see John Coyle and Gregg Polsky, "Acqui-hiring," *Duke Law Journal* 62, no. 3 (2013): 281–346; and Chris Dixon, "The Economic Logic Behind Tech and Talent Acquisitions," cdixon blog, Oct. 18, 2012.

267 **"We're being courted"**: Gozzo, 30 Days.

268 **"split our team apart"**: Lee, "Startup Mortality."

269 **This lawyer is likely**: The suggestion to pay your lawyer up front is from Gabe Zichermann, "How and Why to Shut Down Your Startup," Medium: The Startup, Aug. 2, 2019, which offers other good guidance on the shutdown process, as does Alex Fishman, "How to Shut Down a Startup in 36 Hours," *Medium,* July 2, 2016. More resources are available on The Shut Down, a website created by Abigail Edgecliffe-Johnson.

269 **The next step is to decide**: The three approaches to managing claims in the wake of a shutdown are described in Bethany Laurence, "Going Out of Business: Liquidate Assets Yourself or File for Bankruptcy?" and Laurence, "How to Liquidate a Closing Business's Assets," NOLO website. Other guidance is available on NOLO's "Going Out of Business Page."

270 **For example, Dot & Bo**: Eisenmann et al., "Anthony Soohoo: Retrospection."

271 **According to NOLO**: Bethany Laurence, "Negotiating Debt Settlements When You Go Out of Business," NOLO website.

271 **In the case of Baroo**: Eisenmann and Ma, "Baroo (B)."

Chapter 11: Bouncing Back

274 **Christina Wallace felt devastated**: The first two paragraphs in this chapter are based on Christina Wallace, "What Happens When You Fail?" Ch. 13 in Charu Sharma (ed.), *Go Against the Flow: Women, Entrepreneurship and Success* (independently published, 2019).

276 **"The thoughts of what we"**: Josh Carter, "Failing and Other Uplifting Anecdotes," *Medium,* Jan. 5, 2019.

276 **"My first instinct was to apologize":** Nikki Durkin, "My Startup Failed, and This Is What It Feels Like," *Medium: Female Founders,* June 23, 2014.

276 **Elisabeth Kübler-Ross's:** Elisabeth Kübler-Ross, *On Death and Dying: What the Dying Have to Teach Doctors, Nurses, Clergy and Their Own Families* (New York: Scribner, 1969).

277 **"It just didn't seem real":** Eisenmann et al., "Anthony Soohoo: Retrospection."

278 **Anthony Soohoo, for example:** Eisenmann et al., "Anthony Soohoo: Retrospection."

278 **Notre Dame professor Dean Shepherd:** Shepherd's academic research on entrepreneurial failure is summarized in Dean Shepherd, Trenton Williams, Marcus Wolfe, and Holger Patzelt, *Learning from Entrepreneurial Failure: Emotions, Cognitions, and Actions* (Cambridge, UK: Cambridge University Press, 2016). For general readers, Shepherd's insights are presented in *From Lemons to Lemonade: Squeeze Every Last Drop of Success Out of Your Mistakes* (Upper Saddle River, NJ: Prentice Hall, 2009). Walsh and Cunningham, "Business Failure and Entrepreneurship," summarizes other academic literature on how entrepreneurs recover from their venture's failure.

278 **"Talking about Poppy's failure":** Eisenmann et al., "Poppy (B)."

278 **"Fighting it won't help":** Adi Hillel, "Killing Your Startup and Staying Alive: Four Steps to Entrepreneurial Resilience," *Medium: Hubitus,* Mar. 23, 2016.

279 **After cycling through:** Walsh and Cunningham, "Business Failure and Entrepreneurship," summarizes academic literature on how entrepreneurs learn from their venture's failure. Amy Edmondson, "Strategies for Learning from Failure," *Harvard Business Review,* April 2001, provides an overview of different reasons for organizational failure, barriers to learning from failure, and strategies for overcoming those barriers.

279 **At the other end:** Y. Liu, Y. Li, X. Hao, and Y. Zhang, "Narcissism and Learning from Entrepreneurial Failure," *Journal of Business Venturing* 34 (2019): 496–512, presents survey data that shows that narcissistic founders are less likely to learn from a prior startup failure.

280 **But Jason Goldberg's postmortem:** Goldberg, "On the Rebound," is the source for his quotes in this chapter.

281 **When I examined the career paths:** PitchBook was used to identify U.S.-based startups founded in 2013 or 2014 that shut down in 2015 after raising at least $500,000. CEOs' career histories were based on their LinkedIn profiles. Twenty-five of the fifty CEOs had founded a startup before the one that failed in 2015; the other twenty-five were first-time founders.

282 **Founders interviewed:** Jason Cope, "Learning from Entrepreneurial Failure: An Interpretive Phenomenological Analysis," *Journal of Business Venturing* 26 (2011): 604–623.

282 **"I won't pursue venture capital":** Fishkin, *Lost and Founder,* Afterword.

283 **"What I have learned":** Eisenmann and Ma, "Baroo (B)."

285 **Shai Agassi founded:** "Agassi Turns Environment Friendly Focus to Mass Transport," *Haaretz,* Aug. 7, 2014.

Letter to a First-Time Founder

288 **Y Combinator's Paul Graham says:** Graham, "Startup = Growth."

289 **I truly believe:** Daniel Kahneman, *Thinking, Fast and Slow* (New York: Farrar, Strauss and Giroux, 2011).

289 **So, I wrote:** Alumni founders' responses are presented in Tom Eisenmann, "No

Regrets (Mostly): Reflections from HBS MBA '99 Entrepreneurs," Launching Technology Ventures course blog, Mar. 28, 2011.

Appendix: Early-Stage Startup Survey

299 **My multivariate analysis employs:** My multinomial logistic regression model exhibits good fit with N = 470; chi square difference for likelihood ratio test of model fit = 198.1, with 92 degrees of freedom and significance level = .000; and Cox & Snell pseudo R-square = .344. Ordinal logistic regression yielded broadly similar results, but I used multinomial logistic regression because my data did not satisfy ordinal regression's requirement for proportional odds. That is, the effect of predictors on the odds of moving from low to medium valuation outcomes was not the same as their effect on the odds of moving from medium to high outcomes. More details about the model and regression results are available in a working paper by the author.

Index

ABOUT THE AUTHOR

Tom Eisenmann is the Howard H. Stevenson Professor of Business Administration at Harvard Business School (HBS), where he teaches entrepreneurship and studies the management of new ventures. Eisenmann is faculty co-chair of the HBS Arthur Rock Center for Entrepreneurship and the Harvard MS/MBA, a joint degree program offered by HBS and Harvard's School of Engineering and Applied Sciences. Since joining the HBS faculty in 1997, he's led The Entrepreneurial Manager, an introductory course taught to all first-year MBAs, and chaired the second year of the MBA program. With colleagues, he's created fourteen MBA electives on different aspects of entrepreneurship, including courses on product management, entrepreneurial sales and marketing, marketplace design, and startup failure. Eisenman has co-authored 130 HBS case studies that have sold more than 1.5 million copies for use in business schools and executive education programs across the world. His writing has appeared in *The Wall Street Journal, Harvard Business Review,* and *Forbes.* Eisenmann has coached thousands of students who aspire to be entrepreneurs, has made angel investments in dozens of new ventures, and has served on many startups' advisory boards and boards of directors. He received his bachelor's, MBA, and doctoral degrees from Harvard University. Prior to completing his doctorate, Eisenmann was a partner at McKinsey & Company and co-head of its Media & Entertainment Practice.

Twitter: @teisenmann

ABOUT THE TYPE

This book was set in Sabon, a typeface designed by the well-known German typographer Jan Tschichold (1902–74). Sabon's design is based upon the original letter forms of sixteenth-century French type designer Claude Garamond and was created specifically to be used for three sources: foundry type for hand composition, Linotype, and Monotype. Tschichold named his typeface for the famous Frankfurt typefounder Jacques Sabon (c. 1520–80).